6.30.72

MARITIME ENTERPRISE

1485–1558

WARSHIP, PERIOD 1514–45.
From Cott. MS. Aug. I. i. 18.

MARITIME ENTERPRISE

1485 — 1558

BY

JAMES A. WILLIAMSON

1972
OCTAGON BOOKS
New York

Originally published in 1913

Reprinted 1972
by special arrangement with Oxford University Press, Inc.

OCTAGON BOOKS
A DIVISION OF FARRAR, STRAUS & GIROUX, INC.
19 Union Square West
New York, N. Y. 10003

LIBRARY OF CONGRESS CATALOG CARD NUMBER: 74-159237

ISBN 0-374-98634-7

Manufactured by Braun-Brumfield, Inc.
Ann Arbor, Michigan

Printed in the United States of America

PREFACE

THE subject of English maritime enterprise during the period 1485–1558 falls naturally into two divisions—discovery and trade. The former has engaged the attention of numerous historians in the last thirty years, their works centring mainly on the voyages of the Cabots with subsequent exploring adventures more or less summarily treated. Commerce, on the other hand, has been somewhat neglected as a factor in that great development of the powers of the English nation which made itself evident in the sixteenth century. The only exhaustive book on the *maritime* trade of our country in the period in question is that of G. Schanz,[1] published in German in 1881, and never translated into English. This work stops at the year 1547.

The object of the present work is to present a comprehensive picture of English maritime affairs from the accession of Henry VII to that of Elizabeth; to trace out such lines of policy as are visible in the existing records; and to elucidate certain incidents concerning which disputable ideas, or no ideas at all, are current.

With regard to the Cabot voyages, no new evidence is adduced, but a scientific criticism and analysis of that already known has been attempted; leading, in the author's opinion, to the partial rehabilitation of the character of Sebastian Cabot. The evidence in favour of his independent exploration in the North-West seems,

[1] *Englische Handelspolitik gegen Ende des Mittelalters.*

when properly discriminated from other matters with which it has been unjustly confused, too strong to be neglected.

The later voyages of discovery under Henry VII, and those under Henry VIII, have been as deeply .entered into as the scanty surviving evidence permits. The debt which our maritime expansion owes to the last-named monarch is emphasized by the fact that most of the projects of his reign owed their origin to his initiative, acting in despite of popular apathy.

With the trading voyages to Brazil, the African coast, and the North-East the new era of national expansion was entered upon. On these matters the Record Office possesses numerous documents which supplement the printed sources of information. The negotiations concerning the Guinea voyages furnish an illustrative sidelight on the actual influence exercised by King Philip over the conduct of English affairs.

In the chapters on commerce under Henry VIII and his two successors the development of the various branches of trade, and their relation to diplomacy, have been outlined, but many details have been necessarily omitted. The circumstances attending the fall of the Hansa in England are here fully stated for the first time.

For purposes of reference a chapter on the naval history of the period has been added. The connexion between the naval service and the mercantile marine was perhaps closer in Tudor times than at any subsequent period. Officers, men, and ships served alternately in the one and the other; and the navy itself was more of the nature of a marine militia than of a regular force.

CONTENTS

ILLUSTRATIONS

SUMMARY OF ENGLISH MARITIME AND COMMERCIAL HISTORY, 1485-1558

CHAPTER I

HENRY VII AND HIS COMMERCIAL POLICY

THE reign of Henry VII marks the opening of the modern era in the history of the English nation, the period in which, from being an agricultural and military people, we have become transformed into a maritime and commercial community, with interests stretching far beyond the shores of our immediate neighbours on the continent of Europe. Throughout the Middle Ages all the strivings and ambitions of England were concentrated on the conquest, by force of arms, of the surrounding countries—of the remaining parts of the British Isles at first, and afterwards of France. With a hardy and independent peasantry and a fierce and warlike baronage, it could scarcely have been otherwise. English kings found themselves obliged, for their own preservation, to put themselves at the head of such movements, and those of them who were unable or unwilling to do so were continually menaced by the turbulent elements to which they refused an outlet.

This system of violent expansion, successful in the cases of Ireland and Wales, and not seriously pursued in that of Scotland, proved to be its own destruction when applied to France. Although a military conquest might endure for a time, it was impossible that England could permanently absorb a nation larger than itself, of different blood, language, and manners of thought, in the same way that Wales had been absorbed. When

Henry V commenced his wonderful career of conquest
the sentiment of nationality was already too well established ; and the long struggle, which ended forty years
later in the expulsion of the English from France, consolidated that sentiment, and rendered the renewal of
such an attempt for ever impossible of success. But
just as France had developed from a mere geographical
area into a nation in the modern sense of the word,
so also had England, although much remained to be
done before her development could proceed on truly
national lines. The Wars of the Roses, protracted, with
intervals of peace, for thirty years, cleared away much
of the remaining débris of feudalism ; and at their close
Henry VII came forward as the first king of modern
England. The old ideals, the old national instincts, and
the old social order had gone, or were in process of
dissolution ; and the work of his reign consisted in forming new ones and giving direction to that universal
awakening of the human mind which now first began
to make its influence felt in the practical affairs of the
English nation.

As with all changes of deep-rooted and far-reaching
importance, its results were slow to manifest themselves,
and were scarcely apparent to many of the greatest
minds of the time, bred up to the old order, yet nevertheless working unconsciously in the furtherance of the
new. The king himself, who did more than any other
man to usher in the new era, and whose policy has been
followed, with intervals of retrogression, almost to our
own time, may well have been unaware how greatly he
differed from his forerunners, and there is nothing in
his recorded utterances to show that he realized the
significance of the change that was taking place. In

fact, as compared with many of the more flamboyant
statesmen who followed him, he must have appeared
slow and conservative, a survival of mediaevalism rather
than a man of the Renaissance. Like the evolution of
the natural world, that of imperial Britain has been
largely unconscious, and measures which owed their
origin to expediency and the needs of the moment have
frequently hardened into enduring elements of the
national system. Let us then examine, from this point
of view, one aspect of the reign of the first Tudor—his
commercial policy; bearing in mind that, although he
himself was concerned only with the immediate welfare
of his family and country, his work was of such a character
as to serve as the foundation for an edifice upon which
the passage of four centuries has not yet placed the
topmost stone.

European commerce, down to the age of the great
geographical discoveries, hinged upon two great trade
routes and two great producing areas, the one of manufactured, and the other of raw, material. To these four
dominant factors all subsidiary avenues and crafts owed
their origin and continued existence. The two primary
trade routes were : first, that connecting, by way of the
Levant and the nearer East, the Italian cities with
the vaguely known and fabulously portrayed wealth of
southern Asia ; and second, that by which the hardy
merchants of the Hanseatic League conveyed the produce
of the Baltic shores, of Scandinavia, of the wide plains
of Muscovy, and through them the far-fetched wares of
Persia and Cathay, to western Europe, which region,
stimulated by amenities whence the indolent mind of
Asia drew no profit, inevitably became the centre of the
world's progress. Nothing for nothing being a universal

law, Europe had to find something of her own to exchange for the furs of the North and the spices of the East. The cities of the Rhine delta supplied, in great part, the indispensable *quid pro quo*, by devoting themselves to a variety of manufactures amongst which that of cloth assumed a position of paramount importance. Here, then, arose the first producing area necessary to the balance of the mediaeval trading system ; England constituted the second and equally indispensable one, for she alone, secured by the sea from the worst scourges of war, could supply the raw material for the cloth industry. The generous wool-sacks of England became her title of entry into the ranks of the progressing nations of the world.

Already, before the dawn of the new era, England had begun to manufacture a portion of her wool into rough, inferior qualities of cloth, but, until the awakening under the Tudor dynasty, she cannot be said to have realized the possibilities of her position. The Hanse merchants and the Italians were in possession of the bulk of her foreign commerce, and only a few subsidiary trades were in the hands of Englishmen, whose education and ability in such matters were inferior to those of the foreigners.

A more detailed consideration of the lines of communication with which England was immediately concerned reveals four main commercial avenues, all forming part of the great general system already described : the trade with Germany and the Baltic, chiefly controlled by the great Hansa, whose tentacles spread from Riga to the Rhine ; the export of half-made cloth to Flanders, shared between the Hansa, the Flemings, and the English Merchant Adventurers ; the wool export, to Calais by the English Staple Merchants, and overland to Italy

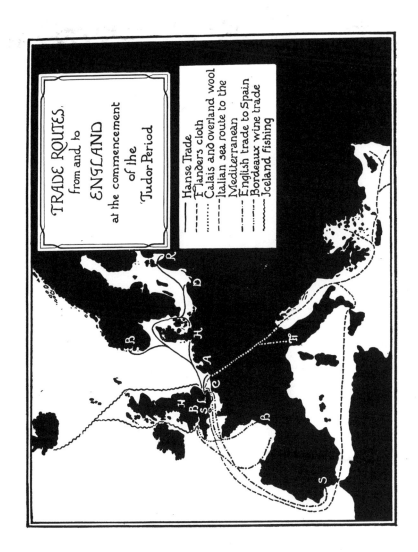

TRADE ROUTES
from and to
ENGLAND
at the commencement
of the
Tudor Period

—— Hanse Trade
– – – Flanders cloth
········· Calais and overland wool
– · – · – Italian sea route to the
Mediterranean
– – – English trade to Spain
– · – · – Bordeaux wine trade
〜〜〜〜 Iceland fishing

P. 16

by the Venetians and Florentines, who maintained business houses for that purpose in London ; and the long sea route for wools, wines, and spices, to and from the Mediterranean, again monopolized almost exclusively by the Italians. In addition there were minor, but nevertheless much frequented, trades to Spain for wines and oils, to Gascony for wines, and to Iceland for stock-fish. The two last mentioned were more exclusively in the hands of Englishmen than any of the others.

These mediaeval trade routes, although destined to be profoundly modified by the great extension of the limits of the world as known to Europeans, remained of paramount importance for more than a century to come, and Henry VII set himself to the policy of ousting foreigners from their control, and of fostering, by every means known to his statesmanship, the mercantile enterprise of his own people.

One of the shrewdest business men who ever sat upon a throne, he had no doubt studied and admired the commercial system of Venice. That state, which existed solely by means of and for the purpose of trade, maintained her ascendancy by a fiscal policy which combined rigorous protection with a species of socialism undefiled by any morbidly altruistic ideas. All the familiar weapons of modern protection—preferential duties on goods from Venetian dependencies, navigation laws to encourage Venetian shipping, retaliatory tariffs against rivals, and reciprocal arrangements with such as were disposed to be reasonable—were to be found in the armoury of Venice, and were applied with an unquestioning assurance as to their efficacy, only possible in an age when the doctrines of free trade were yet unborn.

In addition there was in Venice an absolutely complete

subordination of the individual to the interests of the State. If the export or import of a certain article was considered prejudicial to the welfare of the city, that trade was stopped forthwith ; if the clothworkers of Venice were short of raw material, shipmasters coming from England were ordered to load with wool and nothing else ; if the State galleys for the Flanders voyage had difficulty in completing their cargoes, those who preferred to ship their goods in private vessels were forced to pay half or quarter freights to the official ships as well ; since it was desirable that Venice should possess a large commercial navy, the overland conveyance of certain wares was forbidden or subjected to paralysing duties. Such are a few examples of the working of an undemocratic republic, of a type which may never be seen again, but which was eminently suited to the needs of its time. And the secrets of the success of this unparalleled interference by the State with individual rights ? They were two : first, magnificent discipline, ready obedience enforced by severe penalties ; and second, an elasticity of method, an instant variation of policy to meet varying conditions, which could only have been carried out by an assembly of level-headed, patriotic merchant-statesmen, such as filled the benches of the Venetian senate.

Henry VII, then, had before him a pattern of successful mercantile policy, but he was under no illusions as to his powers of enforcing such a discipline on England. Although he far exceeded him in subtlety of mind, he lacked the ferocious mastery of men which his son was afterwards to display. He had to make up his mind to work slowly and cautiously, to be content to sow that others might reap, to lay sure foundations for the great-

ness of his family and of the country with which its
interests were bound up.

Generally speaking, the policy of the Middle Ages had
been, in the interests of cheapness, to encourage foreign
merchants of all kinds to bring their goods to England,
and to establish factories in her ports ; in many cases,
even, aliens had been granted privileges exceeding those
of native traders, and consequently the trade of England
was largely in foreign hands. Henry soon gave signs
that this policy of cheapness was to be abandoned. His
first Parliament passed an Act [1] prohibiting the import
of Bordeaux wines in other than English vessels, manned
by English crews. To avoid friction, the too sudden
application of this law was mitigated by the frequent
granting to foreign merchants of licences to break it.
But these were exceptions ; the rule remained, and the
grants of licences gradually diminished.

While determined to advance the general interests of
his subjects, he was always ready to conclude commercial
treaties conferring a mutual exchange of benefits ; and
he sought, wherever possible, to draw mercantile advantages from his handling of purely political matters. The
commercial relations of England and the Netherlands
form an illustration in point. In 1493 there was a serious
quarrel on account of the support given to Perkin Warbeck by Margaret, the widowed Duchess of Burgundy
and sister of Richard III. Henry's retaliation to her
vindictive encouragement of his enemies consisted in
ordering the cessation of all intercourse, and the removal
of the Continental head-quarters of the Merchant
Adventurers from Antwerp to Calais. Uninterrupted
trade with England was essential to the prosperity of the

[1] Extended and made permanent in 1489.

Netherlands, where a large proportion of the craftsmen were employed in dyeing and finishing the rough English cloth. There was on both sides great distress in commercial circles, and unemployment due to the loss of trade; but the inconvenience thus caused, while considerable in England, was intolerable in the Netherlands, and the result was the negotiation of the famous *Magnus Intercursus* of 1496, followed by supplementary treaties in 1497 and 1499.[1] By these treaties tariffs were reduced, fishing rights regulated, and many vexatious restrictions abolished; in addition, Henry secured the political object for which he had undertaken the struggle. When the English cloth merchants returned to Antwerp they were received with public demonstrations of joy.

The English king, although willing to make concessions when such were inevitable, showed himself remorseless in seizing an accidental advantage. In January 1506 the Archduke Philip, who had succeeded to the throne of Castile on the death of Queen Isabella in 1504, set out from Flanders to Spain by sea. In the Channel he encountered a furious storm, and, after all on board had given themselves up for lost, his fleet reached the shelter of Weymouth. Contrary to the advice of his captains, he went on shore. The country people, seeing the arrival of strange ships and armed men, gathered to resist an enemy, but, finding him to be a friend, they made him welcome. Sir Thomas Trenchard, a most astute gentleman of the neighbourhood, offered him entertainment, and sent off post haste to acquaint King Henry of the prize which fortune had cast on his shore.

---

[1] *Foedera*, xii, pp. 578-91, 654, 713-20; *Cotton MSS.*, Galba C ii. 249: 'A Brief of so much of the Intercourse of 1499 as concerns Merchant Adventurers, with their opinions touching the same.'

Philip now realized his rashness and would have been glad to depart, but was earnestly entreated by Trenchard and his friends to stay and speak with the king. Fearing that if he insisted their courtesy would give place to force, he put a good face on the matter and professed himself delighted to remain. Henry sent the Earl of Arundel, with many lords and knights, to bring him to Windsor with his wife Juana.

He was paraded through London and, as the price of his liberty, had to agree to a commercial treaty which settled outstanding questions in such a one-sided way, and admitted English cloth at such a cheap rate to the Netherlands, that the defrauded Flemings named it the *Malus Intercursus*.[1] In those times shipwrecked voyagers received scant compassion, and Henry was only taking the same advantage on a large scale as his unscrupulous subjects took on a smaller one when they stole the cargoes from stranded ships. Philip died without ratifying the treaty of 1506, the details of which were not completed until after he left the country, and relations became unsatisfactory in consequence. Margaret proposed to resume trade on the terms of the *Magnus Intercursus*, but Henry was unwilling to forgo his hard bargain. Finally, a compromise between the treaties of 1496 and 1506 was agreed upon, the customs payable by Englishmen in the Netherlands remaining on the basis of the latter. The question of the legal validity of the *Malus Intercursus* remained unsettled, the matter being postponed from time to time by the issue of provisional ordinances for its maintenance. As late as 1538 the Netherlanders were still demanding its abrogation.[2]

---

[1] Hall's *Chronicle*, 1809 ed., p. 500.
[2] *Spanish Cal.* vi, part i, pp. 59–60.

An important trade existed between England and
Spain and, at the beginning of Henry's reign, it was
largely in the hands of Spanish merchants, a number
of whom resided in London. The customs duties
had long been in an unsettled state, and were the
subject of an arrangement included in the Treaty of
Medina del Campo, 1489.[1] It was provided that the
subjects of either country might travel, reside, and
carry on business in the other without a passport,
and should be treated in every way as native citizens.
Customs duties were to be reduced and all letters of
marque (i. e. private reprisal for injuries) revoked. There
were also other clauses intended for the suppression of
piracy, a subject which will be referred to later.

That such treaties were often broken is proved by
their frequent renewal; and indeed, the signing of
a treaty was more often the signal for a commencement
of wranglings as to its interpretation, than a token of
settlement. In the case in point it had been agreed
that customs were to be reduced to what they had been
thirty years before. The intention was plain, but Henry
discovered that the English duties had been *higher* at
the date mentioned than at the time of the treaty, and
he promptly increased them, although the Spaniards
protested that they had lowered theirs. The dispute on
this point dragged on for many years, and references to
it occur at intervals in diplomatic correspondence until
the marriage of the Prince of Wales and Katherine of
Aragon. A curious fiscal argument occurs in a letter
from Henry to the Spanish sovereigns in 1497.[2] He says
that the effect of the high duties is that Spaniards sell
their goods at a high price in England, and so are enabled

[1] *Spanish Cal.* i, p. 21.   [2] Ibid. i, p. 144.

to obtain more English cloth with the proceeds than they could otherwise do. Thus the duties are paid by the English, not the Spaniards. An excellent sermon— for other people—on the disadvantages of protection !

Although anxious to foster English trade and enterprise to the utmost, Henry could not afford to neglect his dynastic interests, and the latter were of paramount importance in his dealings with Spain. His title was weak and his enemies strong, and, during the first part of his reign, it seemed quite likely that he would perish in a feudal revolution as four of his predecessors had done in the space of a century. To remedy the instability of his throne he was sometimes obliged to make use of commerce as a weapon or a bribe, as opportunity offered. An instance of the first was seen in his dealings with the Netherlands ; the negotiations for the Spanish marriage were an example of the second. The proposals and hagglings with reference to this marriage dragged on for years. Henry was eager for it. He was, in a sense, a parvenu among the kings of Europe, and he felt that it was a vital matter for him to establish his family among them. Ferdinand and Isabella, on the other hand, had great hesitation in allowing their young daughter to be exiled among the English, whom the Spaniards regarded as being socially and morally inferior to themselves. In addition to this personal objection they had another. They wished to procrastinate until Henry should have disposed of his pretenders and given proofs of the firmness of his throne. Hence his extreme eagerness to lay Perkin Warbeck by the heels, which embroiled him with the Netherlands in 1493. The marriage being the keystone of his policy, he left no means unused to bring it about, and so we find com-

mercial relations employed by him as a screw with which
to extort the reluctant acquiescence of Spain. In 1496
he declared that he would come to an understanding
on the question of the duties after the alliance and
marriage should have been concluded. In 1497, in the
letter already quoted, he promised that Spanish traders
should have preferential treatment as against the Italians
in celebration of the happy arrival of the princess in
England, an event which was still to be delayed, as it
proved, for more than four years to come. One more
instance of the intimate connexion of politics and trade
may be given. In 1504 the Spanish Government prohibited the export of goods from Spain in foreign vessels
so long as there were any Spanish ships unemployed, but
in consideration of the position of the now widowed
Katherine in England and of their desire to recover her
or her dowry, the English were exempted from the
application of this law.[1]

With Venice Henry VII was never on bad terms,
although for several years a brisk tariff war was waged
between the two powers. It arose from the action of
Venice in imposing an additional export duty of four
ducats per butt on malmsey wines loaded by aliens at
Candia. This was done under pretext of discouraging
the pirates of that region, but in reality for the purpose
of favouring Venetian shipping. Henry retaliated by
making Venetians pay 18s. per butt extra duty on
importing these wines into England, and by fixing a
maximum selling price of £4 per butt. A butt of
malmsey contained 126 gallons, and a gallon of the
wine thus cost about 7½d. in England. The differential

[1] *Spanish Cal.* i, p. 337.

duty and the maximum selling price threatened to squeeze
the Venetians out of the market, but the king went
further. He entered into negotiations with the Florentine Government with a view to the establishment of an
English wool-staple at Pisa.[1] This would have constituted the latter city the distributing centre for English
wool in the Mediterranean, and Venice would have been
deprived at a blow of an important branch of her trade.
The proposal seriously alarmed the Venetians, and they
threatened to discontinue the dispatch of the annual
trading fleet to England. It would have been manifestly impossible for them to bring cargoes of spice to
England if they were debarred from loading wool in
return, especially as the export of specie from England
was prohibited. The Pisa project was probably not
seriously intended and was not persisted in, although
the appointment in 1494 of two English consuls in that
city, with full authority over English merchants, indicates that considerable business was done there.[2] In the
end, after lengthy but quite dispassionate negotiations,
such as befitted business-like powers, Henry carried his
point and the wine duties were reduced.[3]

The prohibition of the export of money, and also of
gold and silver plate, from the realm was typical of the
economic ideas of the time. Gold was looked upon as
wealth in itself rather than as a means of exchange, and
this notion was strengthened as time went on by the
enormous apparent advantages which Spain derived from
her American conquests. It was an error which led Spain
to ruin, and would have been equally fatal to England

---

[1] *Venetian Cal.* i, pp. 185, 186, 188.   [2] *Foedera*, xii, p. 553.
[3] *Venetian Cal.* i, *passim.*

if she had had the same opportunity to go astray. Fortunately, Englishmen found themselves excluded from the gold-bearing regions, and were driven to trade and eventually to colonization instead.

To be successful as a merchant under the conditions which obtained in the days when individual effort was beginning to displace the rigid guild-system of the Middle Ages, a man had need of alert wits, a stout heart, and capital sufficient to enable him to withstand the violent fluctuations of fortune. Even in times of peace the risks were great, although undoubtedly the profits of the successful were proportionate. Shipwrecks were necessarily frequent on unlighted and practically uncharted coasts; the trade routes were infested with pirates and privateers; and commercial treaties were broken almost as soon as made. The cautious trader, before venturing his goods into a foreign country, was careful to procure a licence or safe-conduct from the Government, and even this did not always protect him. If he could obtain the patronage of a powerful person, he might contrive to avoid the payment of customs dues. In 1492, when Henry VII imposed the prohibitive duties on Candia wines, the Venetian merchants in London were advised to distribute forty or fifty butts of the wine, or their cash equivalent, as bribes in getting the matter set right. Even State-owned vessels were not secure from molestation, when sufficiently far from home. In the same year, 1492, we read that Henry, being at war with France, detained the Flanders galleys of Venice to act as transports for his troops.[1] A powerful Government might secure compensation for such an infringement of its neutrality, but private merchants would have stood

[1] *Venetian Cal.* i, p. 213.

little chance of doing so. Conditions such as these caused success to depend entirely on individual qualities ; and when once they took to the sea Englishmen were not slow to develop that character for resource and audacity which stood them in such good stead in the long war with Spain at the end of the sixteenth century.

An incident which occurred in 1505 shows how little reliance could be placed upon treaties by the persons whom they were designed to benefit. On the strength of an undertaking by the Spaniards, already mentioned, that notwithstanding the navigation law the English might freely export goods from Spain, a fleet of English merchantmen went to Seville, with cargoes of cloth, intending to come back with wine and oil. On arriving there, they were forbidden by the local authorities to export anything, and returned professing themselves ruined. Their spokesmen petitioned the king, ' with much clamour ', for redress. Henry sent for de Puebla, the Spanish ambassador, whom he suspected of duplicity in the matter, and subjected him to a storm of furious abuse. De Puebla must have passed a bad quarter of an hour, but, as he remarked, he did not so much mind as there was no witness to the interview. He explained that the treaty, by a mistake, had not been proclaimed in Andalusia. He wrote at once to King Ferdinand and asked him that right might be done. A few days later he reported that some members of the Privy Council had visited him on the same matter and that he had had a most unpleasant interview with them. He again begged Ferdinand to give satisfaction, as the English sailors were such savages that he went in fear of being stoned by them if reparation were not made.[1]

---

[1] *Spanish Cal.* i, pp. 366, 367, 374.

Piracy, as has already been noticed, was of common occurrence, and was a great hindrance to sea-borne trade. Surprising as it may seem, it was cheaper to send goods from London to Venice by the overland route, up the Rhine and across the Alps, than it was to send them by sea. This was partly owing to the huge expenses incurred for defence against pirates. One Venetian captain, reporting his safe arrival in London, mentioned that, fearing to be attacked, he had shipped a hundred extra hands and twenty-two gunners, and that by their aid he had beaten off the attack of a Norman pirate. Perhaps the greatest piratical coup of the time was the capture on August 21, 1485, of the entire fleet of Flanders galleys. They were assailed off Lisbon by a force of French ships, commanded by an officer in the service of the French king. After a desperate fight, lasting twenty hours, in which over four hundred Venetians were killed and wounded, four large galleys surrendered.[1] An enormous booty was taken from them, and no one seems to have been punished for the affair. In fact, the deed was justified on the ground that Venice was under a papal interdict and therefore outside the law. Pirates were particularly active in the Channel and, besides roving the high seas, were sometimes bold enough to enter English harbours in search of prey. In 1495 some Frenchmen sailed up Southampton Water and raided the Venetian galleys which were at anchor off the town. They seized, among others, the commander of the fleet and the Venetian consul in England, and held them to ransom, exacting 550 ducats for each.

Piracy was the more difficult to suppress because there was often a very slight distinction between merchant and

[1] *Venetian Cal.* i, Preface, lxviii.

pirate. Unscrupulous persons frequently combined the two callings as opportunity offered. To check the abuse, a clause was inserted in some of the commercial treaties, to the effect that the owners of vessels, before leaving a foreign port, were to deposit a sum of money as a guarantee of good behaviour, sometimes twice the value of the ship and cargo. Another remedy for the victims of piracy was but an aggravation of the disease. It consisted in the granting of letters of marque or reprisal to the injured parties, thus allowing them to take the law into their own hands. Naturally, the scope allowed them by these letters was very liberally interpreted by the holders, who seem even to have regarded them as negotiable property. An extreme instance was the seizure on the Rhine of certain Milanese merchants, bound for England with their goods, at the instigation of the Emperor Frederick III. This was done on the ground that letters of reprisal against Milan had been granted by a former king of England to a certain merchant, then deceased. His heirs had apparently transferred their rights to the German sovereign.

The extent to which navigation was dependent on the weather is difficult to realize in these days. Communication between England and Spain was almost at a standstill in the winter. A letter of 1496 mentions that during the first three months of that year the seas had been so rough that few vessels had been able to leave Spanish ports. One courier had been detained two months and another three without any chance of leaving. The diplomatic correspondence between England and Spain, which was dispatched almost exclusively by the sea route, was always much diminished in volume during the winter months, and letters sometimes took many weeks to reach

their destination. When Queen Isabella of Castile died
and the Archduke Philip, her successor, proposed to
travel by sea from Flanders to Spain, he was advised
that the voyage could only be made in safety between
May and the middle of August. He chose to undertake
it in the winter, with the consequence already described.
In two months of the year 1498 fifty ships are said to
have been wrecked on the coasts of Portugal and Spain.[1]

When the perils of the sea were so great, the trades
of pilot and chart-maker, often combined by the same
individual, were of great importance. In the absence of
official charts of coasts and harbours, the man with local
knowledge, who could safely guide a ship to port, was
much sought after by merchants, and a pilot of good
repute could naturally command good prices for his ' sea
cards '. In regulating these matters Spain was in advance
of England. When voyages became longer and more
frequent, owing to the extension of American discoveries,
a proper system of examining and licensing pilots was
established. An office for the purpose was instituted at
Seville, and in 1519 Sebastian Cabot, who had by that
time left the service of England, was put in charge of
it with the title of Pilot-Major. All charts and reports
of new discoveries were sent in to this office, and the
information contained in them was embodied in a
standard map, which was thus kept up to date. The
Guild of the Holy Trinity, originating early in the reign
of Henry VIII, represented an attempt to organize the
craft of pilotage on similar lines in England, but it was
long before English pilots attained to the standard of
the Spaniards in theoretical knowledge.

[1] *Venetian Cal.* i, p. 278.

CHAPTER II

MERCANTILE ORGANIZATION

IT was the universal tendency of the Middle Ages for trades and industries to organize themselves, more or less rigidly, for the purpose of mutual defence and assistance. Such organizations accomplished their object by successfully defending the interests of the calling when isolated individuals would have fallen easy victims to tyranny; but the success was concomitant with a stifling of individuality and a stereotyping of personal relations, which were the bane of mediaeval times, and against which the Renaissance was in large measure a revolt.

In England the great London Companies, with their counterparts in other towns, became the arbiters of internal industry; while the greater part of such oversea traffic as was not in foreign hands became grouped into two combinations of which the members were known as the Merchants of the Staple and the Merchant Adventurers.

Of these, the Merchants of the Staple were the first established, dating back to the thirteenth century, a time when raw wool and tin were practically the only exports of England. At the beginning of the Tudor period they formed a close corporation, under royal patronage, and had in their hands the entire business of exporting unmanufactured wool, wool-fells, and hides to Calais, at which place their dépôt or ' staple ' had long been fixed.

Thither the cloth manufacturers of the Low Countries resorted for the purchase of their raw material.

A very heavy export duty was imposed on wool, yielding from one-third to a half of the total receipts from all customs, and serving the additional purpose of fostering home manufacture by making the raw material more expensive to the foreigner than to the Englishman. The entire expense of maintaining the garrison and fortifications of Calais was defrayed from the wool duty. This political tie between the Crown and the Staplers caused the interests of the latter to be well looked after by the king, although their relative importance inevitably declined as the export of manufactured goods increased. Their monopoly gave them the entire handling of the wool export for Flanders and the Rhine, all other persons being forbidden to engage in it. Italian merchants, however, were allowed to export wool to their own states, provided that none was sold north of the Alps; and other traders, both Englishmen and foreigners, were granted licences from time to time to ship wools to the Mediterranean. The export duties were so adjusted that, generally speaking, non-Staplers paid double as much as Staplers. Henry VII's contemplated extension of the Staple system to Pisa, and the alarm occasioned in Venice thereby, have been referred to in the previous chapter.

The Wool Staple was a typically mediaeval device, harsh and inelastic, and its privileges were doomed to be submerged in the rising tide of manufacturing enterprise. The growth of the latter continued to absorb the surplus of wool until none was left for export. Political events assisted the change : the loss of Calais in 1558 was a crushing blow ; and although, by transference to

a Flemish town, it was sought to maintain a foreign
dépôt, the conflict between England and Spain at the
end of the century deprived it of a permanent resting-
place. The manufactures of the Netherlands, and consequently their demand for raw material, also languished
on the outbreak of their struggle for independence under
Philip II. The decline of the Staple was quite appreci-
able even before the death of Henry VII. The average
annual customs paid on wool during the first five years
of his reign amounted to £16,800; for the last five
years the figure fell just short of £10,000.[1] The corresponding averages on all other wares were £17,500
and £29,000 respectively, a very convincing testimony
to the efficacy of the king's policy. There is no evidence that the decreased export of wool was in any
way due to a smaller output. To judge from social
writers on the period the tendency was all the other
way; the conversion of arable land into sheep farms
being one of the gravest domestic problems of the
time, owing to the consequent falling off in the demand for agricultural labour. The unexported wool
must, therefore, have been taken up by the native clothmakers, and the striking increase in non-Staple trade was
the result.

The Merchant Adventurers were a society organized
on similar lines to the Staple, but perhaps not so strictly
disciplined, and including all traders engaged in the
export of cloth to the Netherlands. According to tradition they dated from the reign of King John,[2] but they

---

[1] For detailed figures as to customs payments see Schanz, *Englische
Handelspolitik gegen Ende des Mittelalters*, ii. 37-156.
[2] *Harl. MSS.*, 597, f. 211.

received their first undoubted charter of incorporation
from Henry IV in 1407.[1] This charter, renewed by
successive kings, remained in force until 1505, when the
society was reconstituted by a grant from Henry VII.
The preamble stated that, owing to injuries sustained
abroad by lack of proper governance, new regulations
were necessary. The merchants were therefore empowered to meet and choose a governor and twenty-four
assistant governors from among ' the most sadde, dis-
creete and honest persones' of their number. The
Governor and Assistants were to have full power of
control over the English merchants resorting to the Low
Countries. Thirteen was fixed as the number forming
a quorum for the transaction of business, and any one
refusing to take office when elected was liable to a fine
of £20.[2] An additional grant in the next year gave
power to the Governor and Council to fine and commit
to prison those who disobeyed their commands. This
constitution worked fairly well for the next fifty years,
although complaints were sometimes made of the indiscipline of the merchants. Unlike the Staplers at Calais,
the Merchant Adventurers were resident, when abroad,
under the jurisdiction of a foreign prince, which rendered
them more difficult of control. During the restraint of
the Flanders trade, prior to the *Magnus Intercursus*, they
were ordered to shift their head-quarters to Calais ;
' notwithstanding, the said Low Countries were by dis-
ordered persons so furnished with the said woollen
commodities that very few merchants repaired to Calais,

---

[1] Thomas Gresham, writing to Northumberland in 1553, speaks of
sending a copy of their privileges dated 1296, but the document does
not now exist (*Cal. S. P. Dom.* 1547-80, p. 51).

[2] *Cotton MSS.*, Tib. D viii, f. 37. Printed by Schanz.

either to buy the same or to bring foreign commodities thither to be sold '.[1]   1695047
Shortly afterwards an attempt was made by the richer members of the Company dwelling in London to squeeze out the minor traders by making them pay heavy sums for admission to membership. But it proved a failure, being contrary to the general spirit of the age. The prosperity of the smaller seaports was threatened, and the aggrieved parties complained to the king. An Act was therefore passed in the Parliament of 1497 by which the fee for a licence was limited to ten marks, on payment of which sum any Englishman might trade. Thus the Merchant Adventurers were saved from petrifying into an exclusive band of privileged monopolists such as the Staple had become. With their freer and more elastic organization, they moved with the times, and remained in the forefront of commercial enterprise throughout the Tudor period. The expansion of their business brought them into conflict with the Hanseatic League, whose decline, as far as its hold upon England was concerned, was thenceforward inevitable. The Merchant Adventurers proved unsparing enemies, never letting slip any chance of discrediting their rivals, and instigating the Government to annoy them whenever opportunity offered. The course of the struggle and the final success which crowned the efforts of the English merchants will be described in a subsequent chapter.[2]

It is important to emphasize at this point the difference

---

[1] *Harl. MSS.*, 597, f. 211.
[2] Ancient histories of the Merchant Adventurers : *Harl. MSS.*, 597, ff. 211–15, a general sketch written in the reign of Elizabeth ; *Stowe MSS.*, 303, ff. 99–107, written in the time of Charles II, of very slight value ; *A Treatise of Commerce* (printed), by John Wheeler, 1601, much fuller and better informed than the other two.

between the cloth manufacture in England and in the
Netherlands. The greater part of the cloth at this time
exported by the Merchant Adventurers was of a coarse,
heavy variety, which had not been subjected to the
various finishing processes of rowing, shearing, dyeing, &c.
in which the Flemish craftsmen were more expert. The
Flemish industry was twofold : it consisted in completing
the manufacture of English cloth, and also in making
the lighter and more expensive fabrics such as chamlets,
crapes, and serges, from raw wool purchased at Calais.
This 'light drapery' manufacture was not introduced
into England until late in the sixteenth century, being
greatly assisted by Elizabeth's wise policy of encouraging
Philip's revolted subjects to settle in this country,
bringing the secrets of their craft with them.

The export and import duties of this period form an
interesting subject. Broadly speaking, they fall into two
main divisions : the 'subsidies', otherwise known as
tonnage and poundage ; and the 'customs'. The subsidies were a set of variable duties, granted to the
king for life at the beginning of his reign, and consisting
of tonnage, or import duty per tun of wine ; poundage,
a duty per pound sterling value on most other goods
exported or imported ; and wool duties, levied on
exported wool. The customs, as distinct from the subsidies, were fixed duties of ancient origin, primarily levied
on the strength of the royal prerogative, and were continued without much alteration [1] by the tactful Tudors,
who had no wish to raise a discussion on their legality.
It remained for James I to strain the prerogative by
arbitrarily increasing the old customs rates, and thus to
precipitate a struggle which ended in the abolition of

[1] Some additions were made by Mary.

the levying of imposts by royal authority, and established
the dependence of all duties on parliamentary grant.
The principal and original object of the duties was
undoubtedly the raising of revenue during the wars of
the Plantagenet kings ; but, as time went on, they came
to be used as instruments of protection for those classes
of merchants who were particularly favoured by the
Crown. As will be shown, the royal favour, previous to
Tudor times, was not reserved exclusively for Englishmen. The protective function of the duties was that
which Henry VII sought to develop, in the interests
of English trade ; and modifications were introduced in
the subsidies whenever it seemed expedient.

The following table gives the duties levied on some
of the principal classes of merchandise and payable by

Article.	Englishmen.		Aliens.	
	Custom.	Subsidy.	Custom.	Subsidy.
Wool,[1] per sack [2] . . .	6s. 8d.	33s. 4d.	10s.	66s. 8d.
Woolfells,[1] per 240 . .	6s. 8d.	33s. 4d.	10s.	66s. 8d.
Hides,[1] per last . . .	13s. 4d.	66s. 8d.	20s.	73s. 4d.
Wine, per tun	nil	3s.	2s.	3s.
Sweet wines, per tun . .	nil	3s.	2s.	6s.
Tin, per £ value . . .	nil	1s.	3d.	2s.
Other goods,[3] per £ value	nil	1s.	3d.	1s.

Englishmen and foreigners respectively at the beginning
of the reign. The subject is a somewhat obscure one,
and authorities are contradictory on certain points. The
customs are taken from Arnold's *Chronicle*,[4] where they

[1] Staple articles: in their case ' Englishmen ' means members of the
Staple, and ' Aliens ' includes such Englishmen as exported cargoes of
wool, &c., to the Mediterranean.
[2] A sack of wool contained 14 tods, each of 28 lb. weight, or 392 lb. in
all (*Lansd. MSS.*, 152, f. 239).
[3] Excluding cloth. Cloth duties are given separately below.
[4] 1811 ed., pp. 193–6.

are included in a list of which the exact date is not given.[1]
Since, however, the customs were practically invariable,
the point is not one of great importance. The subsidies
are those granted by the Parliament of 1485.[2] They
remained in force during the king's life, with certain
modifications due to political exigencies.

The wool duties were on exports only and the wine
duties on imports only. The poundage was levied on
exports as well as imports. The following goods were
exempted from paying poundage : woollen cloth exported by Englishmen ; wool, woolfells and hides
exported (taxed by the special wool duties) ; corn, flour,
fish, flesh, bestall,[3] and wine imported ; and victuals
exported for the garrison of Calais. Goods were valued
for poundage on their original cost, on the oath of the
merchant or his servant, and fraudulent declaration was
punished by forfeiture.

The wool duties were by far the heaviest in amount,
and, to lighten the excessive strain on the capital resources
of the merchant, it was provided that half the duty
should be paid within six months after shipment, and
the other half within twelve months. If the wool were
lost at sea, by wreck, piracy, or war, a similar quantity
might be shipped duty free.

By the Act of 1485 which granted the subsidies for
the reign, the Hanse merchants, who had hitherto been
exempt from paying the wine subsidy, were specially
included as being liable to that duty ; but their other
existing privileges, which were considerable, were continued unaffected. By another Act it was provided that
if a foreigner had become a naturalized Englishman he

---

[1] On internal evidence it is probably slightly before the time of
Henry VII.   [2] *Rolls of Parliament*, vi. 269, 270.   [3] Live animals.

should nevertheless continue to pay duties as a foreigner. On the other hand, to foster English shipping it was laid down that if an Englishman shipped his goods in a 'carryke or galley', that is, in a foreign ship, he must pay duties on the foreign scale. A study of these duties shows how great a measure of protection was afforded to English trade.

One of the most important of the colonies of foreign merchants settled in England was the London branch of the Hanseatic League. This, the greatest mercantile corporation in history, originated, like its smaller counterparts in England, in the association of merchants from various German towns for the purpose of mutual protection and co-operation while trading to foreign countries. After many vicissitudes, it attained in the fourteenth century to the status of a sovereign power, maintaining a formidable fleet and waging wars with the northern nations in defence of its interests. The London 'factory' was one of its largest oversea branches, and, during the fifteenth century, saw its pre-eminence threatened by the gradual growth of native mercantile enterprise, as evidenced by the rise of the Merchant Adventurers. The rivalry thus engendered was intense, but the Hanse merchants were able to take advantage of the internal dissensions in England, and a long period of privateering and reprisal was ended by an agreement which they extorted from Edward IV. In 1473 and 1474 treaties were signed by which the rights of the Hansa to trade in England under more advantageous terms than other foreigners, and even, in certain cases, than Englishmen, were recognized. Their group of warehouses and dwelling-places in the Steelyard, 'commonly called Guildhall Theutonicorum', was also secured to them in perpetuity, under the jurisdiction of officers appointed by themselves.[1]

As manufactured woollen goods formed a principal item of their business, it is illustrative to give in detail a list of the duties on those and other articles, in which their privileged position is apparent : [2]

Article.	Englishmen.		Spaniards.		Hansa Mchts.		Other Aliens.	
	Custom	Subsidy	Custom	Subsidy	Custom	Subsidy	Custom	Subsidy
Cloth, without 'greyn', per cloth	14d.	nil	14d.	nil	12d.	nil	33d.	12d.
Cloth, half 'greyned'	21d.	nil	21d.	nil	18d.	nil	49d.	12d.
Cloth 'in greyn' .	28d.	nil	28d.	nil	24d.	nil	66d.	12d.
Single worsted, per piece	1d.	1d.	1d.	1d.	1d.	1d.	1½d.	12d.
Double worsted, per piece	2d.	1d.	2d.	1d.	2d.	1d.	3d.	12d.
Every bed, single worsted	5d.	1d.	5d.	1d.	5d.	1d.	7½d.	12d.
Every bed, double worsted	9d.	1d.	9d.	1d.	9d.	1d.	13½d.	12d.
Wax, per cwt. . .	12d.	nil	12d.	nil	12d.	nil	12d.	12d.
Wines, per tun . .	nil	36d.	24d.	36d.	24d.	nil	24d.	36d.

It will be seen that, although the Spaniards received very nearly equal treatment with Englishmen, the Hansa had in nearly every case more advantageous terms, and was thus enabled to sell its goods at a lower price or at a better profit than native merchants. It must be borne in mind also that the trade in cloth with Spain was comparatively small.

With their position thus strengthened, the members of the Hanseatic League began to oust English traders

[1] *Foedera*, xi. 793–803.
[2] Arnold's *Chronicle*, pp. 193–6. But compare the details of Hanse privileges in 1552 (*inf.* p. 167). There is no evidence that any alteration was made in the duties, and Arnold's figures must therefore be received with caution.

from the Baltic, the German ports, Scandinavia, and even Iceland. The English traffic with the last-mentioned country was further threatened with utter extinction by a quarrel with the King of Denmark, who forbade Englishmen to resort thither, although the prohibition was not made entirely effective.

On the accession of Henry VII public opinion demanded that he should diminish the privileges of the Hansa, wrung, as they had been, from Edward IV at a time when England was weak from a protracted civil war, and certain, if unchecked, seriously to hinder the expansion of native trade. He was unable, however, to denounce the treaty of 1473-4, as he dared not risk open war with a maritime power which could retaliate by assisting his numerous enemies to invade his realm. He therefore adopted a policy which, while ostensibly upholding its legal rights, sought every opportunity to nullify them in practice in favour of his own subjects. Accordingly, in the first year of his reign, in spite of protests, he granted a charter to the Hansa, renewing its privileges as secured by the treaty.[1] The settlement of the Iceland dispute was next effected. In 1489 Henry dispatched ambassadors to Denmark who, in the following year, concluded a treaty with that country, by which peace was restored, trade was resumed on its former basis, and the prohibition of English voyages to Iceland was removed.[2]

This was a blow at the Hansa of which it could not legitimately complain, although it abolished at a stroke its threatened supremacy in the fish trade, which, in pre-Reformation days, was relatively much more important than it has since become. It was

---

[1] *Harl. MSS.*, 306, f. 82.   [2] *Foedera*, xii, pp. 374 and 381.

followed up by a series of annoyances in the matter of
the interpretation of treaties and customs laws. The
Easterlings [1] retaliated with restrictions on English trade
with Prussia. A diet was held to adjust differences at
Antwerp in 1491. A long list of grievances against the
English administration was presented, which may be
taken as illustrative of the policy pursued towards the
Hansa at all times when there was no special reason to
desire its goodwill. Ships and goods, it was alleged,
were robbed in an English port; Hanse vessels were
arrested for shipping cloth to Antwerp and for exporting
unwrought cloths; the Act of Parliament granting subsidies was interpreted as overriding the treaty privileges
of the League; the Lord Mayor arbitrarily fixed prices
in London, and was guilty of other unjust practices;
the Hansa suffered under the Navigation Acts prohibiting the import of Bordeaux wine and Toulouse
woad in other than English ships; unlawful customs
were exacted on certain articles, and the import of
others was forbidden; the privileged duty rates were
only allowed on goods coming from the Hanse towns,
full duties being exacted on goods from other countries;
the customs officers overestimated the value of Easterlings' goods and, when the duties were paid, delayed
clearance so that English merchants might be first
in the market on the other side; arbitrary charges
were made for convoy, the Easterlings being forced
to pay although they had not asked for protection;
and Hanse vessels unlading at Hull were forced to take
in cargoes at the same place, although frequently such
cloths as they wanted were not obtainable there.[2]

[1] The merchants of the Hansa were commonly called Easterlings in
England, and their London dépôt was known as the Steelyard.
[2] *Cologne Archives*, printed in Schanz, ii. 397.

The above practices were plainly unjust, but were of such a nature, proceeding as they did from the universal ill will of all grades of officials and underlings, that only the strongest and most determined of governments could have put them down. That of Henry VII had no desire to exert itself in this direction, and undoubtedly connived at the oppression. The only outcome of the diet was a formal reaffirmation of the treaty of 1474, with a mutual promise of better conduct and a provision for settling damages and stopping piracy.

During the quarrel with Margaret of Burgundy, in 1493, when all trade with the Low Countries was prohibited, the Steelyard merchants were forced to deposit £20,000 as security for their observance of the order.[1] At this time they were so intensely unpopular in London that it was unsafe for a German to walk in the streets alone. A rumour was spread that they were continuing to trade with Flemish ports in spite of the prohibition, and popular hatred rose to boiling-over point. A mob of the unemployed and discontented gathered with the intention of sacking the rich warehouses in the Steelyard. The Easterlings defended themselves bravely, and were partially successful in beating off the assault, although they afterwards claimed that much damage had been done. While the issue was still in doubt the Lord Mayor assembled the magistrates and officers of the city ; and, at the approach of the forces of order, the rioters fled. About eighty apprentices and workmen were captured and locked up in the Tower. They were all subsequently released.

Commercial hostilities continued on both sides, and were the subject of renewed diets at Bruges in 1497

[1] Hall's *Chronicle*, 1809 ed., pp. 467-8.

and 1499.[1] The Hansa brought forward similar grievances to those already enumerated. They complained, in addition, of being subjected to the oppressive jurisdiction of the Admiral's Court, which at that time took cognizance of all marine cases. They also claimed damages for the riot of 1493 and for various piracies. The English retaliated by putting in a much larger bill of damages, and asserted that they had been expelled from the Hanse towns, and that their house at Danzig had been confiscated. The English had more to gain than to lose by the continuance of bad relations, for their interests in the Baltic were not nearly so extensive as those of the Hansa in England. Henry held firm in his contention that legislation, such as that affecting the import of Bordeaux wine and Cologne silk and the export of cloth, was binding on all merchants resorting to England, special privileges notwithstanding. Further than this he did not care to go. The English merchants would have been glad to see him expel once and for all the tenants of the Steelyard, but he never liked to commit himself to a position from which there was no retreat ; and he could not forget that the Hansa, driven to desperation, would be a formidable enemy. He had done enough to set English North Sea traffic on its legs ; and the continued prosperity of the Merchant Adventurers is no bad testimonial to the soundness of his cautious policy.

The Spanish and Italian merchants in London were less unpopular than the Easterlings, and received considerably better treatment. Their competition was not

---

[1] *Cologne Archives, Acta Anglicana*, 1434–1521, ff. 166, 188–9 ; printed by Schanz, ii. 409, 419.

so vital to English interests, and there were political
reasons for dealing with them in a more civil manner.
Harshness and insolence could not be displayed towards
Spain, since the matrimonial alliance with that country
was the keynote of Henry's policy, to which mercantile
considerations had necessarily to be subordinate. However, by careful and persistent pressure, he was able to
place English trade to the south on as satisfactory a basis
as that to the east. He was certainly fortunate in the
choice which the Spanish sovereigns made of a representative in England.

Dr. de Puebla, who filled that office during the greater
part of his reign, was a mean and venal figure, amenable
alike to flattery, bullying, and bribes ; and the king was
able to read him like a book and play upon all his weak-
nesses in turn. His infidelity to his employers made it
easier for Henry to enforce the Navigation Laws, already
referred to, by which the Gascony trade was placed
exclusively in English hands ; and to strengthen the
position of English merchants in Spain by getting the
better of the bargain in most of the tariff negotiations.
De Puebla was so miserly that he lived in a disorderly
house for the sake of cheapness, and was well known as
seizing every opportunity of getting himself and his
servants fed at other people's expense. But in spite of
his conduct he enjoyed the confidence of Ferdinand and
Isabella, who were certainly not ignorant of his short-
comings. Their motive in continuing him in his post
seems to have been that, although Henry VII despised
the man, he had also a certain regard for him, and
occasionally confided intentions to him to which no one
else was made privy. The Spanish sovereigns even went
to the length of investing him with absolute judicial

powers over all the Spanish merchants in London. The
subjects of his jurisdiction hated him, and complained
bitterly that he used his authority to extort bribes.
They asserted further that he could have had the objectionable tariff dues lowered if he had chosen, but that
he had sold their interests to the English Government.[1]
Of the truth of the latter accusation there is no doubt.
In Henry's Privy Purse accounts there are entries of
payments to de Puebla of £66 15s. on two occasions,
and of £20 on another, it being stated that they were
'in reward'. Henry VII was not the man to disburse
such large sums unless in consideration of value received.
Judging by other entries, however, the bribing of ambassadors seems to have been a common practice.

To the merchants of the various Italian cities Henry
was generally gracious in his manner. The fierce competition which embittered relations in the north was
absent, for England was not yet ready to take a preponderating share in Mediterranean trade. On the other
hand, the Italians, and more particularly the Venetians,
were in a position to cut off the supply of certain articles
such as malmsey wines, spices, and other eastern goods,
which had almost become necessaries to England, and
which could not be obtained elsewhere. Friendly relations were established with Milan, and the Milanese
merchants were taken under the king's especial safe-
conduct. In 1488 the Venetians, Genoese, Florentines,
and Luccans petitioned that the export duties on wool
and tin might be diminished. Since there was then
little or no shipment of those articles to Italy in English
bottoms, the king granted their request, and made
alterations in the customs and subsidies amounting to

[1] *Spanish Cal.* i, pp. 161-7.

a net reduction of 10s. per sack on wool and 12d. per £ value on tin.[1]

The Venetian factory in London was never subjected to the treatment which the merchants of the Steelyard received. The organization of this Venetian colony has many points of interest. It consisted of numerous merchants who were permanently resident in England, and were under the governance of a consul whose judicial powers were far more extensive than those of a similar official at the present time. The English law then took no cognizance of the disputes and crimes of foreigners in cases in which no Englishman was implicated. Hence the Italians were left to maintain order among themselves in the same way as the Spaniards and the Germans ; and the Venetian consul represented among his compatriots the full majesty of their country's law. He was also responsible for exacting the numerous fines and dues which, in addition to the English customs, were constantly imposed and varied by the strict regulations of the Venetian Senate.

A very firm control was exercised by the home government, and the consul himself, although he had disciplinary powers over the merchants, was carefully supervised in his turn. A regular service of couriers, travelling overland through Europe, maintained touch with the authorities in Venice, and the captains of the annual fleets of Flanders galleys were also charged with the duty of reporting on the affairs of the colony. In 1491, when it was suspected that certain of the merchants in London were covertly opposed to the policy of the Senate in maintaining a tariff war with Henry VII, the captain of the Flanders fleet was instructed to find out who the culprits were,

[1] *Foedera*, xii. 335.

and to report them in order that the Government might make a notable example of their presumption.[1] The factory had its corporate responsibilities as well as its rights : when some prominent Venetians were captured by French pirates at Southampton, the London factory was commanded to pay their ransoms, a duty which a state less careful of the welfare of its citizens would have allowed to fall on their own families. The consuls were sometimes slack in exacting the payment of dues, such as the additional 5*d.* in the £ which merchants had to pay when they preferred to send their goods to Venice overland rather than by sea. To remedy this, supervisors were appointed to audit the consul's accounts and generally to keep him up to the mark.

In all these matters the strict discipline was apparent which permeated the whole state of Venice. It even extended to the control of the movements of privately owned merchant ships. A decree of 1497 gives detailed instructions to the captains of two such ships. They were to load wool, cloth, and tin in London ; the numbers of their crews and the freights they were to charge were specified ; they were to take no aliens' goods until all the goods of Venetians were shipped ; and they were to sail in close company on the voyage. The masters were enjoined to obey these instructions under a penalty of 500 ducats and ten years' suspension of their licences.[2]

The management of the Flanders galleys, which have been so frequently referred to, vividly illustrates the centralized system of Venice. This fleet, which sailed annually with fair regularity for more than two centuries, consisted of large, oared ships which were the property

---

[1] *Venetian Cal.* i, p. 206.   [2] *Venetian Cal.* i, p. 253-4.

of the State. When the time came for preparing for the voyage a public auction was held, at which the cargo space was disposed of to the highest bidders. The cargoes were thus the property of private merchants, although the conduct of the voyage was in the hands of the Government. The latter appointed the captains and gave instructions as to ports of call, the time to be spent at each, and similar matters. Each galley was manned by about 180 rowers, 30 archers, and numerous officers, merchants, servants, musicians, &c. After making calls at various Mediterranean ports the fleet proceeded to the Channel, where it divided, part going on to Flanders, and the remainder making for London, Sandwich, or, latterly, Southampton. Here the cargoes of Levant wines, silks, spices, and other eastern goods were disposed of, while the crews dispersed over the country to hawk the petty merchandises of their own which they were allowed to carry on board. Return freights of wool, cloth, hides, and tin were shipped ; the English portion of the fleet then awaited the Flanders section, and the voyage home was made in company. The usual time taken was twelve months or a little longer. The Flanders galleys first sailed in 1317, and their last voyage was in 1532 ; towards the end of this period the sailings became very irregular, owing to wars in Italy and the gradual decline of the old trade routes.[1]

Before the close of the epoch now under discussion the great geographical discoveries which ushered in the oceanic era of commerce began to make their effects evident. In the last decade of the fifteenth century Columbus discovered the West Indies, Cabot voyaged to North America, and Vasco da Gama arrived at Calicut

[1] For details on this subject see *Venetian Calendar*, vol. i and Preface.

after the first passage round the Cape of Good Hope
recorded in modern history. The Spanish discoveries
poured into Europe a stream of the precious metals
which upset the economic arrangements of every country,
and, by creating a period of industrial unrest, broke up
the old, stagnant organizations of the Middle Ages, and
released a flood of energy which altered the face of the
world. The Portuguese voyages to India soon proved
that the sea route was far superior to the overland
system of trading with the East, by which the Italian
cities had risen to greatness. The western and northern
nations, with free access to the Atlantic, were now the
nations of the future; and the Mediterranean, which
had for ages been the centre of civilization, began to
decline. It is one of the ironies of history that Genoa
and Venice owe their decay in large part to the achievements of their own offspring, Columbus and Cabot.

CHAPTER III

THE CABOT VOYAGES—JOHN CABOT, 1497 AND 1498

THE subject of the Cabot voyages is one of the most puzzling in history, ranking indeed with the identity of Shakespeare as a battle-ground for the exponents of conflicting theories. The trouble arises from the fact that, while John and Sebastian Cabot actually lived and performed important discoveries in the dim days of England's awakening from the sleep of mediaeval ignorance, few of their contemporaries felt sufficient interest in their exploits to write down a clear account of them for the benefit of posterity. Consequently the contemporary records are vague, ambiguous, and wofully incomplete, leaving (when purged of all uncertainties) little more of absolute truth than that John Cabot made two voyages across the Atlantic in 1497 and 1498, discovering some part of what is now British North America in the course of the first of them.

The progress of discovery in the sixteenth century produced numerous historians to narrate its annals. These men, living for the most part in Spain and Italy, had to turn for their information, in default of access to State archives, to such survivors of the exploits themselves as they were able to get into touch with. John Cabot had died soon after his great discovery, and, since his men were for the most part English, not one of them came in contact with any of the historians of southern Europe. The latter had therefore to seek information

from Sebastian Cabot, his second son, who entered the
service of Spain in 1512, lived in that country for five
and thirty years, and returned to pass the last decade
of his life in England, dying at a great age in 1557.
Sebastian Cabot, then, not only moulded the foreign
version of his story, but also in England was the sole
link between the late fifteenth century, when men of
letters took no interest in ocean voyages, and the mid-
sixteenth, when the country was beginning to realize
that her future lay upon the water. Thus the first
'expansionist' writer in England, Richard Eden, sat at
Sebastian's feet and drank in his stories of ancient discovery, which in this way secured acceptance as the
whole truth and nothing but the truth until the sceptical
nineteenth century began to institute a more searching
inquiry.

Sebastian Cabot was a vain egoist, fond of giving vent
to mysterious, bombastic utterances containing a maximum of self-praise and a minimum of hard fact. So,
when appealed to by the historians for information on
North American explorations, he said nothing of his
father's two voyages of 1497 and 1498, in which he may
have taken part, and the details of which he must have
been familiar with, but described instead a subsequent
expedition, which he had himself commanded, in search
of a north-west passage round America to Asia. The
sixteenth-century histories therefore contain *no mention*
of John Cabot, and the accounts found therein *have no
bearing whatever* on his two voyages.[1] A recognition of
this fact is essential because it has been very generally
believed that there were only two Cabot voyages, whereas
there were actually three ; and that Sebastian, in describ-

[1] An exception must be made of a short extract in Hakluyt.

ing himself as commander of a north-western expedition, was talking of the original discovery in 1497 or of the following voyage in 1498, and taking the credit of them to himself. In reality, Sebastian Cabot was telling the truth in describing his own voyage, and merely suppressing the truth in saying nothing of his father's. In other words, he was not so great a liar as he has been painted.

Turning first to John Cabot's discovery of North America, by him thought to be eastern Asia, in 1497, and his second voyage to the same region in 1498, it will be convenient first to state the sources of information, and afterwards to examine the conclusions to which they lead.

On March 5, 1496, Letters Patent were granted to the Cabot family by Henry VII, to the following effect :

Permission to John Cabottus and to Ludovicus, Sebastianus, and Sanctus his sons to take five ships at their own charges, to navigate in any seas to the east, north, or west, and to occupy and possess any new found lands hitherto unvisited by Christians. They were to voyage only from and to the port of Bristol, and were to be exempt from the payment of customs on goods brought from the new lands. No other subjects of the king were to trade to the new lands without licence from the Cabots. In return for these privileges one-fifth of all profits were to be paid to the king.

News of the project reached the ears of de Puebla, the Spanish ambassador in England, who transmitted it to his sovereigns. His letter to them is lost, but their reply, dated March 28, 1496, was as follows :

' You write that a person like Columbus has come to England for the purpose of persuading the king to enter into an undertaking similar to that of the Indies, without prejudice to Spain and Portugal. He is quite at liberty. But we believe that the undertaking was thrown in the way of the King of England by the King of France with the premeditated intention of distracting him from his other business. Take care that the King of England be not deceived on this or in any other matter. The French will try as hard as they can to lead him into such undertakings, but they are very uncertain enter- prises, and must not be gone into at present. Besides, they cannot be executed without prejudice to us and to the King of Portugal.' [1]

The remainder of 1496 was consumed in preparations or, less probably, an unsuccessful voyage was made in that year. In any case, John Cabot set out in 1497, found land on the other side of the ocean, and was back by the beginning of August. The following letters describe the voyage :

Lorenzo Pasqualigo to his brothers in Venice, August 23, 1497.

' The Venetian, our countryman, who went with a ship from Bristol in quest of new islands, is returned, and says that 700 leagues hence he discovered land, the territory of the Grand Cham. He coasted for 300 leagues and landed ; saw no human beings, but he has brought hither to the king certain snares which had been set to catch game, and a needle for making nets ; he also found some felled trees, wherefore he supposed that there were inhabitants, and returned to his ship in alarm.

' He was three months on the voyage, and on his return he saw two islands to starboard, but would not land, time being precious as he was short of provisions. He says that the tides are slack and do not flow as they do here. The King of England is much pleased with this intelligence.

---

[1] *Spanish Cal.* i, p. 128.

'The King has promised that in the spring our countryman shall have ten ships, armed to his order, and at his
request has conceded him all the prisoners, except such
as are confined for high treason, to man his fleet. The
King has also given him money wherewith to amuse himself till then, and he is now at Bristol with his wife, who
is also Venetian, and with his sons; his name is Zuan
Cabot, and he is styled the Great Admiral. Vast honour
is paid him; he dresses in silk, and these English run
after him like mad people, so that he can enlist as many
of them as he pleases, and a number of our own rogues
besides.

'The discoverer of these places planted on his new
found land a large cross, with one flag of England and
another of S. Mark, by reason of his being a Venetian,
so that our banner has floated very far afield.

'London, 23rd August, 1497.' [1]

Raimondo de Soncino to the Duke of Milan, August
24, 1497.

'. . . Also some months ago His Majesty sent out
a Venetian, who is a very good mariner, and has good
skill in discovering new islands, and he has returned safe,
and has found two very large and fertile new islands;
having likewise discovered the seven cities, four hundred
leagues from England, on a western passage. This next
spring, his majesty means to send him with 15 to 20
ships.' [2]

Raimondo de Soncino to the Duke of Milan, December
18, 1497. From the State Archives of Milan. Printed
for the first time in English in *Narrative and Critical
History of America*, edited by Justin Winsor, Cambridge,
Mass., 1886, vol. iii. The Cabot section is by Charles
Deane, F.S.A.

[1] *Venetian Cal.* i, p. 262.   [2] Ibid., p. 260.

' Most illustrious and excellent my lord :

' Perhaps among your Excellency's many occupations, it may not displease you to learn how his Majesty
here has won a part of Asia without a stroke of the sword.
There is in this Kingdom a Venetian fellow, master
John Caboto by name, of a fine mind, greatly skilled in
navigation, who seeing that those most serene kings, first
he of Portugal, then the one of Spain, have occupied
unknown islands, determined to make a like acquisition
for his Majesty aforesaid. And having obtained royal
grants that he should have the usufruct of all that he
should discover, provided that the ownership of the same
is reserved to the crown, with a small ship and 18 persons
he committed himself to fortune ; and having set out
from Bristol, a western port of this kingdom, and passed
the western limits of Hibernia, and then standing to the
northward he began to steer eastward (sic), having (after
a few days) the north star on his right hand ; and having
wandered about considerably, at last he fell in with
terra firma, where, having planted the royal banner, and
taken possession on behalf of this king, and taken certain
tokens, he has returned thence. The said Master John,
as being foreign-born and poor, would not be believed,
if his comrades, who are almost all Englishmen and from
Bristol, did not testify that what he says is true. This
Master John has the description of the world in a chart,
and also in a solid globe which he has made, and he (or
the chart and the globe) shows where he landed, and
that going towards the east (sic) he passed considerably
beyond the country of the Tanais. And they say that
it is a very good and temperate country, and they think
that Brasil wood and silks grow there ; and they affirm
that the sea is covered with fishes, which are caught not
only with the net, but with baskets, a stone being tied
in them in order that the baskets may sink in the water.
And this I heard the said master John relate, and the
aforesaid Englishmen his comrades say they will bring
so many fishes that the kingdom will no longer have

need of Iceland, from which country there comes a great
store of fish called stockfish. But Master John has set
his mind on something greater ; for he expects to go
further on towards the East (Levant), from that place
already occupied, constantly hugging the shore, until he
shall be over against an island, by him called Cipango,
situated in the equinoctial region, where he thinks all
the spices of the world, and also the precious stones,
originate ; and he says that in former times he was at
Mecca, whither spices are brought by caravans from
distant countries, and that those who brought them, on
being asked where the said spices grow, answered that
they do not know, but that other caravans came to their
homes with this merchandise from distant countries, and
these again say that they are brought to them from
other remote regions. And he argues thus—that if the
Orientals affirmed to the southerners that these things
came from a distance from them, and so from hand to
hand, presupposing the rotundity of the earth, it must
be that the last ones get them at the north towards the
west, and he said it in such a way that, having nothing
to gain or lose by it, I too believe it, and what is more,
the King here, who is wise and not lavish, likewise puts
some faith in him ; for since his return he has made
good provision for him, as the same Master John tells
me. And it is said that, in the spring, his Majesty
aforenamed will fit out some ships, and will besides give
him all the convicts, that they will go to that country
to make a colony, by means of which they hope to
establish in London a greater storehouse of spices than
there is in Alexandria ; and the chief men of the enterprise are of Bristol, great sailors, who, now that they
know where to go, say that it is not a voyage of more
than fifteen days, nor do they ever have storms after
they get away from Hibernia. I have also talked with
a Burgundian, a comrade of Master John's, who con-
firms everything, and wishes to return thither because
the Admiral (for so Master John already entitles himself)

has given him an island ; and he has given another
one to a barber of his from Castiglione of Genoa, and
both of them regard themselves as counts, nor does my
Lord the Admiral esteem himself anything less than
a Prince. I think that with this expedition there will
go several poor Italian monks, who have all been promised
bishoprics. And, as I have become a friend of the
Admiral's, if I wished to go thither I should get an
archbishopric. I humbly commend myself,

' Your Excellency's

' Very humble servant,

Raimundus.'

The next two letters mainly concern the second voyage,
that of 1498 :

Pedro de Ayala to Ferdinand and Isabella, July 25,
1498.

' I think your Majesties have already heard that the
King of England has equipped a fleet in order to discover certain islands and continents which he was informed some people from Bristol, who manned a few
ships for the same purpose last year, had found. I have
seen the map which the discoverer has made, who is
another Genoese like Columbus, and who has been in
Seville and Lisbon asking assistance for his discoveries.
The people of Bristol have, for the last seven years,
sent out every year two, three or four light ships (*cara-
velas*) in search of the island of Brasil and the seven
cities, according to the fancy of this Genoese. The
King determined to send out ships because, the year
before, they brought certain news that they found land.
His fleet consisted of five vessels, which carried provisions for one year. It is said that one of them, in which
one Friar Buil went, has returned to Ireland in great
distress, the ship being much damaged. The Genoese
has continued his voyage. I have seen, on a chart, the
direction they took and the distance they sailed ; and

I think that what they have found, or what they are in search of, is what your Highnesses already possess. It is expected that they will be back in the month of September. I write this because the King of England has often spoken to me on this subject, and he thinks that your Highnesses will take great interest in it. I think it is not further distant than 400 leagues. I told him that, in my opinion, the land was already in the possession of your Majesties, but though I gave him my reasons, he did not like them. I believe that your Highnesses are already informed of this matter, and I do not now send the chart or *mapa mundi* which that man has made, and which, according to my opinion, is false, since it makes it appear that the land in question was not the said islands.'[1]

De Puebla to Ferdinand and Isabella, July 25 (?), 1498. Printed in the Hakluyt Society's *Journal of Columbus,* 1893.

'The King of England sent five armed ships with another Genoese like Columbus to search for the island of Brasil and others near it. They were victualled for a year. They say that they will be back in September. By the direction they take, the land they seek must be the possession of your Highnesses. The King has sometimes spoken to me about it, and seems to take a very great interest in it. I believe that the distance from here is not 400 leagues.'

A second charter, granted on February 2, 1498, also bears upon the second voyage :

Petition of ' John Kabotto, Venetian,' for a charter in the following terms, which was accordingly granted : Authority and power to John Cabot ' that he by him, his deputie, or deputies sufficient ' may take six ships, up to 200 tons burden, and voyage to ' the lande and

---

[1] *Spanish Cal.* i, pp. 176-7.

isles of late founde by the seid John'. All subjects of
the King to give every assistance in their power to Cabot
for the furtherance of the enterprise.

The successful return of John Cabot in 1497 has left
some traces in the records of official business :

Grant from the Privy Purse of Henry VII, August 10,
1497, 'To him who found the New Isle, £10'.[1]

Pension grant of £20 per annum to John Cabot,
December 13, 1497.

'Henry by the grace of God, etc. to John, Cardinal
Archbishop of Canterbury etc., Our Chancellor, greeting.
We let you wit that we, for certain considerations us
specially moving, have given and granted unto our well-
beloved John Calbot of the parts of Venice an annuity
or annual rent of £20 sterling, to be had and yearly
perceived from the Feast of the Annunciation of Our
Lady last past, during our pleasure, of our customs and
subsidies coming and growing in our port of Bristol, by
the hands of our customers there for the time being,
at Michaelmas and Easter, by even portions. Wherefore we will and charge you that under our Great Seal
ye do make thereupon our letters patent in good and
effectual form. Given under our Privy Seal, at our
palace of Westminster, the 13th day of December, the
13th year of our Reign.'[2]

Together with this may be taken the authorization for
the immediate payment of the pension, which would
seem to have been delayed, dated February 22, 1498.[3]
Both these documents are printed by Mr. C. R. Beazley
in his *John and Sebastian Cabot* (1898).

Memoranda of loans of £20 to Launcelot Thirkill of
London, 'going towards the new island', March 22,

---

[1] *Add. MSS.*, 7099, f. 41.
[2] R. O., *Privy Seals*, Dec. 13, 13 Hen. VII, No. 40.
[3] R. O., *Warrants for Issues*, 13 Hen. VII.

1498 ; £30 to Thomas Bradley and Launcelot Thirkill, 'going to the New Isle', April 1, 1498 ; and 40 shillings and five pence to John Carter, ' going to the new isle '.[1]

Launcelot Thirkill's name appears again in a document of 1501, which shows that he returned safely from this voyage (the second), if indeed he actually performed it.

In this category also falls the important discovery made in 1897 among the Westminster Chapter Archives,[2] consisting of the accounts of the Customers of Bristol for the years 1497–8 and 1498–9. These accounts show that John Cabot's pension of £20 was paid during the years named. He is mentioned by name, and the customers deduct the amount of the pension from the total receipts which they hand over to the Exchequer officers.

A manuscript chronicle, of unknown authorship, in the British Museum,[3] contains a reference to the second voyage, ostensibly written before its return :

'This yere (1498) the Kyng at the besy request and supplicacion of a straunger Venisian, which by a chart made hymself expert in knowyng of the world, caused the Kyng to manne a ship w^t. vytaill and other necessaries for to seche an Iland wheryn the said straunger surmysed to be grete comodities. W^t which ship by the Kyng's grace so rygged went iij or iiij moo owte of Bristowe, the said straunger beyng conditor of the said fleete, wheryn divers m'chants as well of London as Bristow aventured goods and sleight m'chandises, which dep'ted from the west cuntrey in the begynnyng of somer but to this p'sent moneth came nevir knowledge of their exployt.'

[1] Add. MSS., 7099, f. 45.
[2] Chapter Muniments, 12243. Printed in facsimile as The Cabot Roll, Bristol, 1897, edited by A. E. Hudd.
[3] Cotton MSS., Vitell. A. xvi.

Stow and Hakluyt both quote from a manuscript
chronicle, then in the possession of the former, but now
lost. Hakluyt says it was written by Robert Fabyan.
Stow's version (1615 edition, p. 481), almost identical
with Hakluyt's except as regards the name of the explorer,
runs thus :

'1498, an. reg. 14. This yeere one Sebastian Gabato,
a Genoa's sonne, borne in Bristow, professing himself to
be expert in knowledge of the circuit of the world and
islands of the same, as by his charts and other reasonable
demonstrations he showed, caused the King to man and
victual a ship at Bristow to search for an Iland, which
he knew to be replenished with commodities. In the
ship divers merchants of London adventured small stocks,
and in the company of this ship, sayled also out of
Bristow three or foure smal shippes fraught with sleight
and grosse wares, as. course cloth, caps, laces, points and
such other. . . .
'1502, ann. reg. 18. This yeere were brought unto
the King three men taken in the new found Ilands, by
Sebastian Gabato, before named, in anno 1498. These
men were clothed in beasts' skins, and eate raw flesh,
but spake such a language as no man could understand
them, of the which three men, two of them were seen
in ye King's court at Westminster two yeares after,
clothed like Englishmen, and could not be discerned
from Englishmen.'

Hakluyt's version adds at the end of the 1498 extract :
'And so departed from Bristow in the beginning of
May, of whom in this Maior's time returned no tidings';
and at the end of the 1502 extract : 'but as for speach,
I heard none of them utter one word'. (The Mayor
referred to was William Purchas, whose term of office
expired at the end of October 1498.) Hakluyt printed
this extract from the now lost Fabyan chronicle in

his *Divers Voyages* (1582), and again in his *Principal Navigations* (1599). The two versions differ in two respects : in *Divers Voyages* the name of John Cabot is omitted, he being simply designated ' a Venetian ' ; while the bringing of the savages to England is placed in the eighteenth year of Henry VII's reign instead of the fourteenth as in *Principal Navigations.* Stow's own extract, as has been seen, calls the explorer Sebastian Gabato. The variations were intentional rather than accidental, as it was the habit of both editors to amend their material where they considered it to be in error, without drawing attention to the fact. The truth probably is that Hakluyt had no warrant for his alteration of the date of the arrival of the savages, other than his ignorance of later voyages and consequent assumption that Cabot must have brought them. It is now known that other expeditions were made in the early years of the sixteenth century, and that these savages were most probably kidnapped by one of them, thus having nothing to do with the Cabots.

The final piece of evidence bearing on John Cabot is that contained in an inscription on a map of the world published in 1544, and attributed, with fair certainty, to Sebastian Cabot himself. An example of this map came to light during the nineteenth century, and is now at Paris. The inscription relating to the Cabots was translated by Hakluyt from a copy of the map which was in the possession of Queen Elizabeth at Westminster. Copies of it were numerous in England in Elizabeth's time.

' In the yere of our Lord 1497 [1494 in Paris copy], John Cabot a Venetian, and his sonne Sebastian (with an English fleet set out from Bristoll) discovered that land which no man before that time had attempted, on the 24th of June, about five of the clocke early in the morning. This land he called Prima Vista, that is to say, First seene, because as I suppose it was that part whereof they had the first sight from the sea. That Island which lieth out before the land, he called the Island of S. John on that occasion, as I thinke, because it was discovered on the day of John the Baptist. The inhabitants of this Island use to weare beastes skinnes and have them in as great estimation as we have our finest garments. In their warres they use bowes, arrowes, pikes, darts, woodden clubs, and slings. The soile is barren in some places, and yeeldeth little fruit, but it is full of white beares, and stagges farre greater then ours. It yeeldeth plenty of fish, and those very great, as seales, and those which commonly we call salmons : there are soles also above a yard in length : but especially there is great abundance of that kinde of fish which the savages call baccalaos. In the same Island also there breed hauks, but they are so blacke that they are very like to ravens, as also their partridges, and egles, which are in like sorte blacke.'

The two Letters Patent granted by Henry VII afford some information as to the Cabot family and the intentions of the king. Owing to their length and verbosity they have been merely summarized here, but they have been frequently printed *in extenso*. In the first of them occurs the only mention of the name of Sebastian Cabot in strictly contemporary documents (contemporary, that is, with the voyages). It has been deduced that, since Sebastian was evidently the second son and at least a year older than Sanctus, and since the name of a minor would not appear in such a charter, Sebastian must have been twenty-two years old at least in 1496. Another point to be noticed is that permission was given to sail to the east, the west, or the north, but not to the south. Henry VII was on friendly terms with both Spain and Portugal, and wished to remain so; he was therefore careful not to allow Cabot to trespass on their routes, although he was quite aware that the end in view—i. e. the discovery of a sea-passage to Asia—was identical with theirs. He was not prepared to risk a quarrel for an unachieved advantage, but was evidently ready to do so if a lucrative trade were proved to be possible; otherwise he would not have engaged in the adventure at all.

The second charter is evidently intended to supplement, but not to supersede, the first. It omits the provisions as to customs, monopoly, and payments to the king, and confines itself to the details of the second expedition. It is valuable as proving beyond doubt that John Cabot commanded on the first voyage, and was successful in finding land. There is no mention in it of any of his sons, and no other document for nearly fifty years associates Sebastian with John's discoveries, the next joint reference to the pair occurring in the map of 1544. This, however, is no proof that Sebastian did *not* sail on these expeditions, and the point must be regarded as doubtful.

It should be noted that the terms of the first charter are such that it holds good for an indefinite time, and that no new grant was really needed for making further voyages. Therefore the fact that no third charter exists does not preclude the possibility of voyages having taken place other than those of 1497 and 1498.

The six contemporary letters, all of them unknown until the latter half of the nineteenth century, are the most valuable authorities remaining for the deeds of John Cabot. The evidence they afford is of the highest class, since they are written by observant third parties, and not by the explorer or his sovereign for the purpose of glorifying their own achievements. In particular, the letters of Pasqualigo and Soncino, which give the greatest amount of information on the first voyage, represent the conclusions formed by intelligent bystanders with no personal interest in the affair, and writing with the sole object of giving useful news to the recipients. They are therefore free from the taint of possible bias and self-interest, which is inherent in the later statements of Sebastian Cabot, and any misstatements they contain are the result of ignorance rather than intention.

The Venetian colony in London was rich and numerous, and its members must naturally have taken a deep interest in the exploit of their countryman. Pasqualigo was an important member of it, and probably became personally acquainted with Cabot or some of his followers. His letter has an air of accuracy, and the details given, although meagre, are not fanciful, with the exception of the distances, which are probably loose statements of members of the crew. Considering that Cabot was only three months on the voyage, it is hardly possible that he could have coasted for 300 leagues.

There is a great contrast between the two letters of Soncino. The first, written soon after the arrival of Cabot in London, is evidently based on hearsay and rumour, and contains no fact of importance. The second dispatch of Soncino is a news-letter written several months after the return of the 1497 expedition, and shows that in the interim the writer has taken great pains to obtain full information on the subject. The letter is a model of clearness and businesslike arrangement. The writer gives authorities for his statements ;

he has talked with Cabot and with members of his crew ; he has listened to the explorer's demonstrations, probably in the presence of the king and the court; he gives some idea of Cabot's character and personality, and the amount of credence which should be paid to him ; and when he falls back on rumour he is careful to insert ' it is said '. He has evidently displayed such an intelligent interest that Cabot has offered him a place in the next expedition. Full value may therefore be assigned to the facts in his letter. When Soncino speaks of sailing to the east, he means of course the west. He had in mind that the new land was thought to be the Far East although reached by a western route.

The letter from Ferdinand and Isabella is useful as showing the jealousy of Spain at the projected enterprise even before it had started. The same sentiment is again strongly expressed in Pedro de Ayala's letter two years later, and, although it does not appear from the available documents that any official remonstrance was addressed to Henry VII, Spanish disapproval must, nevertheless, have had its share in causing the gradual abandonment of American enterprises in the early years of the sixteenth century.

Ayala's letter, written after the sailing of the second expedition, is the only one of the series which contains any positive facts as to that expedition. It has an unsatisfying air of vagueness and, as regards the first voyage, is not nearly so precise as Soncino's long account. This is partly due to the fact that the details of the matter were already known to the Spanish sovereigns, and there was thus no need to enter deeply into them. One point in the letter has been made the basis of a rather revolutionary theory as to the second expedition, namely, that John Cabot was in Seville and Lisbon during the winter of 1497-8, recruiting men for his second voyage. This theory is built upon the general statement that Cabot had sought assistance in those places. An interpretation which makes him do so in 1497-8 is hardly allowable. In the first place we know that he could get plenty of men in England, where also investors came forward readily and the greatest enthusiasm prevailed ; secondly, it is not likely that he would have trusted himself in Seville at that time, having regard to the feelings of the Spanish Government on the subject ; and thirdly, a winter voyage to the Peninsula was a risky undertaking if the traveller were pressed for time. In the then state of navigation he might easily be detained for weeks and months by bad weather ;[1] and John Cabot could not afford to risk the postponement of his expedition for a year, with its possible abandonment, or the appointment of another to command it in his stead. On the contrary, the natural and probable interpretation of the statement is that Cabot had sought a hearing for his plans in Spain and Portugal before coming to England ; and even at that, it is quite a ' by the way ' remark and lacks corroboration. The same may be said as to the caravels annually sent out from Bristol ; Ayala was not in England during the period referred to, and was probably repeating a piece of current gossip.

The few facts he relates of the 1498 voyage rest on surer ground, as having occurred under the writer's more immediate attention. The five ships are mentioned elsewhere, and that number is thus probably correct. The ' Friar Buil ' referred to was possibly a Spanish spy : it is

[1] See Chap. I, pp. 29-30.

singular that his name alone of all the adventurers is thought worthy of mention to the Spanish sovereigns. Unless such an obscure man was an agent of theirs, it is difficult to see what interest they could have had in hearing of him. The assertion that Cabot's charts were falsified entirely lacks confirmation, and there is no ground for believing it. Ayala was suspicious and prejudiced, and ready to impute dishonest intentions to England. It is noticeable that in affairs quite separate from this one he took up a more hostile attitude towards Henry VII than did his superior, de Puebla. He had a great admiration for Scotland, in which country he had been ambassador, and this may have engendered a corresponding hatred of England.

The information, such as it is, afforded by the rewards to John Cabot and the loans to his associates in the second expedition is, of necessity, absolutely trustworthy. The documents in question were written for immediate business purposes, with no idea of their ever being used to elucidate the story of the discoveries.

The unfinished account of the 1498 voyage, given in the anonymous British Museum chronicle, has evidently some near relationship to that contained in the lost Fabyan manuscript copied by Hakluyt and Stowe. It is probable that Fabyan based his account on the former chronicle, adding the note on the savages from his own knowledge, but not troubling to relate the fate of the 1498 voyage. This in itself gives ground for presuming that the expedition in question returned in safety without achieving any striking results. If none of the vessels ever came back, a possibility that has been suggested, Fabyan would hardly have refrained from commenting on such a sensational occurrence. As it is, he merely

records the fact that they had not returned by the end
of October 1498, and there leaves the matter. Existing
editions of Fabyan contain no reference to the Cabots.

The famous map of 1544, of which the only copy
now known to exist is in the Bibliothèque Nationale of
Paris, is generally agreed to be the work of Sebastian
Cabot, or at least, based on information supplied by him.
The inscriptions upon it, descriptive of various countries,
are in Latin or Spanish, the majority in both. Typo-
graphical considerations indicate that it was not printed
in Spain—the printer does not use the Spanish *tilde* over
the n—and Antwerp has been suggested as the most
likely place of origin. The inscription given above,
relating to the Cabot discovery, was translated by
Hakluyt from a similar map which he saw at Westminster,
and Hakluyt's translation agrees very closely with a
modern translation from the Paris map, showing that
they are from one and the same source. The voyage
described is obviously the first one, but the local colour
as to the natives and their habits must have been supplied
from later experiences, as the contemporary letters
expressly assert that John Cabot saw no inhabitants on
the first expedition. The date of the discovery is given
on the Paris map as MCCCCXCIIII (1494), but this
may be explained as a careless error for MCCCCXCVII,
due to bad writing. It should be noted that this inscription is the earliest authority for the statement that land
was sighted on June 24 at 5 a.m., and that the island of
St. John was discovered and named on the same day.
There seems to be no good reason why the statements
on the map should not be believed, other than that
they proceed from a tainted source. Sebastian Cabot's
reputation for veracity is certainly under a cloud, even

when he is acquitted of giving false information about his explorations. In other matters he undoubtedly lied freely and frequently.[1]

The ground being now cleared by a necessary, if tedious, appraisement of values, it is possible to relate what is known of John Cabot's voyages.

It had been owing to a mere accident that Christopher Columbus had not sailed under the English flag on his first epoch-making voyage to the west. In 1485, after vainly attempting to interest the sovereigns of Portugal and Spain in his ideas, he had dispatched his brother Bartholomew to England, to lay his plans before Henry VII. But Bartholomew Columbus had suffered disaster on his journey. After being robbed by pirates in the narrow seas, he was further delayed by sickness and poverty before being able to lay his brother's case before the king. When he was at length successful in doing so, Henry listened with sympathy and promised assistance, but, being preoccupied with other matters, he postponed the adventure until too late. When he did finally make up his mind to take the affair in hand, it was only to hear that Christopher Columbus had already sailed from Palos in the service of Ferdinand and Isabella.

Henry had missed a great chance, partly through his own fault, and must have realized his mistake when news began to spread through Europe of the discovery of rich islands on the western route to Cathay, as all men supposed the new land to be. It was considered at the English court a thing ' more divine than human ' to

[1] See Harrisse's *John and Sebastian Cabot* (1896) for an account of Sebastian's intrigues with Venice, and other discreditable affairs.

have reached the Far East by way of the west, and the anticipations of the advantages of the new discovery must have exceeded even the reality. Throughout the Middle Ages the imagination of all who were capable of thought had been stimulated by glowing accounts of the riches and wonders of the East. The experiences of Marco Polo and many another wanderer of lesser fame had been spread broadcast through Europe; such adventures lose nothing in the telling, and indeed the material civilization of Asia compared not unfavourably with that of mediaeval Christendom; hence to reach Cathay became the ambition of many a restless mind. The Venetians and the Genoese were content to trade with the Asiatic merchants who brought their goods overland to the ports of the Levant. The Portuguese navigators, excluded from the Mediterranean, pushed successively further and further down the coast of Africa in the hope of finding a way round it into the Indian Ocean. They had not yet succeeded when, in 1493, Columbus returned with his report of rich islands to the west, and it was universally believed that he had solved the problem in the simplest possible way.

To the western nations of Europe this news was more especially important, and so, when John Cabot petitioned Henry VII, three years later, for permission to make similar discoveries, he obtained a patent from that king without difficulty. Cabot was of Genoese birth, although a naturalized citizen of Venice, and he had been for some years settled at Bristol. He had taken part in the Venetian trade to the Levant, and had on one occasion travelled as far as Mecca. At that place, a busy centre of exchange for eastern goods, he questioned the merchants as to the source of the supply of spices, drugs,

perfumes, rare silks, and precious stones, in which they
dealt. They replied that these goods were transported
by successive caravans from a vast distance, and that they
themselves had never visited the countries that produced
them. This suggested to Cabot a similar train of reasoning to that of Columbus : it was evident that the long
land journey and the laborious transport and exchange
from hand to hand must immensely add to the original
cost of the produce which Europe valued so highly ;
great wealth was therefore in store for the man and the
country which should first find a practicable sea route
to the orient. Cabot, like Columbus, based his plans on
the sphericity of the earth, and came to the conclusion
that the shortest way to the east was by the west. It
is unknown whether it was in consequence of these ideas
that he came to England. It may well have been so,
for it was evidently of little use to urge such plans in
Venice. The Italian merchants stood to lose instead of
gaining by any alteration of the trade routes, and, moreover, could be cut off from access to the Atlantic at the
pleasure of the power which could block the straits of
Gibraltar. Whatever his reasons, John Cabot came to
Bristol, bringing his wife and family with him. In after
years his son Sebastian, when it suited him to make himself out an Englishman, claimed to have been born in
Bristol ; but as Sebastian cannot have been born later
than 1474, and John was not naturalized as a Venetian
till 1476, it is hardly possible that Sebastian's statement
was true. The year 1476, therefore, is the earliest possible date for John Cabot's arrival in Bristol, and the
probability is strong that he did not settle there for
several years after that.

Bristol was the largest seaport of the west of England,

and, in the fifteenth century, a most important branch
of its trade was with Iceland, whence the Bristol ships
fetched quantities of stockfish. It is possible that traditions of early Norse voyages to ' Vineland ' still lingered
in· northern regions and were picked up by the Bristol
sailors. There were other legends current of lands to
the west : the island of Brasil, marked on many mediaeval
maps ; the blissful isle of St. Brandan, actually supposed
to have been visited by a shadowy Irish saint of anti-
quity ; and the Seven Cities, said to have been founded
by Spanish bishops fleeing from the fury of invading
Moors when the Cross fell before the Crescent on the
banks of the Guadalete. Moved either by these traditions or by the new scientific reasonings of men like
Cabot, the Bristol merchants undoubtedly felt an interest
in the possibilities of the unexplored Atlantic. There
are rumours of their having sent out ships towards the
west before 1497, but unfortunately they rest on no
solid basis of proof.

Things were at this stage when, in the winter of
1495–6, Henry VII visited Bristol, and we may suppose
that John Cabot took the opportunity of petitioning the
king for a charter which should place the enterprise on
a more regular footing. On March 5, 1496, the patent
was drawn out, in the terms already described. For
reasons unknown, more than a year elapsed before John
Cabot started on his first recorded voyage. He set out
in the early summer of 1497 in a small ship with a crew
of eighteen men, mostly Englishmen of the port of
Bristol. In addition to Cabot, and possibly his sons,
there were among the crew two other foreigners, one
a Burgundian, probably a Netherlander, and the other
a Genoese. A document, generally known as the

Fust MS., and now destroyed, gave the name of Cabot's ship as the *Matthew*, and the dates of the voyage as May 2 (departure) and August 6 (return). Authorities are at variance as to the authenticity of the Fust MS. The use of the word ' America ' in a record ostensibly written several years before that name was first invented seems to brand it as an imposture, but it may have been written up in the form of a year-to-year chronicle several years after the date contained in it, and still have embodied true information. The dates given tally approximately with what is known from other evidence.

After leaving Bristol the explorers passed the south of Ireland, and then steered northwards for an indeterminable time—' a few days '—Cabot's intention apparently being to reach a certain parallel of latitude, and then to follow it westwards. He knew that the further north he went, the less would be the distance to be traversed, owing to the decreasing circumference of the earth and the general lie of the land of eastern Asia, which was roughly known. When he had made sufficient way to the north, he turned westwards, and, after considerable wandering, sighted land. The ' wandering ' may simply mean that he sailed westwards for a long time, or that he was diverted to the north or south. In any case the wording is so vague that the actual course cannot be even approximately laid down.

In the map of 1544 it is stated that the landfall was in the neighbourhood of Cape Breton, and that it was made on June 24 at 5 a.m. ; also, that an island near the land was visited on the same day and named the Island of St. John. The doubts cast on the authenticity of this inscription have already been considered. On the whole, Cape Breton seems the likeliest place for the

landfall, although the most learned authorities are hopelessly at variance on the point, some favouring Cape
Breton, others Newfoundland, and others Labrador.
With the knowledge at present available the problem
must be pronounced insoluble. The date, June 24, is
a little late, as it allows less than half the total duration
of the voyage for the coasting and return journey ; but
this is not impossible if the coasting was restricted and
the return was made with more favourable winds than
the outward passage. We know, from an absolutely
trustworthy source, that Cabot was back in London by
August 10, and thus probably at Bristol some days earlier.

The land discovered had a temperate climate. In
view of Sebastian Cabot's accounts, which have sometimes been read as applying to this voyage, it is important
to notice that no mention is made of ice or any extraordinary length of day, points which would certainly
have been remarked by Pasqualigo or Soncino, if they
had been narrated by the returning crew. An immense
quantity of fish was encountered off the coast.

After planting the flags of England and Venice at the
place where he first landed, John Cabot coasted for some
distance. Probably the 300 leagues of Pasqualigo's letter
is a mistake, being incompatible with the total duration
of the voyage. It has been suggested that ' leagues '
should read ' miles '. The direction of the coasting,
whether northwards or southwards, is likewise not stated.
Cabot saw signs of habitation, but no actual inhabitants ;
and doubtless he was not anxious to see any, for a crew
of eighteen all told would not furnish a landing party
with which he could confidently face all comers. This
first voyage was merely for the purpose of reconnoitring
and preparing the way for a greater enterprise. It was

a pity that the reconnaissance was not more thorough, for it might have saved much disappointment afterwards. As it was, Cabot was firmly convinced that he had reached the north-eastern coast of Asia, ' the territory of the Grand Cham ', which the Spaniards were thought to be on the track of, although they had not yet arrived there. However, provisions began to run short, and he turned his ship homewards, passing on the way two islands which he had not time to explore. He arrived at Bristol in the early days of August.

John Cabot travelled at once to London to lay his report before the king. He carried with him his charts and a globe with which to demonstrate his discoveries ; and he was so far successful in convincing the prudent and parsimonious monarch of the value of the new land that the latter made him an immediate grant of £10 from the Privy Purse (ten to twelve times as much in modern money), and later allotted him a pension of £20 a year. The royal sanction, if not a more substantial aid, was promised for a much larger expedition to sail in the following year for the purpose, not only of exploring, but also of founding colonies and trading posts. Cabot and his contemporaries were still under the impression that he had found the east of Asia. He admitted that he had only touched the fringe of the golden land, but he asserted that he had only to sail with a larger and better-found expedition, with provisions to last for a year's voyage, and to follow the coast westwards and southwards to the tropic region, to arrive at the wonderful island of Cipango,[1] the source of the world's supply

---

[1] Evidently Japan. 'Zipangu is an island in the eastern ocean, situated at the distance of about 1500 miles from the mainland or coast of Manji. It is of considerable size ; its inhabitants have fair complexions, are well

of spices and precious stones. He had a persuasive tongue, and his arguments were absolutely convincing to the minds of all who heard them, from the cool and calculating king to the hard-headed merchants of London, and still more to hot-blooded adventurers, whose ears already tingled with wondrous tales of the Spanish Indies. He was everywhere sought after and fêted. He dressed in silk and assumed the title of Admiral. In their own imagination he and all his men were princes and nobles ; to the surgeon of the *Matthew* he gave an island ; to a Burgundian among his crew he gave another.

From London, Cabot went back to Bristol, there to be lionized and to make preparations for the adventure of the following year. On February 3, 1498, the king issued a second patent, made out this time to John Cabot alone, without mention of his sons, empowering him to take six ships and pursue his discoveries on much the same terms as those of the first patent. It is not evident that the State contributed anything to this fleet beyond a cheap and convenient permission to take convicts from the gaols to do the hard work of the proposed colony. Most probably Henry VII was a shareholder in his

made, and are civilized in their manners. . . . They have gold in the greatest abundance, its sources being inexhaustible, but as the king does not allow of its being exported, few merchants visit the country, nor is it frequented by much shipping from other parts. To this circumstance we are to attribute the extraordinary richness of the sovereign's palace, according to what we are told by those who have access to the place. The entire roof is covered by a plating of gold, in the same manner as we cover houses, or more properly churches, with lead. The ceilings of the halls are of the same precious metal ; many of the apartments have small tables of pure gold, of considerable thickness ; and the windows also have golden ornaments. So vast indeed are the riches of the palace, that it is impossible to convey any idea of them. In this island there are pearls also, of a pink colour, round in shape, and of great size, equal in value to, or even exceeding in value, the white pearls.' *The Travels of Marco Polo*, Everyman's Library, pp. 323-4.

private capacity, as he seems to have been as much' convinced as any of his subjects of the profits that were to accrue.

But soon the king was to receive a significant hint of trouble from a quarter whence he doubtless expected it. Even before Cabot had obtained his first patent, in 1496, Spanish jealousy had been aroused at the prospect of a voyage to the west. De Puebla had evidently reported what was going forward to his sovereigns, and in their reply to him occurs the statement that such enterprises ' cannot be executed without prejudice to us and to the King of Portugal '. Evidently they were prepared to take their stand on the Bull of Alexander VI, which divided between Spain and Portugal all the undiscovered parts of the world, and which had been confirmed by the Treaty of Tordesillas between those two nations in 1494. Whether de Puebla communicated this protest to Henry or not we do not know. Probably he did not, as he always showed himself extremely anxious to curry favour with that monarch. But in 1498 Pedro de Ayala, another Spanish agent, was also in London, and to him the king frequently spoke of the new voyages in order to sound him as to the opinion of the Spanish court. De Ayala claimed stoutly that the lands which the English were trying to discover were already in the possession of Spain, and he gave his reasons, which, he says, the king did not like. Henry, however, could not afford to quarrel with Spain, and from this time forward he seemed to become half-hearted in his approval of western projects.

With regard to John Cabot's second voyage, only the intentions of the explorer and the circumstances of his start from Bristol are known. The former were as follows : Sailing with several ships laden with English manufactured goods—'coarse cloth, caps, laces, points, and such other'—he proposed to return to the land which he had discovered on the first voyage, and thence to follow the coast which, as he had observed, trended towards the south-west, until he arrived in the tropical latitudes. There he expected to find, over against the land, the rich island of Cipango—the island replenished with great commodities of the chronicles—and in it to establish, if not a colony in the true sense of the word, at least a permanent trading post. This is evidenced by the proposal to take several priests, and also the convicts, who would be useless on the voyage, but would do the hard work of planting a new settlement. The programme was naturally very distasteful to the Spaniards, since the position of Cipango, in John Cabot's ideas, must have been in the same latitude as their own discoveries, although lying further to the west.

Everything in the contemporary letters, and also in the chronicles, points to the fact that Cabot, in common with every other thinking man in 1497-8, had no suspicion of the existence of the separate continent now called America, and that he intended to make for the tropical region of the coast of eastern Asia. Indeed, it is inconceivable that he, a much-travelled man, who had experience of tropical climates and their products, should have sailed northwards to look for spices, unless we are to assume that he knew that America was not Asia and was consequently looking for a north-west passage. That assumption a careful reading of the evidence renders untenable. This matter of the intended destination of the second voyage is the point at which the commonly received versions of the Cabot problem go astray, the

accepted theory being that the second expedition was
an attempt to force a passage round the north of the
new continent and so into the Pacific. But it cannot
be too strongly emphasized that John Cabot had not
the remotest intention of sailing round the north of
what he took to be Asia, since such a course, if persisted
in, would have brought him, according to his charts,
back to the North Sea and the British Isles !

All preparations being complete, he sailed from Bristol
in the beginning of May 1498. He had with him his
own ship, manned and victualled, if the chroniclers are
to be believed, at the king's private expense, and three
or four smaller vessels fitted out by the merchants of
London and Bristol, some of whom had also been financed
from the Privy Purse. Pedro de Ayala states that the
fleet numbered five in all, and also reports, but only as
a rumour, that one of them put back to an Irish port in
consequence of damage, sustained presumably in a storm.
The ships were provisioned for a year, and Cabot expected
to be home again by September. In the outcome, however, nothing had been heard of him as late as the end
of October.

Here unfortunately our knowledge of John Cabot
leaves the realm of sober fact, and degenerates into mere
theory and speculation. History is totally silent as to
the progress of this voyage, launched with such a great
acclaim ; as to its vicissitudes, as to the date, place, and
circumstances of its ending, nothing whatever is known.
It is only through the cumulative effect of side-winds,
none of them absolutely conclusive, that it can be
deduced that Cabot's squadron reached the American
coast, and that he himself, with part at least of his men,
returned in safety.

First, as to his personal survival. This was always considered extremely doubtful until the discovery of the Bristol Customers' accounts for 1497–9, which prove beyond doubt that, until Michaelmas 1499, the annual pension of £20 was still being paid. It is conceivable of course, that the pension was being drawn by an accredited agent, his wife for example, so that there is no positive proof that he was in Bristol during that year. But it may, as a minimum, be confidently asserted that he was not known to be dead, since in that case no agent could have drawn the pension without obtaining fresh official papers. Hence, either Cabot returned in safety from the 1498 voyage, or else no word had been heard of his fleet for nearly eighteen months. The balance of probability is certainly in favour of the former alternative.

One of the persons to whom loans were granted from the Privy Purse was Launcelot Thirkill, of London, ' going towards the new island '. A later document shows this man to have been in England in 1501. Consequently, if he accompanied the fleet, as he evidently intended, some part of it must have returned in safety.

A still more probable testimony to the return of Cabot's expedition, and to its having coasted extensively on the other side of the Atlantic, is furnished by the map of the Spanish pilot, Juan de la Cosa, drawn up in the year 1500. It is a map of the world as known at the time, and includes a part of the east coast of North America, with flags marking the places visited by the English. The flags are intended to represent the English standard, and some of the names, although translated into Spanish, are such as English explorers might have given ; others are unintelligible. They are as follows, reading from south-west to north-east :

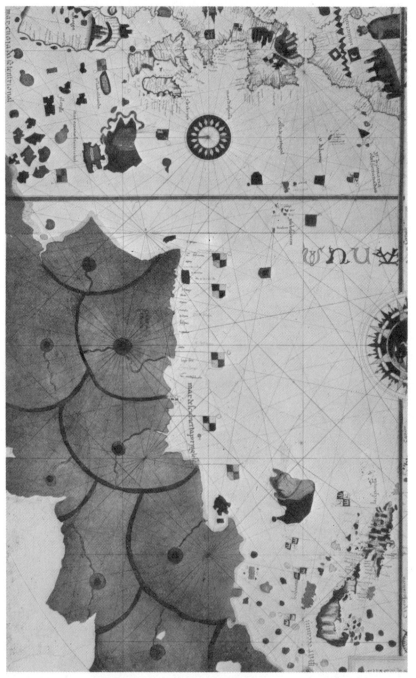

THE NORTH ATLANTIC.

From the map of Juan de la Cosa, 1500.   The earliest map showing English discoveries.

Mar descubierto por Yngleses, cavo descubierto, C. de
S. Jorge, lagofor, anfor, C. de S. Luzia, requilia, jusquei,
S. Luzia, C. de lisarto, menistre, argair, fonte, rio longo,
illa de la trenidat, S. Nicolas, Cavo de S. Johan, agron,
C. fastanatra, Cavo de Ynglaterra, S. Grigor, y verde.

The map is so unlike the real coastline that it is impossible to identify definitely any of the places mentioned.
In addition, there are no lines of latitude or longitude.
The most plausible interpretation is that 'Cavo de
Ynglaterra', the most northerly point marked on the
mainland, is Cape Race, and that the southernmost flag
represents a point on the coast of Virginia or Carolina,
possibly Cape Hatteras. However, this is mere guess-
work, as is shown by the divergent views taken by equally
competent authorities. The only indisputable information obtainable from the map is the fact that the English
did actually coast along a large part of the North
American littoral before the year 1500. It is practically
certain that the map embodies the geographical knowledge gained in John Cabot's second voyage, since the
amount of coasting shown is too extensive for the first
voyage, the southernmost English flag being placed more
than three-quarters of the entire distance down from
the Cabo de Ynglaterra to the point of Florida. The
only fact which weakens the value of the map's evidence
for the 1498 voyage is the possibility that it embodies
information from Sebastian Cabot's expedition, which, as
will be shown, probably took place in 1499. It is possible
that la Cosa had seen the charts of the latter when he
drew his map in 1500.

But the most illuminating light is thrown on the
voyage of 1498 by a careful reading of the descriptions
of Sebastian Cabot's adventure given in the next chapter.

These accounts indicate that Sebastian had grasped the great fact that the transatlantic land was a separate continent, altogether distinct from Asia. From whence did he derive his information ? Without reasonable doubt, from his father's voyage of 1498. It is practically certain, although definite proof is lacking, that John Cabot acted in accordance with his expressed intentions, and sailed westwards to his former landfall. Thence he turned to the south-west and followed the land towards the tropics, exploring the coast, and seeking eagerly for signs of the wealthy and civilized Asiatics whom he expected to find there. The islands of Columbus were considered as merely a half-way house on the route to Asia, and Cabot was confident that his newly-discovered coast would lead him far to the west of their position, which the king's instructions had doubtless enjoined him to avoid. It may be imagined, then, how his heart sank when day followed day and brought no sight of oriental shipping on the sea or cities on the land ; and when no inhabitants could be encountered save wandering bands of savages, who lived by the chase, and had nothing of value to exchange for the goods in his ships' holds. The coast, too, trended more and more to the southwards, taking him in the direction of the Spanish possessions and rendering illusory the hope of finding Cipango, for which there was evidently no room between them and it. Gradually Cabot must have realized that the new land was not a part of Asia, since it corresponded with none of the known facts about that continent ; and, with the realization, the purpose of his voyage was gone. To find a way to Asia by the west would necessitate the finding of a passage through this strange and desolate land, and, until that was effected, all hope of profitable trade had to be abandoned. Whether an attempt was made to discover such a passage, or whether the expedition sailed straight back to England, is unknown. In either case the result, as judged by the shareholders in the venture, was complete failure.

It is easy to understand how, after this great disappointment, involving the shattering of a lifetime's convictions, John Cabot had no heart for further voyages, but lived quietly at Bristol on the king's pension until death overtook him at the close of the fifteenth century.

Such is the theory of the 1498 voyage to which all the ascertained evidence points. It explains the silence of contemporary chroniclers, who did not think such a financial failure worthy of mention ; it explains the cessation of the interest of the London commercial world in transatlantic ventures; and it explains also the motives of Sebastian Cabot in the voyage which has now to be considered, and the meaning of his narrations, which have long been considered to be little more than a collection of impudent falsehoods.

CHAPTER IV

THE CABOT VOYAGES—SEBASTIAN CABOT, ? 1499

THE voyage of Sebastian Cabot is described in narratives of which the details were presumably furnished by himself, in the works of various historians of the sixteenth century. As in the previous chapter, the necessary extracts will be given first, followed by a consideration of the conclusions to which they lead. Many other authors, besides those quoted, mention Sebastian Cabot ; but, since they merely reproduce earlier accounts without providing any new evidence of their own, it is unnecessary to refer to them here.

Peter Martyr, in his *Decades of the New World*, of which the first part, containing the notice of Cabot,[1] was published at Alcala in 1516, says :

' These North Seas have been searched by one Sebastian Cabot, a Venetian borne. . . . Hee therefore furnished two ships in England at his owne charges, and first with 300 men directed his course so farre towards the North pole, that even in the moneth of July he found monstrous heapes of ice swimming in the sea, and in maner continuall daylight, yet saw he the land in that tract free from ice, which had been molten by the heat of the Sunne. Thus seeing such heapes of yce before him, hee was enforced to turne his sailes and follow the West, so coasting still by the shore, that he was thereby brought so farre into the South by reason of the land bending

---

[1] Hakluyt, vii. 150. All references to Hakluyt, unless otherwise stated, are to the edition in twelve volumes printed by Messrs. Maclehose for the Hakluyt Society in 1903. The above passage was taken by Hakluyt from Richard Eden's translation.

so much southwards, that it was there almost equall in latitude with the sea Fretum Herculeum, having the North pole elevate in maner in the same degree. He sailed likewise in this tract so farre towards the West, that hee had the Island of Cuba on his left hand, in maner in the same degree of longitude. As hee travailed by the coasts of this great land, (which he named Baccalaos), he saith that he found the like course of waters toward the West, but the same to runne more softly and gently then the swift waters which the Spaniards found in their navigations Southward. . . . Sebastian Cabot himselfe named these lands Baccalaos, because that in the seas thereabout hee found so great multitudes of certaine bigge fishes much like unto Tunies (which the inhabitants call Baccalaos) that they sometime stayed his shippes. He found also the people of those regions covered with beastes' skinnes, yet not without the use of reason. He also saith that there is great plentie of Beares in those regions, which use to eate fish. . . . Hee declareth further, that in many places of these regions he saw greate plentie of Copper among the inhabitants. Cabot is my very friend, whom I use familiarly, and delight to have him sometimes keepe mee company in mine owne house. For being called out of England by commandment of the Catholique King of Castile, after the death of King Henry the seventh of that name in England, he was made one of our councill and Assistants, as touching the affaires of the new Indies, looking for ships dayly to be furnished for him to discover the hid secret of Nature. Some of the Spaniards deny that Cabot was the first finder of the land of Baccalaos, and affirm that he went not so far westwards.'

Lopes de Gomara, *Historia General de las Indias*, 1554.[1]

' Sebastian Cabot was the first that brought any knowledge of this land for, being in England in the days of King Henry VII, he furnished two ships at his own

[1] Hakluyt, vii. 153.

charges or, as some say, at the King's, whom he persuaded
that a passage might be found to Cathay by the North
Sea. . . . He went also to know what manner of land
those Indies were to inhabit. He had with him three
hundred men, and directed his course by the track of
Iceland, upon the cape of Labrador, at 58 degrees—
though he himself says much more—affirming that in
the month of July there was such cold and heaps of ice
that he durst pass no further ; that the days were very
long, and in manner without night, and the nights very
clear. Certain it is that at 60 degrees the longest day
is of 18 hours. But considering the cold and the strange-
ness of the unknown land, he turned his course from
thence to the west, refreshing themselves at Baccalaos ;
and following the coast of the land unto the 38th degree,
he returned to England.'

Giovanni Battista Ramusio, *Navigations*. Three
volumes published at Venice in 1550, 1559, and 1556
respectively.

(a) In vol. i occurs the following relation by a ' Mantuan gentleman ',[1] whose name has never been discovered
(Eden falsely identified him with Galeacius Butrigarius,
Papal Legate in Spain), speaking to a company of Venetians in the house of Hieronimus Fracastor :

' Finding himself in the city of Seville a few years ago,
and desiring to know about those navigations from the
Castillians, he was told that a distinguished Venetian
was there who had knowledge of them, named Sebastian
Caboto, who knew how to make marine charts with his
own hands, and understood the art of navigation better
than any one else. . . . Caboto said : . . . " My father
died at the time when the news came that the Genoese,
Christopher Columbus, had discovered the coast of the
Indies, and it was much discussed at the court of King
Henry VII, who then reigned, saying that it was a thing

[1] Hakluyt, vii. 147

more divine than human to have found that way never before known to go to the east where the spices grow. In this way, a great and heartfelt desire arose in me to achieve some signal enterprise. Knowing by a study of the sphere that if I should navigate to the west, I should find a shorter route to the Indies, I quickly made known my thought to his Majesty the King, who was well content, and fitted out two caravels for me with everything needful. This was in 1496, in the commencement of the summer. I began to navigate towards the west, expecting not to find land until I came to Cathay, whence I could go on to the Indies. But at the end of some days I discovered that the land trended northwards, to my great disappointment; so I sailed along the coast to see if I could find some point where the land turned, until I reached the height of 56 degrees under our pole, but finding that the land turned eastward, I despaired of finding an opening. I turned to the right to examine again to the southward, always with the object of finding a passage to the Indies, and I came to that part which is now called Florida. Being in want of victuals, I was obliged to return thence to England, where I found great popular tumults among the rebels, and a war with Scotland. So that there was no chance of further navigation to those parts being considered, and I therefore went to Spain to the Catholic King and Queen Isabella, who, having heard what I had done, took me into their service, and provided for me well, sending me on a voyage of discovery to the coast of Brazil. I found a very wide river, now called La Plata. . . ." '

(β) In the preface to the third volume, Ramusio gives the following note on Sebastian Cabot. From Hakluyt's translation.[1]

' It is not yet thoroughly known whether the lands set in fiftie degrees of latitude to the north be separated and divided by the sea as islands, and whether by that

[1] Hakluyt, vii. 149.

way one may goe by sea unto the country of Cathaia :
as many yeeres past it was written unto me by Sebastian
Gabotto, our countrey man a Venetian, a man of great
experience, and very rare in the art of navigation and the
knowledge of cosmographie, who sayled along and beyond
the land of New France at the charges of King Henry
the seventh, King of England : and hee advertised mee
that, having sailed a long time West and by North,
beyond those Ilands unto the latitude of 67 degrees and
an halfe, under the North pole, and at the 11 day of
June, finding still the open sea without any manner of
impediment, he thought verily by that way to have
passed on still the way to Cathaia, which is in the East,
and would have done it if the mutinie of the ship master
and the mariners had not hindered him and made him
returne homewards from that place.'

André Thevet, *Les Singularités de la France Antarctique*,
Antwerp, 1558. Thevet reproduces the outline of
previous accounts, and adds that Cabot landed three
hundred men at some undefined place in the north, to
found a colony. They nearly all perished of cold :

'Vray est qu'il mist bien trois cens hommes en terre,
du coste d'Irelande au Nort, ou le froid fist mourir
presque toute sa compagnie, encores que ce fust au moys
de Juillet.'

Jean Ribault,[1] writing in 1562, mentions 1498 as the
date of Sebastian Cabot's voyage.

Richard Eden, *Decades of the New World*, 1555, preface,
leaf C 1.

'But Cabot touched only in the north corner and
most barbarous part thereof, from whence he was repulsed
with ice in the month of July.'

[1] No French copy of Ribault's work is known to exist. It was published
in English in 1563, with the title 'The Whole and true discoverie of
Terra Florida'. Reprinted by Hakluyt in *Divers Voyages* (Hakluyt
Society's edition, 1850, pp. 91–115).

Antonio Galvano, *Discoveries of the World to 1550*, Lisbon, 1563. Latest edition, Hakluyt Society, 1862. Hakluyt published this translation in 1601.

' In the yeere 1496 there was a Venetian in England called John Cabota [the name is probably an interpolation of Hakluyt's], who having knowledge of such a new discoverie as this was, and perceiving by the globe that the islands before spoken of stood about in the same latitude with his countrey, and much neerer to England than to Portugall or to the Castile, he acquainted King Henrie the seventh, then King of England, with the same, wherewith the saide King was greatly pleased, and furnished him out with two ships and three hundred men : which departed and set saile in the spring of the yeare, and they sailed westward til they came in sight of land, in 45 degrees of latitude towards the north, and then went straight northwards till they came into sixty degrees of latitude, where the day is 18 howers long, and the night is very cleere and bright. There they found the aire cold, and great islands of ice, but no ground in seventy, eighty or hundred fathoms sounding, but found much ice, which alarmed them : and so from thence, putting about, finding the land to turne eastward, they trended along by it, discovering all the bay and river named Deseado, to see if it passed on the other side ; then they sailed back again till they came to 38 degrees towards the equinoctial line, and from thence returned into England. There be others which say that he went as far as the Cape of Florida, which standeth in 25 degrees.'

Alonzo de Santa Cruz, *Islario General de todas las Islas del Mundo*, a manuscript first printed by F. R. von Wieser, Innsbruck, 1908. Writing to Charles V, Santa Cruz says :

' This land was called Labrador because a labrador (ploughman or landowner) from the Azores gave information and intelligence of it to the King of England at the time he sent to explore it by Antonio Gaboto the English pilot and the father of Sebastian Gaboto, your Majesty's present Pilot Major.'

Further on he speaks of the Baccalaos ' first explored by the English pilot Antonio Gaboto, by command of the King of England '.[1]

It will be seen that the principal detailed accounts are those of Peter Martyr, Gomara, Ramusio, and Galvano.

Peter Martyr's account was the earliest published (1516) and has the best right to be considered as correctly reproducing Sebastian's own claims, since it was written by a man who was personally known to him and who was in frequent friendly communication with him. Circumstances of both time and place thus point to Martyr as the most trustworthy witness of Sebastian Cabot's statements during the first years of his residence in Spain. As will be seen from the analysis given below, practically all the important details common to more than one account are found in his work, and it may be safely assumed that every serious historian subsequent to him was acquainted with it, more especially as it was written in Latin and thus accessible to all men of education.

Gomara, writing a few years after Sebastian Cabot had left Spain, repeats the main features of Martyr's account. He may have known Sebastian personally, but does not expressly say so. His attitude is critical and somewhat suspicious, and he shows that he is not a mere

[1] By ' Antonio' Cabot Santa Cruz evidently meant John, as the context shows. His mistake in the name arose from his copying Ziegler's version of Peter Martyr. Jacobus Ziegler (Strasburg, 1532) reproduced Martyr's account of the northern voyage, attributing it to ' Antonio' Cabot. Apparently Ziegler did not know there were two Cabots.

blind reproducer of all he is told by his reduction of
the northern limit of the voyage claimed by Sebastian.
It should be remarked that the latitude of 58° N. is
Gomara's own figure and not Cabot's, because this has
been advanced as proof that Cape Farewell in Greenland
was the point reached. There is no real evidence that
Sebastian's northward wanderings took him far away
from the Labrador coast; and the fact that in early
maps, including that of 1544, Greenland and Labrador
are confused with one another, or rather, represented
as continuous, points the other way, since, if Sebastian
had crossed Davis Strait, he would have known that
they were distinct.

Ramusio's two relations, (a) by the Mantuan gentleman, and (β) in the preface to volume iii, are not of
nearly such high value. In particular, the Mantuan
gentleman's story is quite untrustworthy. It is a report
by Ramusio of a discourse delivered some years before
he wrote it down, and in which the narrator in his turn
was speaking from memory after the lapse of several
years. Ramusio himself admits that his recollection is
confused on the matter, and the consequence is that he
makes the Mantuan gentleman put statements into the
mouth of Sebastian Cabot with which that individual
would never have insulted the intelligence of his hearers.
The assertion that Queen Isabella, who died in 1504,
helped Sebastian to fit out the expedition with which
he explored the River Plate in 1526, does not encourage
much trust in the remainder of the account. Two of
its implications also contradict one another. Cabot is
first made to say that he believed the new land to be
Cathay, and immediately afterwards he speaks of trying
to find a passage through it, because it trended north-

wards. But if it trended northwards it must also have trended southwards if followed in the opposite direction, and, assuming it to be Cathay, he had only to go that way to arrive at the coast of India, his goal. Other obvious misstatements, as to the date of John Cabot's death, and the reasons for the abandonment of the enterprise in England, which have caused so much damage to Sebastian's reputation for truthfulness, occur in this story. Considering the third-hand and 'hearsay' character of the same, it is hardly fair to put its inaccuracies down to his account. It evidently suffered by the carelessness of one or both of the avenues by which it has been preserved.

Ramusio's statement in the preface to volume iii has a slightly better life history, but here again he is quoting from memory, avowedly faulty, of a letter written several years before, and apparently not preserved by him. However, the details given are scanty, the only remarkable one being that Sebastian Cabot could have made the north-west passage, but was prevented by a mutiny. Such a plausible explanation of failure is quite consistent with Sebastian's character. On the whole, Ramusio exhibits very little critical faculty, and has done Sebastian a great disservice by reproducing such nonsense as the Mantuan gentleman's story.

The brief references in the manuscript of Alonzo de Santa Cruz effectually clear up one point, namely, the suggestion that Sebastian tried to deceive his contemporaries in Spain by claiming his father's exploits as his own. There could never have been much probability in such a charge, in view of the number of persons who must have been living during the period 1512–47 with personal recollections of all the circumstances ; and it is definitely and finally swept away by Santa Cruz's allusion, as a matter of common knowledge, to the explorations of John Cabot.[1]

The remaining account of any length is that of Antonio Galvano, published in 1563, but written before 1557, the date of his death. It is not, on any serious point, at variance with Peter Martyr, but includes some details peculiar to itself. Galvano was a man of grave and sober character, and moreover, an experienced voyager. His judgement, in any conflict of evidence, is more likely to be reliable than that of Ramusio.

A correct view of the statements in all these accounts is best obtained by summarizing them and placing the results side by side in the following manner :

Points of Agreement :—

Two ships were employed (Martyr, Gomara, Ramusio a, Galvano).

Three hundred men were carried (Martyr, Gomara, Galvano).

The general direction of the voyage was to the north-west (Martyr, Gomara, Ramusio a and β, Eden). Galvano says they went westwards to land in 45°, and then northwards to 60°.

Ice was encountered in July (Martyr, Gomara, Eden). Ice without mention of date (Galvano).

After making land, the expedition coasted northwards (Martyr, Gomara, Ramusio a and β, Galvano).

It then turned back and sailed along the coast south-wards and westwards (Martyr, Gomara, Ramusio a,

---

[1] The date of this manuscript is generally given as 1560, but, from internal evidence, it must be earlier. F. R. von Wieser, in his preface to the Innsbruck edition (1908), comes to the conclusion that it was completed in 1541.

Galvano). Eden appears to deny this, but probably unintentionally.

Extraordinary length of day was observed (Martyr, Gomara, Galvano).

A passage was being sought *through* the new land to Cathay (Ramusio α and β). The other accounts are not explicit on this point.

Points of difference :—

Highest north latitude attained : 58°, 'he himself says much more' (Gomara) ; 56° (Ramusio α) ; 67½° (Ramusio β) ; 60° (Galvano).

Lowest south latitude attained : 'latitude of Gibraltar', 36° (Martyr) ; 38° (Gomara) ; latitude of 'Florida' —say 25–35° (Ramusio α) ; 38°, 'others say 25°' (Galvano).

The ships were fitted out at Cabot's own charges (Martyr) ; ships fitted out at the king's charges (Ramusio α and β, Galvano). Gomara uncertain.

A north-west passage was discovered (Ramusio β) ; further progress north was impossible (Gomara, Ramusio α, Galvano).

Date of voyage : 1498 (Ribault) ; 1496 (Galvano) ; 1496 (Ramusio α).

Facts inconsistent with what is known with certainty of John Cabot's voyages :—

Sebastian Cabot was in command ; two ships were employed ; the voyage was into Arctic seas primarily, and only turned southwards when further progress north was impossible.

Statements obviously incorrect :—

Ferdinand and Isabella jointly dispatched Sebastian on the River Plate voyage (Ramusio α) ;[1] date of John

---

[1] Isabella died in 1504 and Ferdinand in 1516. Cabot sailed for the River Plate in 1526.

Cabot's death (Ramusio a) ; date of Sebastian Cabot's voyage (Ramusio a and Galvano) ; the American coast trends eastwards at 56° N. (Ramusio a).

In considering the accounts thus summarized, we are struck first by the importance and the inter-corroborative nature of the points on which unanimity is displayed, and secondly by the relative unimportance (so far as concerns the general outline of the story) of the points of difference. It is precisely on such points as latitude and date that men, writing in good faith, would be liable to err from defect of memory. The single serious discrepancy is the statement by Ramusio that a north-west passage was found, while the other writers assert that it was impossible to find such a passage. But Ramusio, as has been shown, was not very careful as to his facts, and Sebastian Cabot may well have been in a boasting mood when he wrote his letter to him. Sebastian was undoubtedly prone to misstatements on minor points, such as the place of his birth and his discoveries in the art of navigation, and in this respect he was neither above nor below the general standard of morality displayed by the adventurers of his time. With this exception, the above analysis shows that Ramusio's ' Mantuan gentleman ' is responsible for practically all the demonstrably impossible elements in the story. The reasons for disregarding him have already been fully entered into.

The conclusion is thus inevitable that the extracts under consideration present a report of a voyage that did actually take place, and that the following were the principal details of it : Sebastian Cabot was the commander ; two ships were employed, with large crews ;

the general direction was westwards and northwards from England ; so much progress was made into Arctic seas, by coasting northwards along the American shore, that quantities of ice were encountered in the height of summer ; the object of the expedition was to find a passage through the American continent to the land of Cathay beyond, and thence to the Indies in the tropic latitudes ; owing to ice, or mutiny, or both, further northern progress had to be abandoned ; and finally, Sebastian Cabot skirted the whole coast of North America, from the neighbourhood of the Arctic circle down to Delaware Bay, or even to the southern point of Florida, and thence returned to England.

It is evident at a glance that this cannot possibly be a description of John Cabot's first voyage. Facts are known with absolute certainty relating to that voyage which are quite incompatible with Sebastian's story.

On reference to the very meagre, but yet undoubted, details in existence with regard to the 1498 voyage, it becomes equally evident that Sebastian Cabot was not speaking of that either, when he furnished material to the sixteenth-century historians. From first-class sources it has been seen that John Cabot sailed in command in 1498 ; that he conducted five ships ; that he imagined the opposite shore to be that of Cathay ; that he intended to make his former landfall, and then sail to the south-west, instead of to the north ; and that his goal was the Isle of Cipango in the tropic seas, and not a by-him-undreamed-of passage in the Arctic.

Undoubtedly, then, Sebastian Cabot's voyage was not identical with that of 1497, or with that of 1498. It must have been subsequent to those expeditions, since its commander was in possession of geographical knowledge which can only have been gleaned by John Cabot in 1498. Two considerations point to its having taken place in 1499 or 1500, with the balance of probability in favour of the former year. On March 19, 1501, Henry VII granted to a Bristol syndicate a new charter for western exploration, in which it was distinctly laid down that no foreigner, under colour of any former grant, should resort to the new-found lands without the permission of the present patentees. This seems to preclude with certainty the possibility of any Cabot voyage for several years to come, for the new company continued its operations until 1505, and possibly longer.

Another indication, from a Spanish source, points to 1499 as the probable date. A Spanish adventurer, Alonzo de Hojeda, put to sea on a voyage of discovery in May 1499. He explored the coast of Venezuela, steering thence to Hispaniola, and returning to Spain in the spring of 1500. On June 8, 1501, he obtained from the Spanish sovereigns a patent for a second voyage, empowering him to take ten ships and prosecute further discoveries on certain conditions, among which appear the following : [1]

'That you go and follow that coast which you have discovered, which extends east and west, as it appears, because it goes towards that part where it has been reported that the English were making discoveries ; and that you set up marks with the arms of their Majesties or with other signs that may be understood, such as may seem good to you, so that it may be known that you have discovered that land, in order that you may stop the discoveries of the English in that direction. . . .

'Likewise their Majesties make gift to you, in the

[1] Navarette, *Coleccion de los Viajes*, Madrid, 1825–37, iii. 85–8 (original patent printed in full).

island of Hispaniola, of six leagues of land . . . for what you have accomplished in discovery, and for the exclusion of the English from the coast of the mainland, and the said six leagues of land shall be yours for ever. . . .'

Navarette, writing of Hojeda's first voyage, says it is certain that the explorer encountered some Englishmen near Coquibacoa on the coast of Venezuela ; [1] but he gives no authority for the statement, and such authority has been searched for in vain. Possibly the patent quoted above was the origin of his assertion. In any case the patent deserves serious consideration, showing, as it does, that the Spanish Government was genuinely alarmed at the progress of English exploration on the mainland of America. If it is to be credited that Hojeda did encounter an English expedition on his first voyage, that expedition must have been Sebastian Cabot's, as the dates do not allow of the possibility that Hojeda ran across John Cabot in 1497 or 1498. If Hojeda met Sebastian Cabot, it is most unlikely, in view of the latter's accounts of his voyage, that it was on the coast of Venezuela. The most probable time and place of the intersection of the routes of the two explorers was in the autumn of 1499 and in the vicinity of the island of Hispaniola. Hojeda seems to have arrived at that place on September 5, staying there for a considerable time before resuming his voyage ; and it is quite possible that Sebastian Cabot touched there on his homeward passage from Florida, although he would naturally not mention the circumstance in after days when in Spanish service.

But, however interesting these possibilities may be,

[1] Navarette, iii. 41 : ' Lo cierto es que Hojeda en su primer viaje halló á ciertos ingleses por las immediaciones de Coquibacoa,'

there is not sufficient proof for them to be regarded as facts, and their truth or falsity does not affect the credit due to Sebastian Cabot for his determination to turn his father's disillusionment to account. A man of good education, and of a subtle, reflective mind, he realized, as did other cosmographers much earlier than is commonly supposed,[1] that the new-found land was veritably a separate continent, and lay as an obstacle between Europe and the coveted spices of the East. Hence his voyage into the Arctic—the first voyage in search of the North-West Passage, a quest which has formed an integral part of English history almost to our own time, and of which the first act has been buried under such an accumulation of misunderstanding and controversy as to pass almost unrecognized. Whether the voyage took place in 1499 or later ; exactly how far north Sebastian reached ; whether he actually entered Hudson's Strait ; and whether he encountered Hojeda in the West Indies after giving up the northern quest, are points which cannot be decided with the evidence at present at disposal. Certain it is, however, that his was the first attempt to pass from the Atlantic to the Pacific, an achievement which Magellan was to accomplish by a different route twenty years later.

Much has been made of Sebastian Cabot's suppression of his father's discoveries. It cannot be denied that he showed a strange want of generosity on the point, his first recorded reference to them being found in the map of 1544. But the neglect to mention a fact which is common knowledge is not so serious a fault as the withholding a secret generally unknown. From the references

---

[1] On this point see Harrisse: *Discovery of North America* (1892), pp. 102–24.

to John Cabot made by Alonzo de Santa Cruz, it would seem that Charles V was perfectly aware that John, and not Sebastian, was the original discoverer, as indeed any one who troubled to inquire into the matter could hardly fail to be when so many contemporaries of the fact were still living. The wretchedly slipshod and per- functory methods of the sixteenth-century historians are certainly as much to blame as Sebastian, who had a financial motive for taking advantage of the confusion when he claimed, in his old age, the gratitude of England for the services of his family.

That Sebastian Cabot was nothing but a charlatan and a ' glib reciter of other men's tales ' is highly improbable. If he had been such, he would surely have appropriated the 1497 and 1498 voyages to his own credit, and would have made his story agree closely with all the undoubted details of those exploits, with which he was necessarily familiar. If he had really intended to represent himself as the sole discoverer of America, what possible motive could he have had in arousing suspicion by altering the number of ships from one or five, as the case might be, to two ; in maintaining the deception well knowing that his master, Charles V, and many others were cognisant of it ; and finally in giving his whole case away and acknowledging himself a liar by publishing the inscription on the map of 1544 ? His real fault was his egotistic silence on achievements which were not his own, a fault which served his turn at the time, but afterwards brought its own punishment by damaging his reputation to an even greater extent than he deserved.

Most modern writers [1] have assumed that he claimed

---

[1] The principal modern works on the Cabots are : S. E. Dawson, *Voyages of the Cabots*, 1894 ; H. Harrisse, *Jean et Sébastien Cabot*, 1882,

to have commanded one or both of the first two voyages, and they have put forward, as an explanation of the discrepancies, the suggestion that he named the Arctic as the scene of his chief efforts in order to please his Spanish masters. The latter were (on this hypothesis) bound to admit that England had made some discoveries, but preferred to have them located in a frigid and comparatively useless region rather than in more temperate zones. The obvious and fatal objection to this reasoning is that Sebastian, while asserting that he had been in the Arctic, also claimed to have coasted down to Virginia or Florida during the very same voyage, thus giving England just as good a title to those regions by right of discovery as if his first landfall had been made there.

The conclusion is, therefore, that there were three distinct Cabot voyages of which evidence has survived ; the first two, under John Cabot, made upon a false conception, and the third, under his son, upon a true conception, of the nature of the newly discovered continent ; and that the search for the North-West Passage was begun by Sebastian Cabot.

and *John and Sebastian Cabot*, 1896 ; G. E. Weare, *Cabot's Discovery of North America*, 1897 ; C. R. Beazley, *John and Sebastian Cabot,* 1898 ; G. P. Winship, *Cabot Bibliography*, 1900 ; H. P. Biggar, *Voyages of the Cabots and Corte Reals*, 1903. Of these authors Mr. Winship is the only one who takes the view that there were three voyages, and he inclines to the belief that Sebastian's voyage took place in 1508-9.

CHAPTER V

AN EARLY COLONIAL PROJECT

AFTER the Cabot voyages, which were, financially,
a failure, nothing more is heard of American enterprises
originating in England until March 19, 1501. On that
date Henry VII granted a patent 'to our beloved
subjects Richard Ward, Thomas Ashehurst, and John
Thomas, merchants of our town of Bristol, and to our
beloved João Fernandes, Francisco Fernandes and João
Gonsalves,[1] squires born in the islands of Surrys (Azores)
under the obedience of the King of Portugal', giving
them authority to explore any regions of the earth
for the purpose of discovering any countries hitherto
unknown to Christians. The patentees were further
empowered to set up the king's standard on all places
by them newly discovered, and to occupy such places
as his vassals and governors, making laws and enforcing
the obedience of all who should resort to those regions.
During ten years following the grant of the patent they
were to have a monopoly of trade with their discoveries,
other persons being forbidden to engage in it without
obtaining their licence and that of the king, and then
only on condition of paying to the patentees one-
twentieth part of the value of the goods shipped. Certain exemptions from customs duties on small quantities
of goods were granted to the masters and mariners
employed by the patentees, who were themselves entitled

[1] One of these three Portuguese is in all probability the 'labrador'
mentioned by Santa Cruz as having taken intelligence of discoveries
to Henry VII.

to import one shipload of merchandise duty free at some time within the first four years after the grant of the patent. If foreigners persisted in intruding into the dominions of the patentees the latter were given leave to expel and punish them at their discretion, even if they were subjects of a friendly power. They were also granted, jointly and singly, the rank and privileges of Admiral, with power to exercise the same in the new lands. A significant clause provided that no foreigner, under colour of any concession formerly granted under the Great Seal, should resort to the new lands without the licence of the patentees. Finally, the three Portuguese mentioned in the patent were to be naturalized and have all the rights and privileges of Englishmen, except that they were to continue to pay customs duties on the same scale as foreigners.[1]

A study of the terms of the charter, the original of which is in Latin and of great length, shows that the foundation of a permanent colony, and not merely the dispatch of a trading expedition, was contemplated. The clauses, much elaborated in the original, relative to the rights of legislation, power to exclude foreigners, and administrative authority of the patentees, all point to this conclusion, although there is very little evidence that they were ever carried into effect. The locality is not mentioned, but it must have been somewhere on the coast of Greenland or North America between the Arctic Circle and the extremity of the peninsula of Florida, limits which are sufficiently wide, but which are necessitated by the extreme vagueness and the contradictory nature of the indications of the site of the

[1] Patent printed in full in introduction to Hakluyt Society's *Divers Voyages*, ed. by J. W. Jones.

projected settlement. The permission to expel foreigners
by force of arms is interesting as showing that Henry VII,
on paper at least, was in a less conciliatory mood than
usual towards the Spaniards, at whom and the Portuguese
the clause was levelled. The express revocation of any
previous grants under the great seal could only apply
to the patents obtained by the Cabots in 1496 and 1498,
which were now annulled, most probably on account of
the failure of those navigators to achieve any commercial
success by their voyages.

The somewhat incongruous combination of Bristol
merchants and Portuguese adventurers may be accounted
for by the assumption that the former provided the
capital and the business management of the affair, while
the latter supplied the navigating skill and experience of
similar enterprises. João Fernandes, at least, possessed
such experience. On October 28, 1499, he had been
granted a patent by King Manuel of Portugal, authorizing
him to make voyages to the North-West and giving him
the captaincy of any islands he might discover; and
certain expressions used in another patent obtained by
him in 1508 imply that he had previously made voyages
in the same direction.[1] The Portuguese, in general, thanks
to their persistent attempts to find an eastern route to
Cathay, were much more advanced in the art of conducting exploring expeditions than were the English of
that period, and they had very quickly followed in the
track of the Cabots to the coast of North America itself.
The two brothers, Gaspar and Miguel Corte Real, as
important in Portuguese history as the Cabots in our
own, perished in the North-West in 1501 and 1502
respectively; while Portuguese fishermen flocked to the

[1] H. Harrisse, *Évolution Cartographique de Terre-Neuve*, p. 41.

Baccalaos, or Newfoundland banks, in such numbers that in 1506 an import tax was levied in Portugal on fish from that region.[1] On the other hand, England was in its infancy as a maritime nation, and its sailors, using inferior ships, charts, and navigating methods, had been hitherto accustomed only to coasting voyages and very short open-sea passages, such as were necessitated by the trade to Iceland and Spain.

It would appear that a commencement of the American enterprise was made in 1501, soon after the granting of the patent. It was usual to set out on such expeditions in the early summer so as to enjoy the maximum of good weather, and also to take advantage of the longest days when examining a new coastline. The only positive evidence of a voyage having been made in 1501 is an entry in Henry VII's Privy Purse accounts [2] on January 7, 1502 : ' To men of Bristol that found the Isle, £5.' Scanty as it is, this entry may be taken as proving conclusively that a voyage was made in 1501. It was customary to make such donations on the arrival in England of the persons concerned : John Cabot had received a similar gift within a few days of his return from his first voyage in 1497 ; and the obvious inference here is that the Anglo-Portuguese syndicate dispatched an expedition in 1501, news of the safe arrival of which came to England at the end of that year. It is uncertain whether a colony was planted and messengers sent back with news to England, or whether the first voyage was made simply for the purpose of exploring and choosing a suitable site. It should be noted that the phrase

---

[1] Harrisse, *Discovery of North America*, p. 174.
[2] *Add. MSS.*, 7099, a manuscript copy of the original accounts, which are not now available.

employed does not necessarily imply that the new land was an island in the usual acceptation of the word; most newly discovered regions were commonly referred to as islands until exploration proved their continental nature.

A series of three documents, all referring to the last week of September 1502, imply the arrival of another ship or fleet from the new land at that time. A Privy Purse entry of September 23 : ' To a mariner that brought an eagle, 6s. 8d.', may or may not relate to the enterprise ; but another of September 30 is more explicit : ' To the merchants of Bristol that have been in the Newfound land, £20.' The third piece of evidence is the grant, on September 26, 1502, of pensions of £10 each per annum to Francisco Fernandes and João Gonsalves, ' in consideration of the true service which they have done unto us to our singler pleasure as capitaignes unto the newe found lande '.[1] Here again the phraseology is tantalizingly vague, and leaves us completely in the dark as to the real nature of the undertaking. It would apply equally well to a colony, a trading voyage, or a voyage of exploration. Two facts may, however, be deduced : first, that something of real importance had been accomplished, as is shown by the unwonted liberality of the king, whose habitual parsimony became accentuated in his later years ; and, secondly, that João Fernandes severed his connexion with the enterprise at this time or earlier, since he is not recorded as obtaining either gratuity or pension.

---

[1] First printed by Harrisse in *John and Sebastian Cabot* (1896). The actual document is an appropriation for the pension and bears date December 6, 1503, but contains a reference to the first grant on the date given above.

Indeed, the next step of which we have evidence is a reconstruction of the whole syndicate and the grant of a new patent by the king on December 9, 1502.[1] The number of the patentees was now reduced to four, namely, Hugh Elyot, Thomas Ashehurst, João Gonsalves, and Francisco Fernandes. Nothing is known of the causes of this change, by which three of the original adventurers dropped out and one new one was introduced; but it may safely be assumed that it was not due to an entire lack of commercial success, since that would probably have resulted in the winding-up of the whole concern.

The new patent was very similar in its terms to the old one, with the following exceptions : In the general licence to conquer and colonize, a special exception was made of the lands of the King of Portugal and any other ' principum, amicorum & confoederatorum nostrorum ' ; the period during which the patentees might have a monopoly of trade was extended to forty years ; two shiploads, instead of one, might be imported duty free ; and Gonsalves and Francisco Fernandes were now placed on a complete equality with Englishmen as regards the payment of customs. Richard Ward, John Thomas, and João Fernandes were expressly debarred from exercising privileges granted in the patent of 1501, which was thus, for practical purposes, cancelled. The clause aiming at the rights of the Cabots was not repeated.

On the whole, the new patent was more favourable than the old, and the contrast seems to be intentionally emphasized between the status of the four new patentees and that of Ward, Thomas and João Fernandes, who

[1] *Foedera*, xiii. 37.

were now excluded. The conduct of the latter had evidently been as displeasing to the king as that of the former had been satisfactory.

An entry in Stow's *Chronicle* with reference to these expeditions has already been discussed in connexion with the Cabot voyages. It states that in the year 1502 three men were brought to the king, who had been taken in the new-found islands. They were clothed in skins, ate raw flesh, and spoke an unintelligible language. Two of them were to be seen at Westminster two years later, when they resembled Englishmen in clothing and appearance. These men must have arrived in the ships which returned in September 1502.

. The new patent granted by Henry VII was followed by a renewal of the energies of the adventurers, and a Privy Purse entry of November 17, 1503, indicates the arrival in England of ships at that time. Like the others, it affords very little information, merely recording the payment : ' To one that brought hawkes from the Newfoundland Island, £1 '. Another entry, ' April 8, 1504, to a prest that goeth to the new island, £2,' points to a fresh sailing soon after that date, although there is no information as to the corresponding homeward voyage in the autumn. The Privy Purse accounts afford only one more piece of evidence, and that is of doubtful bearing on the subject. On August 25, 1505, we find entered : ' To Clays going to Richemount with wylde catts and popyngays of the Newfound Island, for his costs, 13s. 4d.', and on the same date, ' To Portyngales that brought popyngais and catts of the mountaigne with other stuf to the Kinges Grace, £5.' The word ' popinjays ' was generally used to mean parrots, and no clear instance exists of the word being applied to any

other bird.[1] Parrots are not now to be found in the
northern part of North America, but one species at least
existed on the shores of Lakes Erie and Ontario at the
beginning of the nineteenth century,[2] and it is quite
possible that Indians in Newfoundland and Labrador
bartered them to Europeans in the time of Henry VII.
Hence the extract in question need not be absolutely
rejected as applying to the present subject.

The interesting and valuable transcripts of Privy Purse
accounts in Add. MS. 7099 cease at the year 1505.
They are continued to the end of the reign by a manuscript [3] in the Record Office (first entry, October 1, 1505),
but there is no further mention of donations to American
adventurers. At this point, therefore, all contemporary
information ceases. The enterprise may have been continued during the succeeding years, but it was certainly
not very long before it was abandoned, as certain statements of a later date tend to prove.

About the period 1517–19 a play in rhymed verse was
printed, entitled *The New Interlude of the Four Elements*,
of which the only known copy is at present in the British
Museum.[4] The page which should bear information as
to its origin is missing, and the date given above is
arrived at on internal evidence. The following lines
vaguely refer to the early transatlantic voyages (spelling
modernized) :

> This sea is called the great Ocean,
> So great it is that never man
> Could tell it sith the world began,
> Till now, within this twenty year,

[1] See *New English Dictionary*.
[2] *Encyclopaedia Britannica*, 11th ed., art. ' Parrots '.
[3] R. O., T. R. Misc. Book 214.
[4] Reprinted by the Percy Society, 1848, ed. J. O. Halliwell.

Westward be found new lands
That we never heard tell of before this
By writing nor other means,
Yet many now have been there ;
And that country is so large of room,
Much lenger than all Christendom,
Without fable or guile ;
For divers mariners have it tried,
And sailed straight by the coast side
Above five thousand mile !
But what commodities be within
No man can tell nor well imagine,
But yet not long ago
Some men of this country went,
By the King's noble consent,
It for to search to that intent,
And could not be brought thereto ;
But they that were the venturers
Have cause to curse their mariners,
False of promise and dissemblers,
That falsely them betrayed ;
Which would take no pain to sail further
Than their own lust and pleasure,
Wherefore that voyage and divers other
Such caitiffs have destroyed.
O what a thing had been then,
If that they that be Englishmen
Might have been the first of all ;
That there should have taken possession,
And made first building and habitation,
A memory perpetual ;
And also what an honourable thing
Both to the realm and to the King,
To have had his dominion extending
There into so far a ground,
Which the noble King of late memory,
The most wise Prince, the VIIth Harry,
Caused first to be found.

.   .   .   .

Now Frenchmen and other have found the trade
That yearly of fish there they lade
Above an hundred sail.

. . . .

But these new lands by all cosmography
From the Khan of Cathay's land cannot lie
Little past a thousand miles.

In common with all the other evidences of these
obscure transactions, the language here employed is
vague and disputable, although it does undoubtedly
show that the colony, if it ever existed, no longer did
so at the time of writing. The voyage which failed
owing to the cowardice of the mariners was possibly one
undertaken in the early years of Henry VIII, of which
other hints survive.[1] It was entered upon ' by the
King's noble consent ', that is, the then king, Henry VIII,
and not the late one, Henry VII, who is spoken of in
a different manner further on, where the original discovery is attributed to him. The author had seemingly
no detailed knowledge of the successive voyages of the
period 1501–5. His identity is not revealed ; it would
be most interesting to know who he was in view of
the imperialistic notions he expressed at such an early
date.

Robert Thorne, a member of an important family of
Bristol merchants, writing in the year 1527, refers to
his father, also named Robert Thorne, ' which, with
another merchant of Bristowe, named Hugh Eliot, were
the discoverers of the newe found lands, of the which
there is no doubt, as now plainly appeareth, if the
mariners would then have been ruled, and followed their

[1] The evidence that the voyage in question really took place is extremely
doubtful. See Chap. X.

pilot's mind, the lands of the west Indies, from whence all the gold commeth, had been ours. For all is one coaste, as by the carde appeareth, and is aforesaide.' Robert Thorne, the younger, was a strong advocate of the possibility of a northern passage over the pole to Asia, but, in this instance, he is evidently referring to a voyage down the North American coast in the direction of Florida and Mexico ' whence all the gold commeth ', and which his own map, accompanying his book, shows to be ' all one coast ' with the north-western lands. It is impossible to say which voyage it was which thus failed on account of mutiny ; perhaps the last Privy Purse entry, with regard to popinjays and wild cats, had some connexion with it. It is worthy of remark that three separate authorities give stories of early voyages which came to nothing on account of the insubordination of the crews ; namely, Sebastian Cabot as reported by Ramusio, the *New Interlude*, and Robert Thorne ; but it is not necessary to refer all these stories to the same source and make them all apply to the same voyage. The excuse was obviously a convenient one to make, and must certainly have occurred to many a disappointed adventurer whose own lack of constancy had been perhaps as much to blame as that of his men.

A confirmation of the association of the elder Thorne with the American adventurers is furnished by a Record Office paper showing that on January 7, 1502, Robert and William Thorne and Hugh Elyot, of Bristol, were granted a bounty of £20 by the king in consideration of their having bought a French ship of 120 tons.[1]

A consideration of Robert Thorne's map leads to the

---

[1] M. Oppenheim, *Administration of the Royal Navy*, p. 38.

question of the locality to which the Bristol syndicates made their mysterious expeditions. The map shows the whole of the Old World together with South America and the eastern coast-line of North America. It is the last-mentioned part which concerns the present subject. In the latitude of the coast of Portugal, and extending to about the same length, appears a peninsula corresponding, in shape and relative position, to Nova Scotia together with Cape Breton. To the north of it is a long and important indentation, which evidently represents the Gulf of St. Lawrence. Above this the coast extends northwards for about 8° until another gulf is reached of even larger size. Newfoundland is not indicated as a separate island, but is massed with the land to the north of the St. Lawrence. The second or northern gulf is puzzling, and two explanations of it may be given. One is that it represents Davis Strait, separating Labrador and Greenland, and that therefore the land to the north of it is Greenland, wrongly drawn as forming part of the American continent. The other is that it is intended for Hamilton Inlet, a gulf occurring in the Labrador coast in the latitude of 54°. The latter is the more satisfactory explanation of the two, more especially as a land resembling Greenland is shown separately on the map, although much too far to the east. Huge discrepancies in longitude, however, are characteristic of all maps of the period. The size of the gulf, as drawn, gives no help, since it is too small for Davis Strait and too large for Hamilton Inlet. In latitude it corresponds more nearly with the latter. We may take it then that Robert Thorne was not confusing Greenland with America, and that the northern part of his map represents the coast of Labrador. On this land is inscribed ' Nova

Terra laboratorum dicta ', and along the coast, ' Terra hec ab Anglis primum fuit inventa '.[1]

Here is a conclusive solution concerning the destination of the voyages, if only we may assume that Robert Thorne was fully acquainted with the doings of his father and his fellow adventurers.[2] In all probability he was, but, failing definite proof on the point, we must look for other evidence.

Two considerations point to the fact that the English territory was not Newfoundland or Nova Scotia : firstly, that Thorne's map does not recognize the existence of Newfoundland as separate from the mainland ; and, secondly, that the patent of 1502 expressly forbade the grantees to intrude into the lands of the King of Portugal. In the years 1500, 1501, and 1502, the brothers Corte Real, as has been mentioned, made voyages to North America, and explored the coasts of Virginia (taken in its widest sense), Newfoundland, and southern Greenland. On the Cantino map, which was drawn up for the purpose of recording their discoveries, Newfoundland is denominated ' Terra del Rey de Portugall ', and an inscription on the map asserts that the explorers did not land in Greenland, contenting themselves with viewing the coast from a distance. Now, the coast of Virginia was generally agreed to be outside the Portuguese half of the globe as defined by the Bull of Alexander VI and the Treaty of Tordesillas. Consequently, Portuguese energies were concentrated on Nova Scotia and New-

[1] The inscription alone is insufficient to identify the country with modern Labrador, for it is certain that some early cartographers applied the name to Greenland.

[2] Robert Thorne the elder did not die until some time between 1519 and 1526, so that his son, writing in 1527, had had every opportunity of hearing his story from his own lips.

THE NORTH ATLANTIC.

From the map of Robert Thorne, 1527.

foundland, which lay in more easterly longitude, the actual difference also being greatly exaggerated in their maps.[1] These two regions, therefore, must be taken to be the 'lands of the King of Portugal' which the patentees were to respect.

The brief notice, already quoted, in Stow's *Chronicle*, as to the savages brought home by one of these expeditions, may also be used in support of a more northerly site. It is not stated that they were brown or red men, but on the contrary, that after two years' residence in England they resembled Englishmen in appearance. The word Eskimo means an eater of raw flesh,[2] and this is precisely one of the characteristics that observers noticed about them. Both Indians and Eskimos are found in Labrador, but Eskimos do not live in any countries further south. Thus it may be concluded that the ships returning in 1502 came from Labrador or some other northern region. There is no evidence that the English discoveries were anywhere to the south of Newfoundland. No maps can be found which give support to the idea, and the voyages which alarmed the Spanish Government at the time of Hojeda's early expeditions have been shown to have been those of the Cabots. The voyage in which Robert Thorne's father failed to penetrate to the West Indies was thus probably an isolated venture, failing for the reason he gives, and not repeated.

It was quite possible for a fairly lucrative trade to have been carried on in the southern part of Labrador. As far north as 54° the timber is plentiful and well suited for ship-building purposes. In Dawson's work on Labrador, already cited, it is stated that ' Dr. Grenfell

[1] A fine facsimile of the Cantino map is exhibited in the British Museum.
[2] Stanford's *Compendium*, 1897 : ' Labrador ', by S. E. Dawson.

reports trees at the head of Sandwich Bay from which
60 feet spars might be made ', and such trees were not
obtainable in western Europe. Although no agriculture
is possible, the country swarms with game and the rivers
with fish, so that, given friendly relations with the natives,
a trading post would have been able to support life
during the long winter. In addition to timber, furs,
then so much in demand in Europe, might have been
exported. The fishery on the coast is still very important
at the present day, and that of Newfoundland was certainly worked soon after the first discovery by the Cabots.
The English traders may have acted as middlemen,
buying from the fishermen and selling in England, as
they did afterwards in Elizabeth's time. The coast of
Labrador is rugged and forbidding, but at the heads of
the deep inlets the climate is milder and the conditions
more suitable for Europeans. Two of these inlets suggest
themselves as likely sites for a settlement—Sandwich Bay
and Hamilton Inlet. The former is in latitude $53\frac{1}{2}°$;
it is 25 miles long and 6 miles wide, and contains several
good harbours. The latter is in latitude 54° and reaches
150 miles inland, with an average width of 14 miles,
narrowing in one place to one-third of a mile.

The only alternative to Labrador is Greenland, with
which the scanty evidence in some respects agrees. But
for what possible reason could four or five voyages in
successive years have been made to Greenland except for
purely explorative purposes ? It must be borne in mind
that, although a passage to Asia was no doubt the ultimate goal of the adventurers, the expeditions nevertheless
had to pay expenses or the enterprise would have come
to an abrupt end. The Cabot experiences had sickened
King Henry of financing explorers, who came home with

nothing but geographical knowledge in their ships' holds. Greenland provided none of the produce which could be found in southern Labrador, and must on that account be ruled out. The evidence of Thorne's map, as already interpreted, also militates against Greenland. We are therefore driven to the conclusion that the balance of evidence places the English sphere of influence on the coast of Labrador. Whether or not a colony was established is unknown; all that can be said is that the patents contemplated the formation of one. Some sort of merchandise must have been obtained, but the trade was not sufficiently lucrative to warrant a continuation of the business after a few years' experience; for the liability to losses by accident in these northern seas was no doubt considerable.

The mainspring of the whole affair was undoubtedly the persistent belief in the existence of a practicable channel leading to Cathay and India, the discovery of which would have given England the possession of the shortest route and an immense advantage over all rivals. And here is most likely the clue to the colonizing ideas set forth in the patents; for such a 'passage, when discovered, would need to be fortified if its use was to be monopolized by the English.

After preliminary investigations, which held out strong hopes of success, if we may judge from Henry's liberality to the Portuguese and the Bristol men in 1502, insuperable obstacles were encountered, and no clear evidence survives of anything being done later than 1504 or, at latest, 1505. The enterprise had, unfortunately, no chronicler, and the details of its audacities and its heroisms have fallen into complete, though undeserved, oblivion.

CHAPTER VI

THE GROWTH OF COMMERCE

THE death of Henry VII and the accession, in April 1509, of his son, then in his eighteenth year, inevitably caused great changes in nearly all departments of the state. The new king was a typical child of the Renaissance in its most exuberant aspect. Young and enthusiastic, he bubbled with energy both of body and mind, and was at once the champion of the tiltyard and an earnest worshipper at the shrine of the new learning. He was surrounded by nobles whose natures were as fiery as his own and who were impatient of the restraints of a sober and prosaic régime. Thus circumstanced, like a generous rider bestriding a mettled steed, it was natural that he should seize the first opportunity of playing a part in the shifting and treacherous politics of Europe, from which his father had ever remained watchfully aloof.

The old dream of Continental conquest, which seemed to have been finally abandoned by Henry VII, was again revived ; and the country was soon resounding with the noise and rumour of warlike preparations. England, Spain, the Emperor, and the Pope united in an alliance to which the sanctity of the spiritual partner gave the name of the Holy League. Henry was eager to do his share. In 1512 he dispatched the Marquis of Dorset to the Biscayan coast of Spain with an English force which was to join hands with the Spaniards and, advancing

east and north, to achieve the reconquest of Guienne.
The outcome was disastrous. Deserted by its Spanish
allies, the English army fell a prey to its own indiscipline
and lack of experience, and returned without having had
one serious encounter with the enemy. Next year Henry
himself took the field, invaded the north of France,
routed the French at the Battle of the Spurs, and
received the surrender of Tournay and Terouenne. But
in the meantime the other members of the Holy League
had achieved their own objects by expelling the French
from Italy. Having done so, they unhesitatingly made
peace, leaving Henry in the rôle of confiding dupe to
pursue unaided his conquest of France—a task for which
his resources were manifestly inadequate. It was his
first practical experience of the faithless diplomacy of
the time, and the romantic strain noticeable in his earlier
character received a permanent check when he realized
how he had been used as a tool by such a veteran pair
of schemers as Ferdinand of Aragon and Maximilian the
Emperor.

Accordingly, peace was made with France in 1514,
and for seven years Europe enjoyed an uneasy tranquillity
which was but the prelude to fiercer storms. During
the war Thomas Wolsey had climbed to a position of
supreme authority under the king, which he was able
to retain for close on fifteen years. Until 1528 the policy
of Wolsey was the policy of England. In the main he
was mediaeval in his outlook, as befitted the last English
representative of a type which was so essentially a product of the Middle Ages, the statesman-ecclesiastic.
Although advanced in his appreciation of the balance of
power, his ideas were centred rather on royal marriages
and intrigues at Rome than on colonies and maritime

expansion. His outlook was that of a man oblivious of
the marvellous opening-up of the world which was going
on around him and of the part which his country might
play therein. Until quite the end of his ascendancy
there is no authenticated voyage of discovery or attempt
to penetrate new markets with the produce of industry.
In the long run this was not disadvantageous. An
enduring empire was only to be built upon a basis of
consolidated experience and battleworthiness which
England had yet to acquire, and which the reign of
Henry VIII was in large part to supply. In spite of
initial mistakes, Wolsey and his master steadily increased
the prestige of the nation. They trained up a new
generation of diplomatists, able to fathom and cope with
the designs of the continental masters of the craft ; they
increased the navy and encouraged the practice of warlike
exercises by the people ; they strengthened the executive
until treason counted the cost before it showed its head,
and legitimate adventures became the only outlet per-
missible to turbulent spirits.

Meanwhile commerce, no longer the prime object of
governmental care, was allowed to pursue its course
practically without the assistance or hindrance of diplomacy, along the lines which Henry VII had laid down.
The North Sea, the Bay of Biscay, and the Mediterranean
afforded for the time an ample field for the training of
Englishmen in the arts of trade and seamanship. They
saw the world, and rubbed shoulders with the nations
of Europe ; acquiring in the process a pride in themselves
and a talent for dealing with their fellow men, which
have been incalculable but nevertheless important factors
in their subsequent development. The sixteenth century
is the first of the great tradition-building periods of

English history. The tradition which it produced, and
which flourishes in a tarnished form to the present day,
was that Englishmen were unsurpassed as fighters,
explorers, traders, and money-getters by every means,
fair or foul, upon the sea. And this tradition rests, not
only upon the deeds of the great names which History
records in her most lurid passages, but also upon the
accumulated exploits of the infinite number of small
men, but for whom the Drakes and the Hawkinses, the
masters of the sea, would never have been. Hence the
activities of the numerous undistinguished units producing such notable results would, taken in the mass,
appear worthy of study. During the years immediately
under consideration, the commercial side of the story
predominates over the exploring and fighting side.

For thirty years the policy of protection—the efficacy
of which no sane person dreamed of doubting—was
maintained. In the first Parliament of the reign a subsidy Act was passed, granting tonnage, poundage, and
wool duties for the king's life. The provisions were
practically identical with those of the corresponding Act
under Henry VII. The customs, as distinguished from
the subsidy, were continued unchanged. Henry VII's
fiscal system thus passed on intact to his successor. It
is significant that the usual clause was again inserted
providing for the maintenance of the privileges of the
Hansa. There was as yet no thought of the abolition
of the greatest obstacle to England's commercial advancement.

No modification of the imposts occurred until 1539,
although laws were made at various times for the regulation of trade. The Government of Henry VIII, if at
times unjust, was seldom corrupt, and generally sought

to strike a fair balance between the interests of the manufacturer, the consumer, and the trader. Hence we find Acts for such purposes as forbidding the import of foreign-made hats and caps and fixing the prices of the home-produced article, for forbidding the export of food-stuffs, and for ensuring that the more expensive kinds of cloth should not be exported unless fully manufactured. The practice of granting bounties for the construction of new shipping was continued. In 1509 a licence was granted to a merchant to carry a cargo to Bordeaux and bring another home, duty free, in consideration of his having built a vessel of 120 tons, and for the encourage-ment of others to do likewise. Highly detailed legislation, of which the above are examples, although crude and irritating to modern ideas, shows at least that the Govern-ment was taking an interest in the welfare of the classes of its subjects who were affected. No doubt the initiative came usually from the Commons, and the countenance given to it by the king made them more disposed to support him in other matters.

Broadly speaking, English commerce was in the happy condition of having no history until some years had elapsed after the fall of Wolsey. In the year 1534 an innovation of the utmost importance to its constitutional status was appended to an Act relating to the import of French wines.[1] It consisted of a clause stating that the Act in question, together with others relating to export and import, might be contrary to certain treaties; and that the king might therefore repeal such Acts by pro-clamation, and revive them from time to time as he thought fit. This conferred upon the Crown a power which, if wisely used, might be of great advantage to

---

[1] 26 Hen. VIII, c. 10.

England's interests, but which was also capable of abuse by a government actuated by corrupt motives. In any case such facility for suddenly changing the conditions of trade was undesirable, as tending to increase the insecurity which was the bane of the time. The constitutional import of the Act was far-reaching : it implied that a treaty was of superior validity to an Act of Parliament, and consequently gave to the executive, which makes treaties, a power of legislation which it had never possessed since Magna Charta. This Act is not to be confused with the better-known one of 1539 which gave to all the king's proclamations the force of law, and which was repealed by the first Parliament of Edward VI.

The first experiment on a large scale in the use of the power thus acquired was not altogether happy in its results. At the opening of the year 1539 the country was in an extremely critical position. Revolution within and invasion from without were threatening to overturn the Tudor throne. Large sections of the community were enraged at the dissolution of the monasteries, and still more at the desecration of venerated objects like the shrine of St. Thomas at Canterbury, or the numerous wonder-working roods and madonnas which had pandered to the emotions of the superstitious. Open rebellion, it is true, had met with a terrible retribution at the hands of Thomas Cromwell, who now filled Wolsey's place ; but it had been crushed by fraud rather than force, and was ready to burst into fresh flame at the hint of foreign assistance. And seldom had the time seemed more auspicious for the conquest of our island by a foreign coalition. In June 1538 Charles V and Francis I had made a peace having every aspect of solidity ; and six months later they entered into an agreement which was tantamount to a joint rupture of diplomatic relations with England. Scotland would be certain to join such a promising enterprise, while treason at home was to be stirred up by Cardinal Pole, who, armed with the thunders of a papal bull, was moving heaven and earth to procure the ruin of the sacrilegious king and to avenge the slaughter of his own friends and relatives, a large batch of whom had been executed at the end of 1538.

Henry saw that some sacrifice must be made to avert the storm. Besides fortifying the coasts, drilling troops, and terrifying the seditious by an exhibition of the utmost savagery of the law, he determined on a concession which should render peace with England more profitable than an attempt to crush her. On February 26, 1539, proclamation was made that, for the space of seven years from April following, foreign merchants were free to trade with England on payment of such customs and subsidy only as were paid by the king's own subjects.[1] The only branch of trade excepted from the concession was the export of wool, on which the old duties were maintained. Here was free trade at a single stroke, or what practically amounted to it, since the duties paid by natives were very low. Heavy as the sacrifice was, it was justified by the occasion and by the result. Before the lapse of many weeks the international tension was relieved, and the country was able to breathe freely once more. The principal effect of the move was to buy off the hostility of Charles V, whose Flemish subjects were the chief gainers by it. It must be remembered that the change applied to exports as well as imports. The result was that the Flemish cloth dealers were enabled to ship their supplies from England on the

----

[1] *Letters and Papers*, xiv, part i, No. 373.

same terms as the Merchant Adventurers, whose mart
at Antwerp was thus in danger of being superseded by
a similar centre for Flemish buyers in London. In
addition to conciliating the emperor, it is also probable
that the new policy caused some alleviation of the
internal situation in England. The lower total sum paid
in duties and the increased freedom of competition
among importers must have caused a fall in the prices
of foreign products.· But the effect produced in this
direction may easily be exaggerated, since England was
then, in the matter of necessaries, practically self-
supporting.

It soon became evident that the inauguration of a free-
trade policy was intended as a merely temporary expedient
to tide over a difficult situation.[1] The prosperity of
England's rising commerce was threatened, and with it
the fulfilment of her destiny among the nations. Protection was essential to her merchants if they were to
elbow their way to a foremost place amid the jostling
crowd of Flemings, Easterlings, Bretons, Spaniards, and
Italians who thronged the marts of Europe. The serious
effects of the change were immediately evident in the
falling-off of the number of ships engaged in the cloth
export. Flemish buyers in London used Flemish bottoms
in preference to English. Yet a healthy mercantile
marine was vitally necessary to national security at a
period when the regular navy had to be largely supplemented by merchant vessels in time of war. Accordingly,

[1] Cromwell has been credited with the intention of ' stapling ' the
cloth trade in London, i.e. with deliberately supplanting the Merchant
Adventurers' mart at Antwerp by an emporium in London. It is hardly
likely that he would have adopted such a suicidal policy otherwise than
on compulsion. The more probable explanation seems to be as here
stated. Chapuys's letter quoted below (p. 130) appears conclusive.

it was not long before Henry looked round for a convenient pretext for the evasion of his pledge. He was now no longer the chivalrous youth of the Holy League. Hard experience had taught him many a lesson in the game of statecraft as played by the rulers of the Renaissance, and he counted it folly to sacrifice his country's commerce when the need for sacrifice had passed. In fact, to one who reads the history of the sixteenth century, it seems matter for surprise that the great powers should ever have been at pains to make commercial treaties or pledges, their infringement being of almost daily occurrence.

The virtual revocation of the free trade edict of 1539 was effected in the summer of 1540. In the Parliament which sat from April to July of that year—Thomas Cromwell's last Parliament—an Act [1] was passed which had a more important bearing on English shipping than any since the Navigation Acts of Henry VII. Those Acts were cited and re-enacted. In addition, it was provided that, in view of ' the no little detriment and decay that hath and is likely to ensue to the navy ' by reason of the late concession, all foreigners who might wish to avail themselves of its advantages must in future ship their goods in English bottoms. This astute move placed the commercial rivals of England on the horns of a dilemma ; for, if they persisted in trading on equal terms with the Merchant Adventurers, the measure of their success would be also the measure of the growth of a new carrying trade which would be of enormous advantage to our naval resources. The English merchants would also receive some compensation for the loss of their privileged position, since they were themselves the

[1] 32 Hen. VIII, c. 14.

owners of most of the ships which carried their wares, and would thus participate in the new monopoly. The day of the shipowner as a distinct class, with interests opposed to those of the manufacturer, had not yet arrived.

Lest extortionate profits should be exacted by owners of shipping, the Act further proceeded to fix maximum rates of freight from London to the principal ports of Europe, varying for different commodities. From the details given it is evident that, apart from the Staplers' trade of wool, woolfells and hides, the only article of export of any importance was cloth. Cloth, in a partly or completely manufactured state, was sent to Flanders for distribution throughout western Germany, to Denmark, France, the Peninsula, and the Mediterranean.[1] The control of the cloth export to eastern Germany and the Baltic was vigorously contested between the English and the Easterlings. In spite of oft-renewed efforts of the former, their position at Danzig and the neighbouring ports was very precarious, and the Hansa held the bulk of the trade. The imports were more varied : from Flanders came velvet, chamlet, fustian, Cologne hemp or thread, madder, nails, hardware, hops, together with Mediterranean or ocean-borne produce such as sugar, almonds, currants, prunes, dates, and pepper ; Denmark sent wheat and rye, flax, canvas, pitch and tar, ' compters,' ' osmonds ',[2] bowstaves, iron, wax, feathers, and fish ; wines and woad (used in dyeing cloth) were obtained from Bordeaux ; wines, raisins, figs, oil, and salted meats, from Spain ; and sweet wines,

---

[1] Some particulars here given are taken from other sources than the Act of 1540. See Hakluyt, v. 62 ; *Letters and Papers*, xvi, No. 1126.

[2] Iron in pigs and bars ready for manufacture.

spices, carpets, rare textiles, gems, and other eastern goods, from the Mediterranean. When it is remembered that any large transference of cash was forbidden by the laws of almost all nations, it will be realized that the output of cloth and wool must have been enormous to balance such a long list of costly imports. To return to the Navigation Act, one more provision of which is of interest : it was laid down that shipowners were to post a notice in Lombard Street giving, for the information of shippers, the dates of sailing and ports of destination of their vessels.

Loud-voiced indignation abroad was the immediate consequence of the passage of this great measure. The Flemings were the hardest hit, more especially as the Easterlings, rivals of theirs as well as of the English, were exempt from its operation, being enjoined to use English ships only when none of their own were available. Chapuys, the imperial ambassador, wrote bitterly : ' Two years ago, when in fear of war and stoppage of trade, the King issued an edict placing foreign merchants on the same terms as English for customs, etc. Now, seeing no more danger of war, and wishing to increase his own shipping, he has issued an ordinance forbidding merchants to ship goods in other than English bottoms. It concerns most the people of Antwerp.' [1]

A prolonged diplomatic conflict was inevitable, for Henry was not disposed to withdraw from his position unless circumstances should compel him to do so. The threatened internal conflagration had been smothered ; also, the good relations between Charles V and Francis I showed signs of giving place once more to the usual state of hostility habitual to those sovereigns. The

[1] *Letters and Papers*, xvi, No. 13.

financial disadvantages of the free trade policy were
illustrated by a document drawn up in September 1540.[1]
It showed that the loss to the revenue, consequent on
the reduction of foreigners' payments, was £15,450 in
the space of eighteen months. Of this total London
was responsible for £14,000, it being thus evident that
the great bulk of foreigners' traffic passed through the
capital.

Reprisals were immediately resorted to by the Imperial
Government. In the Netherlands an edict was promulgated forbidding the lading of English ships when
any others were available. England retorted by prohibiting the employment of Flemish ships by Englishmen
in any circumstances whatever. Chapuys repeatedly
urged his master to revive the old Spanish laws against
the import of ' untrue ' cloths and the freighting of
foreigners' ships in Spanish ports, but it would seem
that this was only partially, if at all, carried out. Henry
had a yet stronger card to play, and, early in 1541, he
forbade by proclamation the export of wool and undressed
cloth, thus starving the Flemish craftsmen of raw material,
and reviving the evils of the suspension which preceded
the *Magnus Intercursus* of 1496. The dispute dragged
on until the summer of 1542, when the attitude of
France rendered imperative a political agreement between
England and the Empire. Charles could not face the
prospect of a new war with France with England hostile ;
on the other hand, the Queen of Hungary, Regent of
the Netherlands, began to talk of reopening the whole
question of commercial relations between England and
her subjects, which relations still rested on the basis of
the hated *Malus Intercursus* of 1506.

[1] Ibid., No. 90.

Neither side had now anything to gain by being obdurate. Accordingly, Chapuys and Gardiner, Bishop of Winchester, two of the ablest diplomatists of the time, were employed to settle the commercial question as a preliminary to a closer union between the two enemies of France. It was agreed that the objectionable edicts on either side should be revoked, and that the emperor's subjects, both in Spain and the Netherlands, should be exempt from the operation of the Navigation Act.[1] This was certainly a surrender of the main point at issue by the English Government ; it must be remembered, however, that the original free trade concession was not perpetual, but would expire automatically in 1546. When that date arrived, as a matter of fact, it was not renewed. The Flemings were still inclined to cavil at details of the settlement, but commercial interests had now to bow to politics, and ere long Henry and Charles were making war in person on the soil of France. So unbrilliantly ended the fiscal struggle caused by the first departure from the commercial policy of Henry VII.

Apart from the above incident, the record of commerce under Henry VIII shows a steady progress along familiar lines rather than the introduction of any startling innovations. Many factors contributed to this result. Owing to rivalry with France, the country, on the whole, maintained the traditional alliance with the House of Burgundy, of which the emperor was now the heir and the representative. Since he was also King of Spain, the maintenance of amity with him forbade any widespread oceanic enterprises. With the Hansa, too, Henry was unwilling to quarrel, although the extension of the cloth export was certain to bring on trouble with them sooner

[1] *Letters and Papers*, xvii, No. 440.

or later. There were good reasons for deferring the evil day as long as possible : the Hanse community in London was rich and law-abiding, and could be unconstitutionally taxed without making effective protest—towards one forced contribution alone they paid £1,000 ;[1] also they could supply naval stores, the rigging for ships, and even ships themselves in time of need. Thus the English merchants had to be content with a share only of the North Sea trade, together with an increasing interest in the Peninsula and the Mediterranean. The mediaeval commercial system had not, in fact, been developed to the fullest extent of its possibilities. Until that had been done extensions elsewhere were not worth fighting for.

But expansion, although containing no novel elements, was nevertheless extremely rapid within the prescribed limits. The increase of culture and social intercourse with foreign countries raised the standard of living among the well-to-do, and demanded a full share of the luxuries rendered accessible by the progress of discovery. The court of Henry VIII was incomparably more splendid than that of his father, or of any previous king. Many of his courtiers were newly promoted men without sufficient inherited wealth to support their position, and greedy to employ any means of augmenting their incomes. Hence the steady conversion of agricultural land into sheep farms producing England's most valuable raw material. The temporary effect of the change was famine, unemployment, rise of prices, and discontent ; but in the long run the gain was superior to the loss. Labour, cast adrift from the fields, employed itself in the cloth industry, and the very increase of the foreign-bought luxuries of the rich is witness of the growth of the

[1] *Letters and Papers*, iii, No. 2483.

manufactures which were bartered for them. The true significance of the time is observable from the standpoint of the present day. A nation of Boeotians, of plough-men, country squires, and great feudal magnates, could never have founded a colonial empire beyond the seas ; it failed permanently to hold a military empire close at hand in France. A nation, on the other hand, which had transformed some of its ploughmen into craftsmen and mariners, its squires into merchant venturers, and its nobles into fighting admirals and projectors of plan-tations, was fit to seize and possess the waste places of the earth, and to build a world-enveloping power on the proceeds of a world-wide commerce. Of this process the reign of Henry VII was the seed-time ; his son's saw the first pushing of the young plant above the mediaeval clay.

One aspect of the commercial life of the time is par-ticularly striking—the ubiquitous tyranny of officialism. Every transaction, from the greatest down to the most trivial, was the subject of endless regulation and super-vision. The making and selling of cloth, the packing of wool, the times and seasons for shearing and winding, the date and place of vending, the qualifications of persons competent to buy and sell, the sailing of merchant ships, the lading and unlading of the same, were constantly inter-fered with by king, Parliament, Privy Council, and hordes of officials. For the adjustment of such matters statute was piled upon statute, and ordinance upon ordinance. In the period 1485–1558 at least a dozen Acts were passed ' for the true making of woollen cloth '. When made, it had to be sent to London and sold only at Blackwell Hall after passing a theoretically searching scrutiny for quality or ' trueness '. Nevertheless, the very iteration of the statutes shows that they failed largely of their effect. Corruption was rampant in the civil service, and pessimists were always to be found lamenting the steady deterioration of the produce of English craftsmen. Cloths above a certain value might only be exported fully wrought, in order that English dyers, fullers, and shearmen might not suffer unduly from foreign competition ; but changes in the currency and the continuous rise of all prices rendered laws on this subject obsolete very soon after they had been passed, and necessitated frequent amendments. In the same way the sale of wool by the farmers was stringently regulated so that the Staplers might have an advantage over other Englishmen, and they in their turn over foreigners. Maximum selling prices were decreed for wines and other foreign produce : when some Portuguese ships brought cargoes of sugar to the Thames, a paternal Government sent to Antwerp to inquire the retail price of the luxury prevailing there, and, on the strength of this information, fixed it at 7d. per pound in London.

Clearing a cargo from an English port was a complicated process. When the goods were brought down to the wharf they were taken over by the packer and his underlings, whose duty it was to pack them and enter them at the custom-house, giving a true inventory of the contents of the bales. The merchant having paid the duties to the customers, the latter sent ' cocketts ' or tallies for the same to the searcher, who searched the ship to see if they were true. If the searcher detected the presence on board of any goods not accounted for in the cocketts, the goods in question were forfeit, the official himself taking half their value and the State the other half. It was the searcher's duty also to see that

the victuals provided were sufficient for the voyage. He
next mustered the passengers, being empowered to take
4*d.* per head for all such as were aliens. Everything
being satisfactory, he gave a bill of discharge to the
purser of the ship, and charged a fee for his services—
2*s.* 4*d.* for a Flemish ship, 3*s.* 4*d.* for a Hamburger, and
5*s.* 4*d.* for a Spaniard or Portuguese.[1] Each kind of
merchandise—wools, wines, cloth, &c.—had its special
weighers, packers, gaugers, collectors, and overseers necessitated by the wide range of duties, embracing practically
every article of outward and inward trade.

The laws relating to the export of wool and woolfells
limited the trade to the merchants of the Staple and to
Italians exporting direct to the Mediterranean. Other
persons wishing to take wool out of the country had to
obtain licences from the Crown, and to pay heavily for
the privilege. Such licences were freely granted, particularly for the south of Europe, and formed a lucrative
source of revenue. For example, in 1514 the sum of
£800 was paid for a licence to ship 1,000 sacks of wool.
Other licences were granted for the entire or partial
evasion of duties : £1,200 was paid for the right to ship
6000, broadcloths at a reduced rate ; and two Florentine
capitalists secured freedom from customs on all their
merchandise for five years by paying £1,000 down at
a time when the king was pressed for money.

This over-regulation of trade was in accordance with
the ideas of the time. The science of administration was
in an early stage of development, and it was a prevalent
delusion that a theoretically perfect system was the thing
to aim at, without much regard being paid to the practical possibility of working it. Thus the administrative

[1] *Cotton MSS.*, Galba B x, ff. 246, 251.

machine staggered under a load of complications which
would have taxed the resources of the most ideally honest
and industrious officials, and the result was that jobbery
and corruption flourished on an extensive scale. To the
men of the sixteenth century all this seemed perfectly
natural. They cheerfully submitted to inquisitorial
tyrannies which would be revolting to moderns with
their hypersensitive ideas of personal liberty. There was
no demand for real freedom of trade (in the non-fiscal
sense), and no realization of the enormous waste caused
by the existing system. From its very extravagance, the
red-tapeism of the sixteenth century failed to produce
the effects on national character which are so justly
feared from a similar cause at the present day. On the
contrary, the principal characteristic of the subjects of
the Tudors was a very healthy spirit of initiative, paying
scant respect to the undoubted terrors of the law, and
only held in check on English soil by the most ruthless
of governments, while it rendered the sea a happy
hunting ground for unscrupulous adventurers.

The twin evils of the time, as far as legitimate trading
was concerned, were piracy and the arbitrary behaviour
of practically all governments towards the merchants
trading in their ports. Both were largely due to the
constant wars between France and the Empire, in which
struggles England occasionally took a share. As the
sixteenth century progressed, religious strife also played
its part in stirring up international animosity and providing a pretext for evil-doing on the sea. A period of
nearly fifty years elapsed between the accession of
Henry VIII and that of Elizabeth. During twenty-five
of those years either England, France, Spain, or the
Empire, and at times all four, were at war. Moreover,

the wars were so distributed as to leave comparatively short intervals of peace between them, so that there was not time for international order to be fully re-established before the next contest began. In addition to the rivalries of the greater powers, there were struggles between England and Scotland ; between the Hanseatic League and the north-eastern nations ; and between the advancing wave of Mohammedan conquest and the Christian powers in the Mediterranean. The insecurity arising from the above causes constituted an enormous impediment to maritime commerce. The operations of regular warships were supplemented by the devastations of privateers. Letters of marque were freely issued, and merchantmen perforce went armed, becoming belligerents themselves on the slightest provocation. Very early in the century we find that it was customary for English vessels trading to Aquitaine to be equipped with artillery. Embargoes and restraints of trade, unjust taxes and extortions of all kinds, were everyday occurrences. The most harmless merchandise was regarded as contraband of war, so that a neutral ship became a fair prize if suspected to contain so much as an ounce of goods belonging to a merchant of a hostile nation. When once a vessel had been seized, even on the most flimsy pretext, it became a tedious and almost hopeless task to secure its release.

As a consequence, the tendency towards individualism, characteristic of the Renaissance, was largely checked in the sphere of international commerce, and incorporated trading in European waters secured a fresh lease of life. The merchantmen, on all frequented routes, sailed in large fleets for mutual protection, this custom extending even to the short voyages of the Merchant Adventurers to Antwerp and of the Staplers to Calais, although in their cases there were additional reasons for the practice. But although the great organizations maintained their sway, and a new one—that of the English merchants in Spain—was formed, the principle began to show signs of disintegration. In the reign of Edward VI the Government found it necessary to issue an order prohibiting from the Flanders trade all who were not members of the Merchant Adventurers' Company. Later, the aid of the Privy Council had to be invoked to put down a schism in the Company itself, caused by the impatience of central control displayed by the younger members.[1] The same period saw the virtual ruin of the Steelyard, the head-quarters of the Hansa in England. Its privileges were revoked in 1552 and were never permanently restored. The trade of Bristol and the now rising western seaports had always been more or less free. And finally, the fall of Calais in 1558 sealed the doom of the Staplers, whose monopoly failed to take root when transferred to a Flemish town. The great corporations of the future were for oceanic, not European, trade; they were rendered necessary by the same causes as their more local prototypes, and, like them, decayed or disappeared when they had played their parts as pioneers, and the conditions were ripe for individuals to take their place.

Merchants as a class advanced greatly in power and consideration under Tudor rule. It became a common thing for them to be admitted to the honour of knighthood, and to be employed in political and diplomatic

---

[1] *Acts of the Privy Council,* iv. 279, 280. This affair, obviously relating to the Merchant Adventurers, is referred to in the preface as concerning the Steelyard owing to a mistaken interpretation of the word ' Hanze ', here used in its generic sense of a corporation or union of merchants.

positions of trust. The records of such families as the
Thornes, the Gonsons, the Hawkinses, and the Greshams
show that the career open to talents was a well-established
possibility of sixteenth-century life. Naturally, the
representatives of the old order were jealous of the
advance of the new. The old nobility hated the upstarts
at court and council whom the Crown delighted to
favour in order to dissipate the last remnants of feudal
power. Even Thomas Cromwell, himself of the merchant
class, recognized the force of this feeling when at the
height of his power. In his ' Remembrances ' for the
year 1535 occurs an entry : ' That an act be made that
merchants employ their goods continually in trade, and
not in buying land. That craftsmen shall use their
crafts in towns, and not take farms in the country. That
no merchant shall purchase more than £40 worth of
land a year.' Another entry shows that the same idea
was running in his mind in 1539, and throws an illuminating side-light on the state of political science when
the cleverest politician of his time thought it possible to
change the current of a vast social tendency by means
of an Act of Parliament. In 1554 a worthy conservative,
basking in the genial warmth of Mary's rule, wrote of
the Merchant Adventurers : ' To such a pride are those
kind of men become by reason of the disorder of Princes,
as all seemeth to them reason that necessity maketh to
be sought for at their hands ; so as, contrary to nature
and all God's forbode, the merchant is now become the
prince, and who needeth aid at their hands shall so pass
therein, as he shall feel the tyranny they have. . . .'
He seemed indignant and surprised at the change in the
balance of social forces, yet, almost at the same time,
a Venetian observer remarked that there were among

the Merchant Adventurers and the Staplers many individuals worth from fifty to sixty thousand pounds
sterling.[1]

In spite of increasing intercourse, hatred of foreigners
lurked always in the English mind. Early in the reign
of Henry VIII a petition begged the king that the
swarms of aliens—' Frensshemen, Galymen, Pycardis,
Flemyngis, Keteryckis, Spanyars, Scottis, Lumbardis, and
dyvers hother nacions ', a truly terrifying list—be
restrained from trading with England ; and in 1517 the
same sentiment blazed into action with even greater
fierceness than on the occasion of the assault on the
Steelyard in 1493. Inflamed by the sermons of a popular
preacher, the London mob attacked the foreign quarters
of the city on the night of April 30. Although fore-
warned, the Government failed to prevent the outbreak,
and considerable damage was done to the French and
Flemish colonies. The Italians, having taken measures
for their own defence, suffered little harm. The rioting
was finally put down by the Lord Admiral and his
father, the Duke of Norfolk, who gathered troops outside the city, forced the gates which the rioters had
locked, and scoured the streets, taking numerous prisoners.
According to one account, some sixty persons were hanged
for their share in this affair. A Portuguese ambassador,
arriving in London in the midst of the tumult, narrowly
escaped with his life. The severity of Henry VIII on
this occasion, which was known as the Evil May Day,
is in striking contrast with the clemency of his father
in 1493.

The commercial and maritime sections of the community did not escape the far-reaching effects which

---

[1] *Venetian Cal.* vi, p. 1045.

the Reformation exercised on all phases of the national life. In fact, those effects were developed in a more striking manner among the seafaring class than perhaps in any other. The constant intercourse with the Low Countries, and, through the medium of the Hansa, with Germany, caused an importation of the new ideas into the south-eastern districts of England long before any suspicion had fallen upon the orthodoxy of the king. Indeed, throughout the reign of Henry VIII, the revolution in the religious ideas of the above-mentioned classes constantly outran that in the official views. At the outset a champion of the Pope, Henry never departed very far from the old beliefs so far as ritual and clerical practice were concerned. He had no love for the spiritual motives of the Reformation, and merely desired, for secular reasons, to substitute his own authority for that of the successor of Peter, while maintaining everything else as little changed as possible. If there had been no contemporary reformation on the Continent, Henry VIII would scarcely have been reckoned by history as more uncatholic than Henry II of England or Louis XIV of France. Circumstances, however, caused him to tolerate Protestant teachings at times, and before his death the new doctrines, superposed on the still surviving remnants' of Lollardism, had gained a firm hold on the country.

As long as Wolsey retained his supremacy there was no indication of change from above. On May 12, 1521, there was a great burning of Lutheran books by the hangman in St. Paul's Churchyard. The king and the principal dignitaries of the Church were present, and the popular mind was so impressed that some years elapsed before open advocation of reform was heard. The spread of Protestantism was specially to be looked for in

London and the other ports trading across the North Sea, and the Steelyard was early a centre for its propagation. In February 1526 Wolsey instituted an inquiry into the spiritual condition of that establishment. Various German merchants were examined. Among other questions the suspect was asked whether he had ever read or possessed any books by Martin Luther, and, if so, what he thought of them ; whether he believed the Pope to be head of the Church ; whether he had eaten flesh on prohibited days ; and why a certain mass was no longer celebrated in the Steelyard.[1]

By his long and obstinate struggle with Rome Henry alienated the feelings of the Catholic nations, and was insensibly drawn into sympathy with the Lutherans. The results were out of all proportion to the cause. Rigorous Spanish orthodoxy began a persecution of Englishmen in Spain. Merchants were imprisoned, tortured, and fined for asserting the royal supremacy. The centuries-old alliance with the Netherlands and Spain was gradually undermined, and the seeds were planted of that bitter hatred between Englishman and ' Dago ' which ultimately emboldened the former to challenge the claim of Spain and Portugal to the monopoly of Asia and the New World. The more immediate results of the cleavage were to be seen in the threatened invasion of 1538-9 and in a generally increasing ill will in international relations, augmented by the audacity of English sea-rovers. Gone were the suave correspondence and fawning ambassadors of Henry VII and Ferdinand ; in their place were tariff wars, wilful misunderstandings, and carping, querulous diplomatists like Chapuys, leading by natural development to the assassination plots of Alva

[1] *Letters and Papers*, iv, No. 1962.

and Mendoza. That affairs might have followed such a course without the intervention of the Reformation is probably true ; but this was not evident to contemporary thinkers, and at least it may be said that religious hate embittered the struggle and rendered it more desperate in its character. The extent of the feeling against the reactionary power of the Hapsburgs may be gauged by the intensity of the indignation against Mary's Spanish marriage.

In another aspect the Reformation produced effects on the future expansion of England. It undoubtedly modified for the better certain national characteristics. When information became current in England as to the nature of the Spanish administration in America, the cruelty with which the natives were treated was emphasized and possibly exaggerated. The barbarities of the Spaniards provided a moral sanction for the privateering adventures of the English, and, to mark their abhorrence of the practices of their enemies, it became a point of honour with the better sort of Englishmen to be just and humane in their dealings with native races. This effect, however, was scarcely evident during the period now under consideration, and belongs more properly to the age of Elizabeth.

Before his death Henry VIII made certain arrangements for the carrying on of the government during his son's minority. He wished that his own policy, intermediate between Catholicism and Protestantism, and averse from any violent breach with past traditions, should be maintained ; and his will provided for the establishment of a council of regency in which adherents of both parties should find a place. No sooner was the breath out of his body, however, than the Protestants asserted their ascendancy and, under the leadership of the Earl of Hertford, uncle of the new king, proceeded to achieve the Reformation with the utmost violence and lack of foresight. Hertford assumed the titles of Duke of Somerset and Lord Protector of the Realm, an office the creation of which Henry, mindful of sinister precedent, had been desirous to avoid.

Somerset, although bold and ambitious, was essentially a weak ruler. After the first glamour of a military triumph over Scotland, which brought in its train a political defeat, his true character began to appear. He had no power of control over his unscrupulous subordinates, and his best personal quality, a natural kindliness and reluctance to punish, enhanced the evils of his rule. Authority was everywhere weakened ; industrial and religious discontent were stirred up by the greed of the new nobility, who plundered the Church and enclosed common lands to the detriment of the poor. In commercial life corruption began to increase. The new Government, unlike that of the late king, was accessible to the demands of the various ' interests ', irrespective of damage to the common weal, and the need of money made it particularly partial to the views of the Merchant Adventurers.

On November 9, 1547, the Council decided to suspend the statutes relating to the export of unwrought cloths above a certain price, and to permit the free export of all cloths by Englishmen, and also, for a limited period, by the Hansa. The effect was, of course, to benefit the trader at the expense of the craftsman. That this was not part of a settled policy, but merely the prompting of expediency, is shown by another decision to repeal the Navigation Acts of Henry VII with regard to the

importation of Bordeaux wine and woad. Owing to the
high price of those commodities it was decreed that the
trade should be open to aliens between February and
October of each year. The Merchant Adventurers were
not interested in the Bordeaux trade, and the inference
is obvious that they brought pressure to bear on the
Government to secure a privileged position for themselves, while the western shipowners, having no incorporation and no collective power of bribing the Council, saw
their interests go to the wall. Both these changes were
injurious to the general welfare of the country. It was
particularly injudicious at a time of economic stress to
remove any measure of protection to native industry ;
and the same may be said of the weakening of the mercantile marine by the reversal of a policy which had
been successfully maintained for over half a century.
The proverbial spice of good, however, was intermingled
with the evil, and the way was prepared, by the same
means, for the overthrow of the Hanseatic monopoly,
again at the instance of the Merchant Adventurers.
This was done, not by Somerset, who shrank from such
a far-reaching stroke, but by his successor, Northumberland, the friend and patron of Thomas Gresham, now
rising to the leadership of the forward party in the English
mercantile world.

One of the worst effects of the corruption of the
administration was the steady depreciation of the coinage
throughout the reign of Edward VI. It placed Englishmen at a disadvantage abroad, and, by lowering the
rate of exchange, involved the Government in the very
financial difficulties for which it was intended to be the
remedy. One of its consequences was a rapid rise of
prices, that of wool increasing threefold in the space

of six years.[1] In spite of tardy reforms the tendency could not be checked. The price of wool was a governing factor of that of cloth and, indirectly, of all other commodities. The result was that cloth was ' falsified ' to a greater extent than ever before, a new Act to the contrary notwithstanding, and foreign competition began seriously to affect the prosperity of English industry. We read that trade with Flanders decayed, that much cloth was now made in other countries of Spanish wool, and that crowds of workmen were thrown out of employment. One remedy proposed was the holding of free marts in England on the lines of those in the Flemish and German cities. Southampton and Hull were suggested as suitable places, also London and Calais ; but nothing was done before the death of Edward, and the idea was then allowed to drop.

The keynote of the reign of Edward VI is unrest and chaos, religious, political, and economic. In the latter connexion it should be noted that the country was now with difficulty finding sufficient supplies of food. As early as 1533 it had been necessary to pass an Act forbidding the export of corn, cattle, pigs, sheep, &c., unless for the garrison of Calais or by special licence. The extension of the wool and cloth trade was thus being paid for by some loss of economic independence. Already a large part of the food supply consisted of fish brought by the Iceland fishing fleet and the ships of various foreign nations ; and by the end of Henry's reign England was importing corn with fair regularity from the German and Baltic ports. In 1550 a scheme to obtain 40,000 quarters of wheat from Danzig alone is mentioned in Edward's diary. At the same time it would seem that

---

[1] *Cal. Dom. S. P., Addenda, 1547-65*, p. 420.

the Peninsula was more in need of foodstuffs than was England. In spite of the Act of 1533 a considerable illicit export of grain went on from Bristol. A letter from Cadiz in 1538 mentioned that much victual was received there from the west of England and that the price of wheat was 20s. a quarter—certainly a much higher figure than the average price in England at the time. To remedy this leakage a new Act was passed in 1542–3 with the special intention of regularizing the Bristol export, followed by another in 1554–5 of more general application. By the latter it was enacted that corn might be exported without special licence only when the price of wheat did not exceed 6s. 8d. per quarter, rye 4s., and barley 3s. It is probable that actual prices were seldom as low as these.

One symptom of the great commercial changes which the sixteenth century was unfolding in its progress was the gradual falling-off in the once active intercourse between England and the Mediterranean. That sea itself, once the most distant goal of English ambition, was beginning to lose its pre-eminence as the centre of the world's activities. Two causes accounted for its decline. The more obvious was the extension of Turkish power, which destroyed the trading posts of Venice, and slowly but surely closed the old trade routes through Egypt, Syria, and the Black Sea. The Turks as a nation had no genius nor appreciation for commerce, and, although certain contemptuous exceptions were made, their general attitude was that of non-intercourse with Christian nations. The power of Venice was thus cut off at its source ; that of Genoa had already fallen at the hands of the Adriatic city, and Italian traders came less and less frequently to northern seas. The less

immediate, but in the long run more effective, cause
of the decay of the Mediterranean was the increasing
volume of the Portuguese traffic to Asia round the Cape
of Good Hope. Once this route was established—and
it became regularly frequented very soon after its discovery—its superiority was evident, and the track of the
most important commerce in the world was permanently
changed. Antwerp, whither the Portuguese forwarded
their cargoes, became the entrepôt of the north, to be
succeeded in its turn by London when the fires of
religious fury had devastated its wharves and warehouses.

During the early years of Henry VIII the Flanders
galleys visited England with fair regularity. In 1522
they were arrested at Southampton, partly in consequence
of complications arising out of the war with France.
Complaints were made that the galleys now came to
England empty, owing to the scarcity of spices in late
years, that the merchants would not pay ready money
for wools, and that their wine measures were smaller than
formerly. Henry required the Signory to give an undertaking to send the fleet annually, and the Venetians professed willingness to comply.[1] But the truth was that
their commerce was languishing. The great galleys could
no longer find cargoes. A futile effort was made to
revive their old importance, and then, after 1532, they
are heard of no more. Privately owned Venetian ships
occasionally found their way to England after that date,
and English vessels still continued to voyage through the
' Straits of Marrok ' until the beginning of Elizabeth's
reign. The sea-borne trade then died away for a generation, to be precariously renewed towards the close of the
century.

---

[1] *Venetian Cal.* iii, Nos. 440, 441, 608, 877.

The remnants of Anglo-Venetian commerce were mainly conducted by the overland route. The Venetian colony in London was principally occupied in dispatching wool in this way, paying the enormous duties exacted from foreigners rather than buy from the Staplers at Calais. The latter practice was contrary to the policy of the Senate; in 1532 they severely censured some citizens who were guilty of it.[1] The influence which the Merchant Adventurers and the Staplers were able to exert on the Government during the period following the death of Henry VIII seriously affected the Italian merchants in London. In 1557 Giovanni Michiel, the Venetian ambassador, reported that they were in a fair way to being forced to quit England altogether, owing to the prohibition of the export of wools through Flanders. A similar matter had in the previous year elicited a complaint from the whole of the Italians resident in London. They had been in the habit of exporting, via Antwerp, a considerable quantity of cloths and kerseys for the Levant. The Government, in the interests of the Merchant Adventurers, had ordered them to desert Antwerp and make Bergen their entrepôt. The English shipowners, indeed, contended that they ought not to trade overland at all, but to ship through the Straits of Gibraltar. Finally a grudging permission was given for a certain amount of cloth to be sent through Antwerp, provided that none of it was sold this side of Italy.[2]

The accession of Mary, in 1553, followed by the execution of Northumberland, produced no permanent changes in commercial policy. The tonnage, poundage, and wool duties granted for the reign by the first Parlia-

[1] *Venetian Cal.* iv, No. 751.
[2] *Lansdowne MSS.*, 170, f. 131 et seq.

MAP OF BRITISH ISLES, NORTH SEA, AND BALTIC. Venetian, c. 1489. From Egerton MS. 73, f. 36.

ment differed scarcely at all from those of Edward VI
and his two predecessors. The Hansa recovered its
privileges for a short time, only to be again deprived of
them before the end of the reign. Relations with the
Netherlands, strained during the Protestant régime,
improved after the marriage of the queen with Philip
of Spain. But these affairs are of little interest compared
with the projects for more extended enterprise which
now began to be seriously entertained for the first time.
The really significant events of the period are the voyages
of Sir Hugh Willoughby and his successors in search of
a North-East Passage to Cathay, the opening up of an
important trade with Russia, and the expeditions of
English merchants to the Gold and Ivory Coasts in
search of a more lucrative traffic than home waters could
offer them. In fact, the old pelagic system of commerce
was now developed as fully as foreign competition would
admit ; and the sky was white with the dawn of the
oceanic era, with the progress of which the greatness of
the Anglo-Saxon race has marched hand in hand.

CHAPTER VII

THE FALL OF THE HANSA

DURING the reign of Henry VIII the Hanseatic League enjoyed its last days of prosperity in England. Its ancient privileges, confirmed and regularized by treaty with Edward IV, and precariously maintained in face of the unsparing encroachments of Henry VII, continued to be enjoyed in practically undiminished form throughout the life of the second Tudor ; being, in fact, justified in the king's estimation by the services, and still more by the potential disservices, which their possessors had it in their power to render to the English State.

In the first Parliament of the reign, therefore, a short Act was passed for the maintenance *in statu quo* of the rights of the Steelyard ; and similar Acts were repeated at intervals by succeeding Parliaments. In practice, however, the general privilege thus conferred was not held to be immune from modification by the operation of statutes dealing with particular branches of trade. Of this order were the laws governing the manufacture and export of cloth, which were to the following effect : In the session of 1511–12 the old Acts [1] forbidding the export of any but fully-wrought cloth were resuscitated, with the proviso that they should not apply to the cheaper qualities below the value of four marks per piece. Two years later the law was amended by a new Act, of which the preamble set forth the interests of the various

[1] Of 7 Ed. IV and 3 Hen. VII.

parties concerned : the weavers, scattered over the face
of the country, and producing in their cottages the raw,
undressed fabric ; the dyers, fullers, shearmen, and other
craftsmen who, as the names of their callings imply,
completed by their several processes the manufacture of
the finished article, and in whose interest the prohibition
of the export of unwrought cloth had been made ; and
the exporters, merchants who stood to lose by the
restrictions imposed. But let the statute-book speak for
itself and throw light on the most ancient of our manufactures as practised four centuries ago :

‘ Which act, [that of 1511–12, fixing the limit of cheap
cloths at 4 marks] put in execution, shall not only turn
to the abatement of the King's customs, but also grow
to the utter undoing of his subjects the clothmakers and
merchants conveyers of the said cloths, forasmuch as
wool is risen of a far greater price than it was at the
making of the said act ; for where a cloth was then
commonly sold for 4 marks, it is now sold for 5 marks ;
and also, by the said act, the merchants should be bound
to dress every white cloth above the value of 4 marks
on this side the sea after they have bought them ; which
white cloths so dressed when they be brought into the
parts beyond the sea and there by the buyers of them
dyed and put in colours, then they must be newly dressed,
barbed, shorn and rowed ; and so they shall be less in
substance by themself, and the worse to the sale, and
sold for less price by 10 or 12 shillings apiece beyond the
sea, than if they were at first undressed.’

Accordingly it was now enacted that every white cloth
under the price of five marks might be exported undressed, but that all of greater value must undergo
complete manufacture at the hands of English craftsmen. The continuous increase in the bulk of the precious
metals in circulation, and the consequent rise in prices,

rendered a new alteration necessary in 1535. An Act of that year repeated the above preamble almost word for word, but fixed the price limits of 'cheap cloths' at £4 for white cloths and £3 for coloured.[1]

The Easterling merchants, in common with other exporters, were included in the scope of these Acts. That they considered them as an infraction of their liberties is proved by a complaint on the subject addressed to King Henry from Lubeck in 1517.[2] But it was idle for them to expect exceptional redress in a matter which affected English merchants as hardly as themselves. Economic change was producing terrible problems of beggary and unemployment, and it was essential to maintain a certain amount of protection for English industry.

Of more importance was another grievance exposed in the same complaint. This was that the Easterlings were only permitted to import, at their privileged rates of duty, the merchandise of their own cities. The dispute arose from the ambiguity of a phrase in a Latin treaty which gave the Hanse merchants the right to import *suae merces*. The English contention was that the words applied only to articles actually produced in the Hanse towns; the Hansa, on the other hand, claimed that the phrase covered all goods, however acquired. The matter was of some moment and considerable sums were involved, since barter, rather than manufacture, was the essence of the existence of the League. Its cities were rich and powerful, not because they gave shelter to thousands of skilful artisans, but because they formed the European extremity of a trade route which passed through Poland into Russia, and thence tapped the products of the Near

---

[1] A mark = 13s. 4d.   [2] *Letters and Papers*, ii, No. 3435.

and Middle East. But the time was unfavourable for the League to commence a serious controversy with England. A period of European peace had succeeded the war of the Holy League, and bade fair to continue indefinitely. Henry VIII was thus in no pressing need of ships or naval stores, and was disposed to be obdurate rather than compliant. German merchants were imprisoned in connexion with marine depredations dating back as far as 1511. On renewed protests by the Magistrates of Stralsund, backed by some neighbouring potentate, Wolsey said to their ambassador in the presence of many notable persons : ' Your reverence has presented to us the letters of an unknown prince. He may be most Christian and powerful, as you say, but he is unknown to us, and we do not wish to have anything to do with him.' [1]

The Easterlings, however, were stubborn men, and were not prepared to submit tamely to such arrogant treatment. They were determined to maintain their privileges, which, as they said, they had bought with their money and blood. The dispute dragged on until 1520, when a diet was appointed to meet at Bruges to negotiate for a settlement. One of the English commissioners was Thomas More ; another was John Hewster, Governor of the Merchant Adventurers at Antwerp. In September the diet met, but the representatives of the League offered excuses for being unready to begin business. Discussion of their privileges was not what they desired, since any modification would almost certainly be to their prejudice ; what they asked was a sweeping reaffirmation of all their claims, however obsolete. Such was not the intention of the English commissioners, who

[1] *Letters and Papers*, iii, No. 1082.

took the initiative, presented extensive claims for injuries inflicted, and pressed the Easterlings to state exactly the names of the towns belonging to the League when the privileges were first granted. The latter demand touched the Hansa in its weakest spot. It was basing its claims on grants of privileges of very ancient date ; yet it was undeniable that the scope of the League had been vastly extended since that date, and therefore that the whole of its relations with England ought in justice to be reconsidered. Its representatives at the diet had no answer to make ; they could only profess themselves much shocked at the League's integrity being doubted, and declare that such a suggestion had never been raised before. With such irreconcilable motives on either side a final settlement was impossible. The same questions continue to recur at intervals throughout the remainder of the history of the Hansa in England. Some minor concessions were agreed upon and the acerbity of the dispute was smoothed down.[1] A new European war was by this time looming on the horizon, a fact which rendered free access to the naval resources of the Baltic essential to England. The commercial question was of secondary importance, and could wait.

As may have been seen, the relations between Henry VIII and the Hansa depended, broadly speaking, on the fluctuations of foreign politics. When the prospect was peaceful and the country seemed secure, he was inimical to the Easterlings and openly favoured Englishmen at their expense ; when danger threatened, he had to conciliate them on account of their strength in ships and seamen. There was at that time little structural difference between warships and merchantmen,

---

[1] *Foedera*, xiii, p. 722 ; *Letters and Papers*, iii, part i, Nos. 974, 979.

VII   THE FALL OF THE HANSA   157

and it was a simple matter to convert the one into the other. Hence on military grounds alone the enmity of the League was not to be despised.

Thus, with alternations of calm and storm, the denizens of the Steelyard pushed their fortunes, ever ready to seize an advantage and, if we are to believe jealous English accounts, steadily increasing their business and pressing hard on the younger and more tender commerce of England. As time went on, it is evident that the shackles on their activities, feeble as they were, were nevertheless gradually tightened. An Act of 1523 forbade the sale of white cloth to aliens except under certain conditions. In 1526 the Easterlings resident in London were proceeded against for heresy; and, in times of peace, all the oppressive laws in the statutebook were sharply enforced against them. Towards the end of 1535 they were subjected to a temporary restraint and sequestration of property, by reason, as Chapuys says, of the seizure of some English ships by the Swedes. After a few weeks, however, the matter was arranged and trade was resumed.[1] In 1540 the Council of Lubeck forwarded an extensive list of grievances to Henry, of which the following were the most important :[2]

1. Contrary to ancient grants they are now forbidden to load undressed cloth.
2. Whereas they were formerly free to export to England whatever they pleased (wines excepted), special licences are now demanded.
3. They are held responsible for losses sustained by English subjects within their princes' territories.
4. Contrary to the treaty of 1474, they are subjected to the jurisdiction of the Admiral's Court.
5. Unjust and dishonest conduct of customs officials.

[1] *Spanish Cal.* v, pp. 550, 563, &c.   [2] *Letters and Papers*, xvi, No. 392.

As was usual in time of peace, the English exporters had the ear of Henry and his Council, and strained relations continued for some time longer. In September 1540 it was rumoured that the entire privileges of the Easterlings were to be revoked and that they were on the point of leaving the country.[1] But the time was not ripe for such a step, and Henry held his hand. In the great Act ' For the maintainance of the Navy ', passed in the summer of the same year, wherein it was laid down that foreigners wishing to trade on payment of reduced customs must ship in English bottoms, it was expressly provided that nothing in the Act should be construed to the prejudice of the Hanse merchants. In their case it was merely enjoined that they should lade in English ships when none of their own were available. Whatever benefits the Act conferred on English merchants were also shared by the Easterlings, for, while leaving their own privileges intact, it curtailed those of other foreigners, thus leaving them in a relatively better position. In spite of this, charges and countercharges continued for some time to pass between England and the League. In 1542 some Englishmen complained to the Privy Council of injuries sustained at the hands of the inhabitants of Danzig. Representatives of the London Easterlings were summoned to answer the complaint, and alleged, first, that the charges were untrue, and secondly, that there were no Danzig men in their company. But corporate privileges were naturally held to entail corporate responsibility ; and it was pointed out to them that, even though there might be no Danzig men in the London Hansa, as members of the same company they were liable, and must induce the Danzig authorities

[1] *Letters and Papers*, xvi, No. 12.

to make restitution.[1] Although this system of corporate responsibility bore hardly on individuals, it was the only available check on arbitrary proceedings, and maritime trade would have been an impossibility without it.

By this time there was on both sides a sufficient accumulation of grievances to warrant the holding of another diet to clear the air. It was fixed to take place at Antwerp in 1542. But the League made the customary excuses when it came to the point. What they feared most was a searching discussion of their whole position. They were conscious that, whatever a parchment signed and sealed seventy years before might say, their privileges were an absurdity in the light of common sense, and that any modification could only be in one direction. Accordingly the Consuls and Senators of Lubeck wrote to Henry thanking him for appointing a day for the diet, but begging to be excused from sending representatives as the wars rendered Antwerp an unsafe meeting-place.[2] This persistent evasion of discussion shows the weakness of their position. The morale of the attack was with the English merchants and, even in an age when morality went for very little in public matters, their sense of injustice rendered the reduction of the preposterous advantages enjoyed by a company of aliens only a matter of time. For the moment, however, the inevitable conclusion was again postponed. A new war was in progress with Scotland and in prospect with France, and, as usual, naval and military necessities rendered peace with the Hansa indispensable.

The fact that the League's naval power was never used against Henry VIII must not be allowed to obscure

---

[1] *Proceedings of the Privy Council*, vii, 301, 308-9.
[2] *Letters and Papers*, xvii, No. 736.

the fact that it could have been so used, and that, if it had been, the consequences to him would have been most serious. As it was, in this last French war of his, the navies on either side of the Channel were practically equal ; the French, indeed, were superior in material strength. Thus the king simply could not afford to quarrel with the League, and, instead of pressing the matter of the diet, he appears to have made extensive concessions. Such is the implication to be derived from a letter from Lubeck dated April 6, 1543, in which it is stated that the Hanse towns are greatly indebted to Henry and will never do anything to his prejudice.[1] Two years later several Hanse vessels served in his fleet against the French.

So ended the last passage of arms between the League and Henry VIII. Friendly alliance persisted thenceforward to the end of the reign. In 1544 a large consignment of ships, rigging, and stores was received from Danzig for the use of the Navy.[2] Henry was treacherously treated by the emperor, who made an unexpected peace with France in 1544. The hostile relations which resulted between England and the Imperial Government placed the Merchant Adventurers in difficulties in the Netherlands. Oppressive taxes were imposed on them and, for a time, they and their goods were under arrest.[3] From these troubles the Hansa made its profit, and was soon absorbing an ever-increasing share of the cloth export to Antwerp, a trade which the Merchant Adventurers had always regarded as peculiarly their own. When Henry died the prosperity of the London Hansa was at

[1] *Letters and Papers*, xviii, part i, No. 376.
[2] *Cal. Cecil MSS.*, i. 44.
[3] *Letters and Papers*, xx, part i, No. 164.

its highest point, and formed a striking contrast to the ruin which overtook it a few years later. Broadly considered, it seems surprising that such an undoubted anachronism should have survived so far into the noonday of Tudor rule. The explanation, as has been shown, is to be found in the wars of Henry VIII and the relative weakness of his navy as compared with the demands he made upon it. His personal position was so elevated and commanding that he seldom needed to stoop to ignoble truckling with factions, as did the rulers who immediately succeeded him. From his lofty standpoint he viewed the interests of the nation as a whole, and placed its safety above the more sectional desire of the merchants to score off their foreign rivals. Consequently he seems to have been over-generous in his treatment of the Hanseatic League, to have failed to realize that it must be crushed before England could take a leading place among the maritime nations. But it is doubtful if precipitate action would better have advanced the interests of English commerce than did the policy actually pursued. When the time was ripe the inevitable happened, and our trade was free to expand without the drag of privileged competition within our gates.

The accession to power of the Duke of Somerset did not produce any immediate change in the position of the Hansa, although doubtless the Merchant Adventurers were quick to see that their chance had come with the troublous times of a minority. The Act granting tonnage and poundage for the reign contained a clause in favour of the ancient privileges of the Steelyard, but with a proviso for their maintenance during the existing Parliament only. For the time being the prospect of trouble with Scotland and France forced Somerset to hold his hand, if indeed he had any intention of yielding to the demands of the League's enemies. The Protestant sympathies of the new Government tended rather towards alliance with the German powers. Within two months of Henry's death a proposal was on foot to lend 50,000 crowns to the Duke of Saxony and the Free Towns, to be repaid by the latter in cables, masts, anchors, pitch, and other naval stores;[1] and in the same year the suspension of the statutes limiting the export of un-wrought cloth, and the permission of the free export of the same by Englishmen, was extended to the Hansa also for a limited period. This favourable treatment continued even after the deposition of Somerset, during the two years from the autumn of 1549 to the autumn of 1551, in which Warwick was consolidating his power. Thus, when the Hanse establishment at Hull was being oppressively used by the civic authorities, letters were addressed to the Mayor and Jurats enjoining them to cease their aggressions and to refrain from imposing new imposts.[2] Hitherto the only measure suggestive of hostility to the Hansa had been an Act passed in 1548 to suppress 'colouring'. This was a method of defrauding the customs and consisted in the passing of the property of others through the custom-house as their own by those who paid reduced duties, as did the Easterlings. The offence was extensively charged against them, probably with good reason.

Apparently, therefore, the death of Henry had made no difference to the position of the Hansa; and their privileges, which even he had never seriously challenged, seemed more strongly rooted than ever. During these

[1] *Acts of the Privy Council*, ii. 61.
[2] In June 1548, and June and September 1551.

years their business, by all accounts, increased to an enormous extent. It is to be hoped that they made some sacrifice to Nemesis, in the shape of insurance against the evil times that followed. The very weakness of the Government, which seemed their best guarantee, was in the end to be the cause of their ruin. By the year 1551 the administration was in serious financial difficulties, and was resorting to such desperate measures as the wholesale debasement of the coinage. English credit diminished abroad, and the rate of exchange at Antwerp fell alarmingly. Thomas Gresham, a protégé of Warwick's, was sent to the Low Countries to exercise his business genius in remedying matters ; [1] at the same time the Merchant Adventurers were called upon for extensive loans, and, backed by Gresham, they were clamorous for the revocation, in return, of the privileges of the Hansa. That momentous step was accordingly resolved upon by Warwick, not as the culminating act in a piece of patriotic diplomacy, but as a stake thrown on the table by an irresponsible gambler, risking what is not his own. That the consequences were not immediately disastrous may be admitted, but the country was scarcely in a strong enough position for such a risk to be taken, as the feebleness of the fleet in subsequent actions was to demonstrate. The suppression of the Hanse privileges was necessary and desirable ; but it should have been deferred to a time when the English navy was strong enough to maintain unaided the command of the narrow seas. Such undoubtedly would have been the policy of Henry VIII.

Warwick was now on the point of consummating his triumph over the rival faction of Somerset, crippled,

[1] *Dict. Nat. Biog.*

though not destroyed, two years before. In October
1551 he was created Duke of Northumberland by the
pliant young king. The second and final arrest of
Somerset followed, and his trial on fabricated charges
began on December 1. On January 22, 1552, Somerset's
head fell on the scaffold and Northumberland was henceforth, in fact though not in name, supreme ruler of
England.

Meanwhile the tragedy of the London Hansa was
proceeding concomitantly with that of the great protector. The first hint of its impending fate was contained
in an order sent on December 12 to the Clerk of Chancery
to search for the last letters patent granted by the king
to the Steelyard men, 'about January was twelvemonth',
and to send a copy of the same for immediate consideration.[1] As compared with the prolonged diplomatic
struggles which the Hansa had already survived, its suppression was accomplished with surprising rapidity. On
the 29th the alderman and some of the merchants of
the Steelyard were summoned before the Council.[2] The
information laid against them by the Merchant Adventurers was recited and a copy delivered to them in
writing. Briefly, the charges were as follows : That
there was no definition of the exact extent of the League,
and that thus it was enabled to admit whom it liked to
its liberties, to the detriment of the revenue and of the
trade of the English merchants ; that the Steelyard men
'coloured' foreigners' goods extensively ; that their
export of English cloth to the Low Countries and elsewhere, and the import of goods from neutral countries,
constituted an infraction of their original privileges,
which provided only that they should deal in *suae merces*,

---

[1] *Acts of the Privy Council*, iii. 441.   [2] Ibid. 453.

a phrase interpreted by the English as meaning the produce solely of their own territories ; and that the treaty
of 1474, providing that Englishmen should enjoy similar
privileges in German ports, had not been adhered to.[1]

It is probable that, although they had been living
under the shadow of some such crisis for over half
a century, the blow fell unexpectedly at last. No preliminary warning of a categorical nature is discoverable
in the surviving evidence, and it is natural to suppose
that Northumberland, Gresham, and the governing
clique of the Merchant Adventurers concerted their
measures in secrecy. The whole process of trial and
judgement certainly reads like a foregone conclusion.
The Easterlings took nearly three weeks to consider their
reply, which they presented on January 18, 1552. The
Solicitor-General and three other lawyers were appointed
to deal with it, and the matter was before the Council
on January 25 and February 9. The advocates of the
rival corporations argued their several cases, the Hansa
showing ' divers writings and charters ', which, however,
were not thought to be of sufficient force. The hearing
was adjourned to the 18th, when the Merchant Adventurers made their retort to the defence and nothing
remained but for judgement to be pronounced.[2] Judgement was not slow to follow, since the case had been
decided before ever it was opened, and it was desirable
to make an end before the arrival of ambassadors known
to be on their way from the Baltic towns. These latter
must, in bare courtesy, be listened to, and their eloquence
would but delay the inevitable result.

---

[1] R. O., State Papers Dom., Ed. VI, vol. xiv, No. 10, and other R. O.
MSS.

[2] Journal of Edward VI, pp. 59, 61 ; A. P. C., iii. 460, 475.

Accordingly, on February 24, 1552, the decision was promulgated in a document which still rests among the Public Records, endorsed in Cecil's hand as ' The Decree against the Styllyard '. The *Calendar of Foreign State Papers* gives the pith of it as follows :

1. The pretended privileges are void because the merchants have no sufficient corporation to receive the same.

2. These privileges extend to no certain persons or towns, but they admit to be free with them whom they list, to the annual loss to the customs of nearly £20,000.

3. Even were such privileges good according to the law of the land, which they are not, they had only been granted on condition that the merchants should not avow or colour any foreign goods or merchandise ; a condition which the merchants have not observed.

4. For more than a hundred years after these alleged privileges were granted, the Hanse merchants exported no goods except to their own countries, nor imported any but the produce of the same ; whereas now they do so to the Low Countries, Flanders, and elsewhere, contrary to the terms of a recognisance made in the time of Henry VIII.

5. These privileges, which were at first beneficial to the merchants, without any notable injury to the realm, have now by their exceeding of the same grown so prejudicial to the state that they may no longer without great hurt thereof be endured.

6. The treaty of reciprocity, made after the forfeiture of the alleged privileges by war, in the time of Edward IV, whereby the English should have similar liberties in Prussia and other places of the Hansa, has been daily broken, especially in Danzig, by the prohibition of Englishmen to buy and sell there : and though divers requests for redress of such wrongs have been made, no reformation has ensued.

Wherefore, until the merchants can prove better and

more sufficient matter for their claim, all their liberties
and franchises are seized and returned into the king's
hands ; reserving to the merchants the ordinary privilege
of trading, common to those of other nations.[1]

The privileges thus lost were considerable, arising
principally from the adjustment of the duties. On all
foreign wares coming into the country, wines excepted,
the Easterlings paid only 3*d.* in the £ as subsidy or
poundage, while Englishmen paid 12*d.* and other
foreigners 20*d.* For the export of cloth Englishmen
paid no subsidy, the Easterlings paid 12*d. per piece*, and
other foreigners as much as 6*s.* 4*d.*[2] Here the English
exporters had a slight advantage, but insufficient to
neutralize the discrimination of 9*d.* in the £ on imports.
The 12*d.* per cloth paid by the Hansa was not very
ruinous when compared with the value of the goods—
the average price of a piece of cloth for export being
about £5. To the other foreigners the cloth duties
proved almost prohibitive, with the result that in one
year the Hansa shipped 44,000 cloths out of England as
against 1,100 shipped by all other aliens.[3]

The great offence of the Easterlings was undoubtedly
this successful competition of theirs with the Merchant
Adventurers in the cloth export to the Low Countries.
It would seem that, although they had practised it to
some extent as far back as the time of Henry VII, they

[1] This document is assigned in the Calendar to the year 1553, but it
obviously belongs to the sequence of events of 1551-2. At the end of
the original (*R. O., S. P. For. Ed. VI*, vol. xi, ff. 147-9) occur the words :
' This decree was made and given at Westmr. the xxiiii of February in
the sixt year of the reign.' The sixth year of Edward VI extended from
January 29, 1552, to January 28, 1553. See also the *Journal of Edward VI*
and *A. P. C.*, iii. 487-9.

[2] *R. O., S. P. Dom., Mary*, vol. iv, No. 36.

[3] *Edward VI's Journal*, p. 61.

had enormously increased their operations during the
last years of Henry VIII and throughout the reign of
his son, a period in which the English had been in bad
odour with the Imperial Government. But the Merchant
Adventurers claimed a monopoly in this direction quite
as ancient as that of their rivals—dating back, in fact, to
the reign of Edward I, if we are to believe Thomas
Gresham—and they can hardly be blamed for striking
hard when the turn of political intrigue put it into their
power to do so. The numerous lists of grievances against
the Easterlings all emphasize the unprecedented increase
of this branch of their business, and when, under Mary,
their liberties were partially restored, it was with special
safeguards against their selling cloth in Antwerp. If
they had been prepared to recognize that their day of
power was past, and peaceably to forgo this traffic,
they might long have continued unmolested in London,
dealing on favourable terms in the special products of
Germany and the Baltic. But their obstinate insistence
on a treaty close on a century old, and embodying
privileges more ancient still, granted when social,
economic, and national conditions had all been widely
different, was certain not to pass unchallenged in the
new age of national awakening.

The new edict was rapidly put into execution. On
February 27 the Council sent letters to the customers
of London and Hull ordering them to exact from the
Easterlings the ordinary customs as paid by other aliens.
No trace can be found of similar instructions being sent
to Lynn, from which it would appear that the Hanse
dépôt at one time existing in that place had already been
abolished. On the following day the expected ambassadors arrived from Hamburg and Lubeck to plead their

cause, the task of dealing with them being committed to the Lord Chancellor and a committee of nine. On May 1 an answer was delivered which confirmed the former judgement in all points. The Government was determined to stop the Hanse export of cloth, and strict injunctions were issued to prevent any one else from 'colouring' their goods. Later, after renewed representations from the ambassadors, or 'orators' as they were styled, they relented so far as to allow the export at the old rates of a certain quantity of cloths, not exceeding 2,000 in number, which had been purchased before the restraint.[1] An entry in the king's journal noting the above concession, concludes with the following words, which seem to signify that the Government was still disposed to negotiate : '. . . in all other points the old decree to stand, till by a further communication the matter should be ended and concluded.' Again, in October, it was resolved by the Council, 'that the matter (of the Hansa) shall be more fully heard in the Exchequer'. Second thoughts were evidently giving rise to misgivings as to the possible disadvantages of open war with the League.

The Hansa, in fact, never accepted defeat nor relaxed their efforts to secure a reversal of the decree. On September 7, 1552, Sigismund Augustus, King of Poland, wrote to Edward VI on behalf of the citizens of Danzig, setting forth the intolerable burdens to which they were subjected and desiring the restoration of their ancient liberties.[2] But on the main point the Government held firm. No agreement was arrived at, and the 'restraint'

---

[1] For this embassy see *Edward VI's Journal*, pp. 61, 62, 66, 73 ; and *Acts of the Privy Council*, iv. 32, 43, 93, 98, 141.

[2] *Cal. For. S. P., Ed. VI*, p. 220.

continued until after the death of Edward, which event
took place in July 1553.

With the opening of Mary's reign the prospects of the
Hansa brightened for a short time, only to be extinguished
again before its close. The queen was naturally not
prejudiced in favour of any policy of Northumberland's,
and she found good reasons for treating the Easterlings
more leniently. Gresham, as a strong adherent of the
duke's party, fell under a cloud, from which he only
emerged when found to be indispensable to the new
Government. He was not reinstated in his position at
Antwerp until the middle of November.[1] The emperor,
with whose son Mary was already contemplating marriage,
was opposed to the infliction of extreme penalties on those
who were theoretically his subjects. His Flemings also
were afraid that if the Merchant Adventurers were freed
from all competition they would raise their prices at
Antwerp. Influence was accordingly brought to bear upon
the queen, with the result that orders were given for the
restraint to be removed in September 1553, after a duration of nineteen months.[2] In spite of this the usual
Act granting tonnage, poundage, &c., for the reign,
passed in October, made no mention of the restoration
of the Hanse privileges, and the customers of London
continued to exact from them the usual duties payable
by aliens. On complaint being made to the queen, she
issued definite instructions that the Easterlings were to
pay no more than in the time before the restraint. She
further ruled that they should be allowed to export
unwrought cloths up to the value of £6 per piece, the

[1] *Dict. Nat. Biog.*
[2] *R. O., S. P. Dom., Mary*, vol. v, No. 5.

suspension of the statutes on this matter, which took place in 1547, having lapsed.[1]

The Hansa was now better off than it had been for many years, but the improvement was destined to be fleeting. The Merchant Adventurers did not accept the reversal of their good fortune without a struggle. They accumulated evidence of the malpractices of their enemies and clamoured their discontent with a vigour and pertinacity which showed that the Easterlings would never again enjoy an unchallenged supremacy in the North Sea trade. In December 1554 an indictment was drawn up, setting forth in detail the injuries suffered by the Crown and the merchants of England by reason of ' the usurped trade and traffic which the Easterlings many years have used and yet do use '. It is typical of numerous complaints current at the time, and contains most of the stock charges and arguments against the Hansa, amongst which the question of the cloth export holds a preponderating place. Some of the details must be accepted with reserve : party statements, even in our own moral age, are not apt to be over-scrupulous in the handling of figures :

Beginning with a specification of the reduced duties restored since the lifting of the restraint, it went on to deplore the ' decay ' of English shipping and mariners caused by the carrying trade of the Easterlings : where, in former times, thirty or forty large English ships would have been freighted at once, now only three or four small crayers were required. Next, the decay of the cloth manufacture, the diminishing sales at Blackwell Hall, the rise of prices of all commodities, the fall of the rate of exchange on Antwerp Bourse, and, in fact, all

[1] *Foedera*, xv. 364.

the commercial evils of the time, were ascribed to the same ' usurped ' trade. The English merchants trading to the Low Countries were, in common with everything else in this gloomy screed, ' much decayed ', and likely within few years to be utterly undone. The resident Germans being, by the rules of the Steelyard, bachelors, and the Englishmen having wife and children to support, the latter were again at a disadvantage. Their grievances beyond the seas were still more bitter. The Hansa, paying lower import duty, could afford to undersell them everywhere. Severe laws and exactions had driven out those Englishmen who formerly had warehouses in various German and Baltic ports. Not content with that, the Easterlings had followed them into the Low Countries, and had made great sales of English and foreign wares there. At Hamburg they had established a rival mart for English cloth which they caused to be dressed in that city, thus throwing English craftsmen out of work. The Hamburg mart, being nearer than Antwerp to the interior of Germany, was threatening to do away with most of the English trade to Antwerp.

Figures were then given in support of the foregoing and other charges. Thirty-one Hanse merchants had between them shipped 11,200 cloths to Antwerp in eleven months of the year 1554; thirty-four had in the same period sent 23,250 cloths to Hamburg, Lubeck, and other German towns. Twenty-seven persons, being only ' shippers (skippers) and mariners ', had brought cargoes to England, but had taken no merchandise away in return; they must, therefore, have taken money out of the realm. Thirty-eight Dutchmen, not members of the Hansa, were mentioned, who had exported largely from England during the restraint, but who had not since shipped a single cloth ; from which it was deduced that the Easterlings must now be colouring their goods. The charge of colouring was further supported by a tabulation of exports and imports showing that the Hansa had sent out of the country in eleven months goods to the value of £154,366 more than those they had brought in ; since it was certain that they had not brought specie to anything like that amount, it was concluded that they must have coloured cloths for the Flemings and other heavily taxed aliens. But for this, the same cloth would have been purchased from the Merchant Adventurers at Antwerp. To cap the whole indictment, it was urged that the Easterlings studiously avoided chartering English shipping : during the period named they had freighted about forty vessels, not one of them English.[1]

The complaint was backed by a petition from the Merchant Adventurers to the Council, deploring the falling-off of their trade and asking for the following remedies : that the Hansa be forced to define precisely its own extent ; that it be allowed to export to its own cities, only coloured cloths, ' dyed, rowed, barbed, shorn, and fully dressed unto the proof ' ; and that its trade in English goods to the Low Countries be prohibited.[2] The petitioners pointed out that it was not sufficient merely to restrain the traffic to Antwerp, but also that in white cloth to the North German ports. The finishing of such cloth was becoming a rising industry in that region, while English and Flemish craftsmen were losing work. The inclusion of the Flemings in the argument was possibly a bid for the favour of King Philip, who, however, consistently supported the Hansa. But Philip

---

[1] R. O., S. P. Dom., Mary, vol. iv, No. 36.
[2] Ibid., vol. v, No. 5.

had by no means an overwhelming influence in the conduct of English affairs. The queen, no doubt, usually gave way to him, but the Council, while rendering unlimited lip-homage, generally contrived to thwart his desires when they ran counter to their own ; and, as time went on, their independence increased. Such at least was the case with regard to maritime and commercial matters.

The efforts of the Merchant Adventurers were crowned with success. On March 23, 1555, the Council issued orders that, pending the holding of a diet, the Hansa should export no cloth whatever to Antwerp, and to other places only one white cloth for every three coloured ones.[1] If they wished to make any shipments in excess of the above limits they were to pay the ordinary aliens' customs rates. With regard to imports, they might import £1 worth of ' foreign ' goods for every £3 of the produce of their own countries. This order was to continue in force until a diet should otherwise determine the matter.[2]

Thus, after eighteen months' unrestricted enjoyment of their old privileges, the Easterlings found them once more virtually suppressed by an edict almost as severe as that of 1552. There could be no mistake as to the intention of the proposal for a diet. Its only result would be to tear up the treaty upon which their position was based, and to regularize their reduction to the status of ordinary aliens. They therefore refused to have anything to do with it. Yet they did not despair of securing a modification of the latest sentence and, twelve months

---

[1] Other evidence points to a total prohibition of the export of white cloth (see p. 176). The point is doubtful.
[2] *Lansdowne MSS.*, 170, f. 155.

later, an embassy arrived in London with proposals for a settlement. The ambassadors pointed out that their own cities produced little or nothing which could be sold in England, most of their merchandise being brought, by the travail of their merchants and sailors, from the remotest regions of the North and East. Accordingly they asked that the term ' foreign goods ' (*exoticae merces*) might be interpreted to mean the goods of France, Spain, and Italy, and that they might be free to import other merchandise without restriction. With regard to the export of cloth from England, they declared that the distinction between white and coloured cloth was intolerable and, if persisted in, would exclude the majority of Easterlings from commerce with this country. They asked therefore for the restoration of their ancient liberty of exporting to their own cities any cloths, white or coloured, and, if under the value of £6, unwrought. The emphasis laid upon this demand makes it evident that cloth finishing was indeed a growing industry in North Germany, as the Merchant Adventurers had alleged, and that a supply of the rough fabric, obtainable only in England, was indispensable. In return for the above concessions the Hansa was willing to undertake to abstain altogether from selling English cloth in the Low Countries, merely reserving the right to export via Antwerp to its own cities without opening the packages in transit. The letter to Sir William Petre, in which the above proposals were enclosed, ends with a half-threatening recommendation that moderation and friend-ship would prove the better course, and that the English would do well not to make themselves unpopular on the Continent.[1]

[1] R. O., S. P. For., Mary, vol. viii, No. 481.

The Hanse demands were countenanced by King Philip [1], who, as Regent of the Netherlands, was by no means satisfied that his subjects' interests were identical with those of the English. In deference to her husband, Mary determined to make a show of concession, although it would seem that she had by this time been entirely won over to the Merchant Adventurers' point of view. An answer was returned to the following effect : That Their Majesties were mindful of the ancient friendship between England and the Hansa, and were desirous to increase the same, but that the rights claimed had not in former times been generally admitted. As long as they had been used in moderation it was not a matter of much importance, but of late they had been excessively used, to the great prejudice of the revenue and merchants of England, and could no longer be tolerated. Therefore Their Majesties' proposal was that a diet should be held in London within one year, for the settlement of all questions in a manner useful to both parties. In the meanwhile the absolute prohibition of the export of white cloth should be removed, the liberty of exporting one white cloth for every two coloured ones being substituted.[2] Nothing is here said about Antwerp, but it is evident from other sources that the Hansa was held to its offer to abstain from trading there.[3]

An agreement was concluded on the above lines on March 23, 1556, exactly a year after the second revocation of the privileges. It was to endure for one year only, or until the conclusion of the diet if held sooner.

---

[1] *Cotton MSS.*, Titus B ii. 129b. Letter from Philip to Mary in support of a Hanse petition (Dec. 1555).

[2] *R. O., S. P. For., Mary*, vol. viii, No. 491; *Lansdowne MSS.*, 170, f.156.

[3] Report of Paget and Petre to King Philip, *R. O., S. P. For., Mary*, vol. viii, No. 492 ; and *A. P. C.*, vi. 33, 34.

At the same time the Easterlings of the London establishment were granted relief from certain oppressive proceedings of the Lord Mayor, and were given the right to buy cloth in warehouses adjoining the Steelyard instead of at Blackwell Hall.[1]

In spite of all losses and interruptions the trade of the Hansa showed a wonderful vitality. By the end of 1556 they were shipping cloth through Antwerp in such quantities that their enemies could not help suspecting that they meant to ' utter ' some of it there. The Council threatened to bind them over in the sum of £20,000, but they begged off and escaped with a strict admonition to do nothing fraudulent.[2] The drawback to all such agreements as that under which they were working was that the resources of the administration were insufficient for the supervision of intricate mercantile processes. Consequently it was as easy to evade—or be suspected of evading—a commercial treaty, as it became in later days to smuggle goods without paying duty. The fires of hatred and suspicion were now thoroughly kindled, and it was not long before England and the League were again at variance.

As always, the Hansa was strongly averse to the proposed diet for a final settlement, and the allotted year in which it was to be held slipped by without any steps being taken. Conscious that the diet was a trap which would mutilate still further their diminished privileges, they postponed the evil day as long as possible, trusting doubtless that international complications would arise to save them, as had happened so often on previous occasions. The year elapsed and no delegates appeared. Nevertheless, on April 12, 1557, the Council resolved that,

[1] A. P. C., v. 252-7.   [2] Ibid., vi. 33, 34.

notwithstanding the expiry of the last settlement, judgement should be suspended for five weeks longer, during which period they might export 2,000 cloths, on the understanding that the diet should commence without delay.[1] This produced yet another embassy. It arrived before the end of the same month, and we read that Sir James Tregonwell was appointed to conduct the negotiations. They were hopeless from the first; the points of view of the two parties were irreconcilable, and in less than a month the ambassadors were taking their departure, leaving the business on the same footing as before.[2] Again, in October, the queen was corresponding direct with Lubeck, still pressing the question of the diet. The concessions of March 1556 had long expired, but the Easterlings were still carrying on a languishing trade on the same terms as other aliens. It was a situation their pride could not submit to, and by the end of the year all intercourse was at an end between England and the League.

The first hostilities emanated from the latter. During the summer all English ships arriving at Danzig were arrested, compelled to land their cargoes, and to pay extortionate duties on the same, forbidden to load anything in return, and only allowed to depart on the merchants taking oath that they would go home in ballast without purchasing grain anywhere else. It was alleged that fifty-five English vessels were served in this way. At Hamburg also the English were molested. Finally, on August 24, a decree of the Council of the Hansa at Lubeck proclaimed the banishment of all English ships, men, and goods from the Hanse towns.[3]

---

[1] *A. P. C.*, vi. 73.   [2] *Lansdowne MSS.*, 170, f. 156 b.
[3] Ibid., ff. 200, 217 b.

Negotiations were still continued by letter, but the
expulsion was enforced, as is shown by a missive from
the Duke of Schleswig to the queen.   Writing on
January 1, 1558, he suggested that several places in his
dominions might be found suitable for the trade of
English merchants, in consequence of the suspension of
intercourse between England and the Hansa.
The quarrel threatened to entail serious consequences
to England and Spain in their war with France.   A
shortage of corn in England emphasized the closing of
the Baltic marts and increased popular discontent against
the Government.   Serious fears were entertained [1] of
a maritime league between the Hansa, Denmark, and
the French ; and King Philip was unceasing in his
recommendations of peace.   But he had shown only too
thoroughly his utter callousness towards English interests,
and no attention was paid to his advice.   Another
embassy from the Hansa appeared in March 1558, but
failed as the others had done.   No permanent agreement
was to be expected before the conclusion of a general
European pacification, in which all the international
questions which had been ripening for half a century
might receive consideration.   England and Spain had
for the past two years been fighting France.   As far as
England was concerned, the war represented the last
chapter in the history of the great Burgundian alliance,
which, after enduring for a century and a half and
bringing numerous benefits, was now ending in shame and
ruin.   France had indeed been worsted on the Flemish
frontier, but England had sustained the disastrous loss of
Calais.   On all sides there was a genuine weariness of strife.

[1] Kervyn de Lettenhove, *Relations Politiques des Pays-Bas et de l'Angleterre*, Brussels, 1882, i. 128, 144, 161, 184, &c.

The peace congress opened at Arras and concluded its labours at Câteau Cambrésis, from which place the treaty took its name. To the conferences the Hansa sent representatives,[1] and the English envoys received instructions to conclude a peace with them if terms could possibly be arranged.[2] But still both sides remained obstinate. The larger questions were settled or in process of settlement, while the commercial matter seemed insoluble. At this juncture the death of Mary introduced fresh factors into the problem, which proved not to be auspicious to the Hansa. One of the promoters of the original revocation of the Hanse privileges, Sir William Cecil, was called to a prominent position in the counsels of the new queen. Acting doubtless on his advice, Elizabeth maintained a firm attitude, resolving to secure once and for all the equitable treatment of English commerce in the North Sea.

In the ' considerations ' delivered to the Parliament of 1559 it is recommended that ' the Queen's Highness in no wise restore to the Steelyard their liberties ; for they not only intercepted much of the English merchants' trade but, by concealment of strangers' goods, robbed the Queen of customs 10,000 marks a year at least, which was so sweet to them that, as some of them confess, they gained in Queen Mary's time among solicitors above £10,000 in bribes '.[3] Elizabeth pursued the line of policy here indicated. On July 2, 1559, she wrote to the Council of Lubeck saying that she had consulted the councillors of Queen Mary, who had informed her that, during the reign of Edward VI, the privileges had been withdrawn by the Crown in consequence of abuse.

---

[1] *Foreign Cal.*, 1553–8, pp. 393–4.   [2] Ibid., p. 396.
[3] *Cal. of Cecil MSS.*, i. 164.

Although Queen Mary, out of regard for them, had introduced certain just modifications, they had neglected to observe them, and had behaved with great cruelty to England, publicly forbidding intercourse. The late queen might have retaliated, but did not, satisfying herself with imposing certain reasonable conditions on the intercourse of the Hanse towns with England. These regulations had again been violated, and the former acts of ingratitude and inhumanity repeated. She (Elizabeth) would not proceed to interdict all intercourse, but would continue things as Queen Mary left them. If they had reasons against this they were to declare them.[1]

Here was obviously an invitation to the Hansa to come to terms, although the terms must be those formulated by England. Accordingly, after further delay, the long struggle was finally settled in 1560. The Easterlings were given the liberty of exporting cloth to their own states at the same duty as paid by Englishmen, provided that they sent none to the Low Countries or Italy. Goods imported by them into England from other than their own states were to pay 1d. less in the £ than those imported by other foreigners ; while cloths exported by them to other than their own states were to pay 12d. per cloth less. Counter-balancing privileges were secured for Englishmen in the Hanse towns.[2] Thus the two great questions of the cloth export and the carrying trade were settled substantially in favour of England, an auspicious opening to a reign which was to witness a hitherto unprecedented expansion of her maritime interests. Shorn of a great part of their ancient privileges, and with their pride humbled by defeat in a long-contested struggle, the

[1] *Foreign Cal.*, 1558-9, No. 922.
[2] *Cotton MSS.*, Claud E vii. 240, f. 250.

tenants of the Steelyard lived peaceably in London for
nearly half a century more, until their final expulsion
in 1598. By that time England had become so relatively
great and the Hansa so small that the eviction of the
Easterlings was accomplished with no more stir than
would have accompanied the seizure by the bailiffs of
a private debtor's house.

CHAPTER VIII

THE ENGLISH IN THE NORTH SEA

THE first half of the reign of Henry VIII was undoubtedly the palmiest time in the history of the Merchant Adventurers. Under Henry VII their position in the North Sea had been firmly established by the series of treaties which that monarch had concluded with the Netherlands and by his unbending attitude towards the Hansa. Their constitution had also been settled on a permanent basis by the failure of the attempt of the ring of London capitalists to form a small and exclusive society and by the new charter of incorporation granted in 1505. Thus at the outset of the new period which commenced in 1509 they had only to push on their expansion along lines already laid down, and to gather strength for the culminating struggle with the Hanseatic League which has been described in the previous chapter.

The earlier wars and politics of Henry VIII had little, if any, prejudicial effect on the North Sea merchants. French sea-power did not often manifest itself east of the Straits of Dover, while that of Scotland was so vastly inferior to the forces it had to face that it constituted little hindrance to English trade. It is true that the piracies of Andrew Barton and his associates created a great stir at the time; but it is probable that the actual damage done was small in proportion, and English warships were able to make the occupation of the rovers much more risky than was that of their quarry. The

cardinal point of Henry's policy, previous to the Reformation, was friendship with the Empire. As long, therefore, as this state of affairs endured, Englishmen enjoyed
comparatively favourable treatment in the Netherlands.
The ties of self-interest united the two countries;
England requiring a market for her surplus produce of
cloth and wool, and the Flemings needing raw or semi-
manufactured material for the refined products of their
craftsmen, who supplied the wealthy of the whole of
northern Europe with delicate garments, velvets, tapes-
tries and metal ware. The cargoes shipped into England
from the Low Countries were now also beginning to
include the spices, drugs, sugar, and other oriental
luxuries [1] which had hitherto been brought by the carracks and galleys of the Italian merchant states.

The warlike preparations consequent on Henry's entry
into the Holy League were largely furthered by supplies
drawn from the Netherlands. The craft of gunfounding
was in its infancy in England, and most of the heavier
weapons were obtained from the foundries of Mechlin.
Hans Popenruyter of that town supplied forty-eight
heavy guns in 1512, the largest weighing nearly two
tons.[2] At this time the ships of the Merchant Adventurers sailed as usual, proceeding in company for greater
safety, and being convoyed or 'wafted' by warships
detailed for the purpose.

When peace was restored the good relations between
England and the Netherlands continued until 1515, when
a dispute with reference to the interpretation of treaties
arose. The intercourse between the two countries was

[1] The Portuguese shipped a considerable quantity of their East Indian
merchandise to Antwerp, which formed the distributing centre for
northern Europe.   [2] *Letters and Papers*, i, p. 464.

still based on the great treaty of 1496, supplemented by
later ones, and more especially that of 1506, which was
so unpopular with the Flemings. The young Prince
Charles, afterwards the Emperor Charles V, who succeeded Margaret of Savoy as Regent of the Netherlands
in 1515, determined to better the position of his subjects,
and denounced the validity of the treaties on the ground
that they terminated with the death of the contracting
parties. New duties were imposed and English merchants
complained that they were worse treated in the Low
Countries than in Spain and Portugal. Charles, or rather
his guardians and councillors, attempted artificially to
revive the decaying prosperity of Bruges by so arranging
tolls and dues as to compel the English to resort only
to that place. However, the English, as had been
abundantly shown in the reign of Henry VII, had in
the last resort the whip-hand, and rumours of a new
cessation of intercourse brought about an agreement in
July to postpone the whole matter for six years until
Prince Charles should come of age, and in the meantime
to maintain the operation of the original treaties. In
spite of this, the unfriendly treatment of the English
continued, and a complaint of 1516 mentions that tolls
were exacted at different places on the same goods,
damage was done by customs officers in examining goods,
and that Englishmen were hindered in buying and
generally obstructed by officials. Some of the disputes
were settled in 1517, and others were provided for in
an agreement between the English merchants and the
town of Antwerp, signed on June 1, 1518. In 1520
a general commercial treaty, to endure for five years,
was signed between England and the emperor. It provided, in the main, that intercourse and duties should

continue on the former basis. The vexed question of the *Malus Intercursus* of 1506 was again left unsettled.[1]

The inconveniences of trade above described were normal to the time and, in spite of them, the relations between England and the Netherlands during the first part of Henry's reign may be described as good. In 1525, however, owing to the overwhelming success of Charles in his war with Francis I, culminating in the capture of that monarch at Pavia on February 24, the balance of Europe was in danger of being upset, and a change of policy was initiated in England which entailed far-reaching consequences. Wolsey's new plan was an alliance with France, to be sealed if possible by a royal marriage. The idea of a divorce from Katherine of Aragon was taken up eagerly by Henry, but received in his mind a direction totally unforeseen by Wolsey. Henry was soon intent, not on a marriage with a French princess, but on a union with Anne Boleyn, a lady of his own court. When it is remembered that Charles V was a nephew of the king's existing wife, it will be seen that the divorce proposals could not fail to have a bad effect on the relations between England and the Imperial dominions.

Moreover, owing to the course which affairs took, the whole question of the religious position of England was opened up, to the detriment of the papal power. Charles was committed to the pope's side in religious affairs in Germany, while Spain, also under his rule, was fanatically Catholic. Hence a fresh cause of strife appeared between him and England. The divorce case began in the middle of 1527, and, from the first mention of it, the emperor

---

[1] *Letters and Papers*, ii, Nos. 540, 649, 723, 724, 2738, 3647, 3649, 4210; *Cotton MSS.*, Galba B ix. 69; *Foedera*, xiii. 714.

showed himself violently hostile. A hint of the possibilities of retaliation on the English side to any imposition
of commercial disabilities was contained in a proclamation
by the mayor of Calais on July 13. It was announced
that English and foreign merchants might trade at Calais
on the same terms as at Antwerp, and that the governor
and Fellowship of the Merchant Adventurers should have
the same jurisdiction at Calais as formerly at Antwerp.[1]
This could not fail to recall to the Flemings their sufferings during the restraint of 1493 when a similar transference had taken place. The prospects, however, became
worse instead of better, and in March 1528 a panic was
caused by reports of the detention of all English merchants in Spain and Flanders. There was a general
paralysis of trade, workmen were discharged, and large
stocks of cloth remained unsold at Blackwell Hall. It
required all the skill of the Government to ' quench the
bruit ' and restore confidence.[2] The crisis slowly passed
away and the Merchant Adventurers returned to Antwerp. A diet for settling grievances was held at Bour-
bourg, near Dunkirk, in 1532. Another similar period
of depression and fear of war with the emperor occurred
in 1535. The worst crisis of all, that of 1538–9, has
already been considered in a previous chapter.

The organization of the Merchant Adventurers was
of political as well as commercial importance. Their
colony at Antwerp, with its governor and council of
twenty-four, constituted an English outpost in the Low
Countries almost if not quite as valuable as Calais, and
without the disadvantage of requiring a large military
outlay for its maintenance. Just as the possession of
Calais enabled English wool to be sold at a vast profit

---

[1] *Letters and Papers*, iv, No. 3262.   [2] Ibid., No. 4044.

to the Crown, so, until the competition of the Hansa became severe, the produce of English craftsmen was disposed of at Antwerp on more favourable terms than could have been obtained by a less centralized organization. The merchants themselves were an intelligent and respected class, and their governor was usually selected for the possession of such qualities in the highest degree. Consequently it is frequently found that there was the closest understanding between him and the home Government, to which he was able to make himself useful in many ways. Valuable information was sometimes acquired by the merchants and transmitted before it reached the ears of the regular diplomatic representative. They were also especially well placed for keeping a watch on the movements of political exiles and traitors of all kinds. In 1533 John Coke, the Secretary of the Merchant Adventurers, was in constant correspondence with Cromwell, sending him information as to disloyal books and speeches about the king's marriage with Anne Boleyn. A few years later John Hutton, the governor, acted as Cromwell's political agent at Antwerp, while in the troubled times of Edward VI and Mary the tie became closer, and financial aid was commonly rendered by the one party, to be paid for by official attacks upon its rivals by the other.

The circumstances of the time required the maintenance of strict discipline in the Company, and for this purpose the governor was by the charter of 1505 endued with full powers. In 1536 a merchant was condemned to pay a fine of £150 for ' misshipping' cloths; and in the following year William Castlyn, one of the most prominent members of the Company, was fined 100 marks for shipping certain kerseys to Flanders in ships

other than those appointed to be used.[1] Here it may be
remarked that it was usual for the merchants to accu-
mulate their stocks of cloth in London until the date
of the mart at Antwerp was at hand, and then to ship
all their cargoes at the same time in certain ships specified
for the purpose. As many as sixty vessels sometimes
composed one fleet, although they seldom exceeded 100
tons in burden. This dispatching of merchantmen in
large fleets was a characteristic of all branches of maritime
trade and afforded a convenient means of protection and
supervision.

In spite of the powers to fine and imprison enjoyed
by the governor, discipline was not easy to maintain,
and the misfortunes due to the growing hostility between
Henry and the emperor did not conduce to the better
conduct of the English in the Netherlands. In 1542
a letter from the deputy governor complained of the
growing decay of good order and the violation of their
privileges, showing that internal dissension went hand in
hand with attacks from without. The office of governor
was vacant, and there was a difference in opinion between
the merchants at Antwerp and those in London as to
the filling of the post. Two successive appointments
made by the Antwerp section were annulled by the
London head-quarters, who finally called in the aid of
the Privy Council. The latter addressed a strongly-
worded letter to the refractory brethren at Antwerp.
The London party were described as 'ancient, grave
and substantial men' to whose choice the young and
inexperienced at Antwerp ought to submit. The latter
were further upbraided for wishing to have as their
governor 'one most unfit' (John Knotting), who had

[1] *Letters and Papers*, xii, part i, No. 415.

been living as a naturalized citizen of Antwerp and abjuring his own nationality. The letter concluded by charging them to accept William Castlyn, the London candidate, without demur, in default of which John Knotting and the secretary were to repair to London for an investigation of the case.[1] The chief leader of the older or London party in this affair was Sir Richard Gresham, father of Thomas Gresham, the future founder of the Royal Exchange. The division of the Company into two factions, here indicated, became more or less chronic, and it was perhaps inevitable that such should be the case. In a period of change the interests of the older men, whose fortunes were made, lay rather in keeping things as they were and resisting any alteration of the rules of the game, while the young members, impatient to be rich, must frequently have been guilty of actions offensive to their more conservative seniors.

As will be remembered, the critical state of international politics in the years 1538–9 caused Henry VIII to proclaim that for the space of five years foreigners might trade with England on payment of the same duties as were exacted from native merchants. This edict was modified in 1540 by an Act of Parliament which stated that foreigners availing themselves of the privilege must ship their goods in English bottoms. The resulting quarrel with the Imperial Government prejudiced the position of the Merchant Adventurers, more especially as, in the end, Henry was obliged to exempt the Flemings from the operation of the Act. Scarcely was this dispute settled than another arose owing to the imposition by the Regent of the Netherlands of a new duty of 1 per cent. on the value of all

[1] *Letters and Papers*, xvii, No. 1055, also Nos. 990 and 1062.

exports, payable in addition to existing duties. The new
tax—called the *centième*—was for the purpose of defraying
the expenses of the war against France, and at first the
English Government was not inclined to cavil at it. The
merchants, however, viewed the matter differently and
made strenuous protests. Finally, since an alliance was
in process of formation between England and the Empire,
the matter was compromised by the Merchant Adventurers paying a benevolence of £1,000 and being excused
from the duty on goods sent into England.[1] The new
alliance was not of long duration ; in 1544 Charles made
a separate peace with France, leaving Henry to continue
the war alone. The English were furious at the trick
played on them, and English warships and privateers
exercised little discrimination in making prizes of any
vessels suspected of carrying an ounce of French goods.
The Flemings complained of the damage thus done to
their shipping and, in retaliation, all the Merchant
Adventurers at Antwerp were placed under arrest on
January 6, 1545.[2] The arrest lasted for some time, and
the Easterlings improved their opportunity by obtaining
a firm grasp on the cloth export, from which it was
afterwards found so difficult to dislodge them. It is
true, of course, that they had exported cloth to the Low
Countries before, but it was during these years of hostility
between Henry and Charles V that their competition,
coupled with the disadvantages under which the English
merchants laboured, threatened in the end to extinguish
altogether the trade of the latter. As early as August
1538 a letter from Antwerp complained that, although
money was plentiful and good sales had been made, the

[1] *Letters and Papers*, xviii, part i, Nos. 196, 259, 331, 773 ; *Cal. of Cecil MSS.*, i, No. 38. [2] *Letters and Papers*, xx, part i, No. 32.

Easterlings had been beforehand with cloth shipments,
' which hath skatched us in our sales more than two
thousand pound '.[1] In any case English cloth, by whom-
soever sold, was able to hold its own against anything
of the same sort which the Netherlands could produce,
because it could be sold ready finished at Antwerp for
less price than the Flemings had to pay for a proportionate amount of the raw wool at Calais.

The arrest of the Merchant Adventurers in 1545 seems
to have done more harm than good to the Flemings.
An English emissary, writing to the Council from Antwerp,[2] describes the consternation produced, all the
merchants remaining ' in a marvellous stay, the Bourse
unhaunted, their hearts damped and made cold with
fear that they had never to recover again such things as
were taken upon the seas. All the inhabitants of this
town shrunk at it, fearing the utter decay of their traffic.
Great numbers of fullers, shearmen, dyers, and others
thought their livings were utterly bereaved from them,
so that if it had continued a little longer it would have
brought a wonderful alteration of things here. This
little arrest hath made many to confess to me that it
were better for this country to have twenty years' war
with France than one with England, in so great fear
were they of it '. The arrest was over and cloth was
again being dispatched to Flanders by the middle of
May.

The course of events and the financial necessities of
the Government in the reigns of Edward and Mary
threw considerable political power into the hands of the
Merchant Adventurers. The way in which they availed

[1] *Cotton MSS.*, Galba B x. 82.
[2] *Letters and Papers*, xx, part i, No. 65.

themselves of it to secure the downfall of the Hansa has
been described in the previous chapter.
The strife of factions among the Adventurers at this
time became accentuated. On account of a dispute with
the city of Antwerp they were ordered in 1547 and
1548 not to resort to that town, but to make Bergen-op-
Zoom their temporary head-quarters. Some of them
disregarded the injunction and even talked of electing
a new Governor and Secretary, a sharp reprimand
from the Privy Council being necessary to bring them
to order.[1] A letter from Thomas Chamberlain, the
Governor, in this connexion, is worth quoting :

'And thus it is to be seen that the very folly and
rashness of our merchants is our disturbance, who do
daily bring over clothes to Bruges by stealth, notwithstanding my lord's grace' (Somerset) prohibition and
stay of their ships ; and also do buy at Antwerp contrary
to their own statute and ordinance, whereby they have
forfeited large sums, of the which the King's Majesty
ought to have his third part ; and till his highness do
take the same and make them smart, they will never
keep order, but for their own private lucre undo, if they
might, the common weal ; for their fashion is even when
they make their statutes and swear to observe the same,
even forthwith by collusion and colour to break the same,
generally saying, that every man transgressing shall cause
a general pardon among them, and thus they mock with
God and the world and are perjured daily, that it is
pity to think thereon, and that any such should have to
do with them. . . .'[2]

In 1553 the quarrel broke out afresh, and representatives of the two factions, called respectively the

[1] *A. P. C.*, ii. 545, 556.
[2] *Cotton MSS.*, Galba B xii, f. 28.

'Old Hanze' and the 'New Hanze',[1] were before the
Council, which sided, on Thomas Gresham's recommendation, with the former.[2] The New Hanze were
convicted of behaving in a disorderly manner, trying to
subvert the government of the Fellowship, and endanger-
ing its privileges. They were commanded to make
humble submission to the Governor and the ringleaders
to receive punishment.[3] Gresham, although himself a
member of the Company, was acting primarily in the
financial interests of the Government. For that purpose
his principal object was to raise the rate of exchange,
expressive of the state of English credit, on the Antwerp
Bourse. To attain it he sought to handicap the foreign
capitalists, his adversaries, by manipulating the cloth
export, restraining or permitting it as occasion demanded.
Hence he was all in favour of maintaining strict discipline
among the Adventurers. In a letter to Northumberland
in 1553 he deplored their lack of experience and suggested a rigid insistence on an eight years' apprenticeship.
He himself, he continued, had been made to serve that
time by his father's wisdom, although he might have
evaded it.[4] Gresham's character had much of the masterful audacity typical of Tudor statesmanship, and he used
his authority with a high hand when the unruliness of

---

[1] See *Transactions of the Royal Historical Society*, vol. xvi (1902),
pp. 19–67. In an article by W. E. Lingelbach on the organization of
the Merchant Adventurers the suggestion is put forward that the Old
Hanze and the New Hanze were two separate grades of merchants with
differing privileges. Certain not very precise indications point to such
an arrangement, but, on the other hand, there is no hint of any such
thing in the Charter of Incorporation of 1505 or in any other document
of the same type.

[2] In the previous autumn the Council, on receiving a loan of £30,000
from the Company, had promised to suppress disorders (*R. O., S. P. Dom.,
Edw. VI*, vol. xv, No. 13).   [3] *A. P. C.*, iv. 279, 280.

[4] *Foreign Cal.*, 1547–53, No. 655.

the merchants threatened danger to his plans. He succeeded in raising the exchange for the £ sterling from
16 to 22 shillings Flemish, and at the latter figure
liquidated debts contracted at the former.[1]

Although the Merchant Adventurers had succeeded
in ousting their rivals of the Steelyard from the Low
Countries, their own position was by no means secure
during the reign of Edward VI. There was continual
friction with the Imperial Government, whose conduct
became so irritating at one time that Sir Thomas
Chamberlain, English agent at Brussels and a former
Governor of the Company, advised that the merchants
should be withdrawn altogether from the country, ' for
truly these people will never know what they have of
us until they lack us,' although he remarked elsewhere
that the English misfortunes were chiefly due to their
own insatiable greed and disorder. The anti-Protestant
policy which Charles V instituted in 1548, and the severe
measures by which he enforced it in the Netherlands,
formed another disturbing factor in his relations with
England.[2] In 1550 a rupture was thought to be imminent
on this account, and the merchants were advised to
withdraw their goods little by little from the country.
With the accession of Mary, however, the danger temporarily passed away, although it was destined ultimately
to cause a profound modification of England's industry
and of the direction of her maritime expansion. The
merchants themselves were not very deeply imbued with
Protestantism ; or, if they were, means were found of

[1] *Dict. Nat. Biog.*
[2] John Wheeler, however, in his *Treatise of Commerce* (1601), states
that the Emperor refrained from establishing the Inquisition at Antwerp
in 1550, for fear it should drive the English out of the city.

converting them, since a report of 1556 mentions that all those then at Antwerp were Catholics with the exception of four, against whom proceedings were to be taken.[1]

The marts of the Low Countries had for long provided a sufficient outlet for England's surplus products, but circumstances were presently to arise which should drive English enterprise farther afield. The civil troubles in the Netherlands, which began soon after the death of Mary and the overthrow of the Catholic régime in England, and became ever more acute until they exploded into a war of eighty years' duration, did much to blight the commerce and industry of the southern provinces. The northern or Dutch states which rose to pre-eminence in their place with such astonishing rapidity were not a manufacturing community, and had very little need of English cloth and wool. At the same time the German ports and the Baltic became more accessible owing to the decay of the Hanseatic League and the opening up of relations with Russia by Chancellor and Jenkinson. Thus the death of Mary, though not of itself of immediate importance, may be conveniently regarded as synchronizing with the relative decline of the old Flanders trade. That trade, while still extensive for many years, was no longer of primary importance. The capital and energies of the bolder mercantile adventurers were henceforth to be employed in penetrating the farther limits of the North Sea, and still more in oceanic enterprises to the West and the tropic East.

Long before the opening up of communications with Russia—in fact, throughout the period now under dis-

[1] *Domestic Cal.*, 1547–80, p. 87.

cussion—a regular trade was maintained with Sweden, Denmark, and Danzig, and also at intervals with the north German ports. This traffic was free to all English merchants and was not subject to the jurisdiction of the Company of Merchant Adventurers. The latter, it is true, sometimes exerted their influence to induce the Government to secure better treatment for the English at Danzig, but only because certain individuals of their Company were trading in their private capacity to that place. The principal article of English export to the above-named regions was cloth. In return many articles of absolute necessity to an increasingly maritime nation—canvas, hemp, ropes, pitch, and spars—were obtained, together with supplies of grain and fish, for which there was a growing demand as food prices steadily rose in England.

At all times the traders encountered hostility from the Hansa, which, as they were not effectively incorporated, they were less able to cope with than were the merchants in the Low Countries. On the other hand, they suffered less from arbitrary exactions and oppressive restraints imposed for political reasons, since England, until the end of Mary's reign, took practically no interest in the international dealings of the northern powers. The English dépôt at Danzig was always of considerable importance, as is evidenced by the trouble they took to maintain it in the reign of Henry VII. The damage mutually suffered by the reprisals which then took place convinced both parties that tranquillity was more profitable to them, and peace was maintained for nearly fifty years. Danzig was the principal source of the supply of naval stores, and furnished on occasion not only

materials but ships ready built. One such consignment
was received during the war of 1544.[1] Again in 1556
a large quantity of naval stores was procured at that
place. A letter from the Council to the English merchants on this occasion is interesting as showing the
extent of their operations. Whereas, it pointed out, they
had bought up all the hemp and cable yarn in that city,
and had also secured the promise of the rope-makers to
work exclusively for them during the next six months,
they were commanded to desist from such practices until
such time as William Watson, who was coming to buy
for the navy, should be furnished with what he required.[2]
The possibilities opened up by the employment of capital
in large masses were evidently well realized, as indeed
other instances prove.

During the cessation of intercourse with the Hansa in
1557–60 the Duke of Schleswig wrote to the queen to
point out the suitability of various places in his dominions
for English trade. Some communication with North
Germany was essential owing to the scarcity of grain
in England, and a deputation of merchants went to
Schleswig in the summer of 1558 to inspect the ports
and make arrangements for commerce.

The reopening of the communications with the Hanse
towns early in Elizabeth's reign placed the North Sea
and Baltic trade on a far more favourable footing than
had ever before been the case. For the first time the
English could do business in the northern ports on
something like equitable terms and with some assurance
of security ; a steady increase of the volume of traffic
was the result.

---

[1] *Cal. Cecil MSS.*, i. 44.   [2] *A. P. C.*, v. 236.

An important source of food supply was the Iceland fishery, which in the sixteenth century was regularly frequented by English vessels, mainly from the east coast ports. Bristol, which in the Middle Ages had had a foremost share in the traffic, seems to have dropped out altogether in Tudor times. The Bristol fishermen, like those of Normandy and Brittany, preferred the Newfoundland banks—the Baccalaos of the Cabots—which, although more distant, produced more plentiful supplies of fish. No mention of Bristol ships going to Iceland is to be met with under Henry VIII or his two successors.

It was customary for the fishing fleet to rendezvous at some point on the east coast before the end of April and to proceed in company past the Scottish coast, and thence through the Pentland Firth or between the Orkney and Shetland Islands. The ships were laden with food to last the crews for the summer, supplies of salt for the preservation of the intended cargoes, and possibly also with cloth and other manufactured articles for trade with the natives. In time of war with Scotland it was necessary for the fleet to be wafted or convoyed until clear of the coasts of the northern kingdom, and even then stragglers were frequently snapped up. On arrival at the destination fishing for cod and ling was carried on throughout the summer or until the holds were full, and the return voyage was made before the end of September with the same precautions as before.

The English had by no means a monopoly of the fishery, and the various nations of the North Sea which sent out competing squadrons found them troublesome neighbours on the coast. In 1552 an extensive affray occurred between the English and the Hamburgers, and, in this or other affairs of the same kind, forty or fifty

Englishmen were slain. On remonstrances being made to Frederick of Denmark, who, as sovereign of Iceland, was apparently expected by Henry VIII to preserve order on the coast, he replied by charging the English with being the authors of all the trouble. They claimed a fishing-place which had never been theirs ; they reduced the people to bondage ; they refused to pay tribute, and stole fish.[1]

Olaus Magnus, in his *History of the Goths and Swedes*, has a paragraph on the same subject :

' Of the mutual slaughter of the merchants for the Harbours of Iceland.

' It is a miserable spectacle of factors that fall foul one upon the other, either at home or abroad, and kill one another for gain, or put all their merchandise in danger to be lost, or to revenge their Kindred. . . . Amongst these the chief, as it is supposed, are the Bremers, or the cities of the Vandals, the Rostochians, Vismarians, and Lubeckers. And lastly the merchants of England and Scotland, who so stifly contend for the primacy and privilege of the Iceland ports to ride in, as if they fought a fight at sea ; and so wound one another for gain, that whether one or the other gets the Victory, yet there is always ready one of the officers of the Treasury, who knows how to correct them both sufficiently, both in their moneys and bodies, either by ordinary or extraordinary Exaction.' [2]

The Scots, too, had need to look to their defences when the fleet was passing along their coast ; for the fishermen, as James V complained in 1535, were in the habit of plundering the islands and catching the unfortunate inhabitants on the way north, to serve as slaves

---

[1] *Letters and Papers*, v, Nos. 1417 and 1633.
[2] English translation, 1658, p. 127.

during the fishing season, and be landed again on the
homeward voyage in the autumn.[1] The suggestion of
slave-hunting is supported by an existing indenture of
apprenticeship to an east-coast mariner of a boy, nine
years old, brought from ' Lowsybaye ' in Iceland. It
was a rough trade with more than the usual maritime
hardships of those times. In 1542, Norfolk, writing to
the Council on some proposal to utilize the returned
Iceland fleet for Government service, remarked that when
the cargoes were discharged the vessels stank so horribly
that no man not used to the same could endure it.

An interesting letter is preserved from the commissioners at York to the Council during the Scottish war
of 1542. A design was on foot for a raid on the Orkneys
and Shetlands, an idea which the commissioners wrote
to discourage. Touching the isles of ' Shotland and
Orkeney ', they said, they were informed that Shotland
was so distant that Englishmen who went yearly to Iceland dared not tarry on those coasts after St. James's tide.
They must pass through the Pentley Firth, the most
dangerous place in Christendom, and Scottishmen who
knew it best dared not venture to pass it at this season
(October). Orkney was also very dangerous and full of
rocks ; the people lived by fishing and had little to
devastate save oats and a few beasts, which were so wild
that they could only be taken by dogs. The enterprise
would not quit a tenth part of its cost, besides the
danger of losing the ships.[2]

An accurate estimate of the extent of the Iceland
trade is obtainable from certain lists which still exist
of ships engaged. In 1528, 149 ships sailed for Iceland,

---

[1] *Letters and Papers*, viii, No. 1153.
[2] Ibid. xvii, No. 893.

exclusively from east-coast ports, which contributed as follows : [1] London, 8 ships ; Harwich, Ipswich, Manningtree, Dedham, Sudbury, and Colchester, 14 ships ; Woodbridge, 3 ; Aldborough, Sysewell, and Thorpe, 6 ; Dunwich, Walderswick, Southwold, Easton, and Covehythe, 32 ; Lowestoft, 6 ; Yarmouth, 30 ; Claye, Blakeney, and Cromer, 30 ; Wells, 6 ; Lynn, 10 ; and Boston, 4. Another list [2] shows that, in 1533, 85 ships returned from Iceland, belonging to the same ports, of which the southernmost was London, and the most northerly, Boston. These vessels were all small, ranging from 30 to 150 tons, although the latter figure was exceptional, 100 tons being the usual limit. In July 1557, owing to the naval activities of the French, it was necessary to furnish a squadron to protect the homeward-bound Iceland fleet. In addition to nine queen's ships, twenty private vessels were demanded from ports on the east and south coasts as far westward as Dartmouth and Plymouth.[3] A force of this strength, in the then debilitated state of the national defences, would only have been employed to protect a convoy of the highest value.

On the other hand we find, in the lugubrious times of Edward VI, a complaint of the decay of the fishing industry. Whereas, it runs, in the twentieth year of Henry VIII (1528) 140 ships went to Iceland, now only 43 go, and a proportionate decrease is indicated in the fishing in the North Sea itself.[4] The causes assigned are non-observance of fish days owing to the progress of Protestantism, lack of enterprise on the part of the fishermen, and burdensome regulations as to sales.

---

[1] *Letters and Papers*, iv, No. 5101.   [2] Ibid., vi, No. 1380.
[3] *R. O., S. P. Dom., Mary*, vol. xi, No. 38.
[4] *Domestic Cal.*, Addenda, 1547–65, p. 426.

The Catholic reaction under Mary caused a revival of the trade, which special legislation in the next reign attempted to maintain by enjoining the eating of fish on certain days, although the religious incentive no longer existed. As has been indicated, the Bristol mariners preferred to do their fishing on the coasts of Newfoundland and Labrador, and desisted from the Iceland voyage after the opening up of the new regions. There is no categorical authority for this view, but it may be deduced from the non-appearance of Bristol in the documents quoted above and from the undoubted presence of English craft on the American coast quite early in the sixteenth century. The obscure operations of the Bristol adventurers subsequent to the Cabot discoveries have already been considered. The *New Interlude*, of approximately the date 1519, also refers to the Newfoundland fishery, while John Rut, in 1527, although he found only foreigners fishing there on his arrival, spoke of fishing as a matter of course and no novelty to the English. The first statutory mention of an English fishery in Newfoundland is contained in an Act of 1541–2 for the prohibition of the practice of buying fish at sea instead of catching it, which was alleged to be deleterious to the common weal. This Act was not to extend to the buying of fish in Iceland or 'Newland'. In a map drawn up for Henry VIII, in 1542,[1] Newfoundland is inscribed : 'The new fonde londe quhar men goeth a fisching.' Again, in an Act of 1548, there occurs a reference to fishing by Englishmen in 'Newefounde-lande'. Thenceforward the traffic was well established, and has given to the Newfoundland and Labrador coasts

[1] *Royal MSS.*, 20 E ix.

the claim to be the oldest of English settlements beyond the seas. From the beginning, however, the French, Spaniards, and Portuguese were keen competitors. In 1542 a French fleet of from 80 to 100 small vessels, returning from the fishery, were nearly all taken by the Spaniards; and to the present day St. Malo and other western ports of France send out every year wooden sailing craft which fish all the summer on the Newfoundland banks and return to divide the spoil in the autumn, the men being paid according to the profits of the trip.

A few notes are necessary with reference to the affairs of the Staplers. During the reign of Henry VIII the Staple continued to conduct its business in the time-honoured manner. All wool for the consumption of the north of Europe was exported to Calais from London and other ports, while that intended for the Mediterranean was sent, at double duties, by the Italian merchants of London into the Low Countries, and thence via the Rhine to Italy. Occasionally English subjects, not belonging to the Staple, obtained licences to export wool 'beyond the Straits of Marrok', the duty payable being usually the subject of special arrangement with the Crown.

It would seem that, in 1544, an attempt was made by some of the Staplers to export wool to Italy themselves, probably by the overland route, and that this was stopped by the Company. This at least is the most probable inference to be drawn from a curious letter written at Venice by one Henry Bostoke to John Johnson, merchant of the Staple of Calais.[1] The writer refers to the success

[1] R. O., S. P., *Henry VIII*, § 195, f. 176; digest in *Letters and Papers*, xix, part i, No. 85.

of the voyage, ' having long since made wholesale of our
goods to an honest reckoning as the occasion required ;
not perceiving but that we should have made better
reckoning hereafter if the laudable ordinance of our
Company had permitted the continuance of this said
voyage, whereof the impeachment, I beseech Jesus, may
not in process of time be more prejudicial to the whole
generality than now disprofit to our masters in par-
ticularity '. The letter is very vague, the writer refraining
from stating the nature of his commodities and the route
by which they had reached Venice ; but the reference
to ' our ' Company addressed to a merchant of the Staple
is fairly conclusive, and indeed there was no other
company which could have exercised jurisdiction over
Englishmen in Venice. The Merchant Adventurers
concerned themselves only with the Low Countries and
did not interfere with the doings of their members
elsewhere, while the Englishmen who traded in general
cargoes to the Mediterranean were free-lances without
any incorporation.

The keystone of the whole system of the Staple was
the retention of Calais, so conveniently placed for buyers
from France, the Netherlands, and Germany. An Act
of 1515 provided that the Mayor and Fellowship of the
Company should retain the customs and subsidies on all
wools from England, paying the king £10,000 yearly in
lieu of the same. The Company were to defray the
expenses of the Staple, the town, and the fortifications,
while the king was to pay the wages of the garrison. This
Act, which was to endure for twenty years, superseded
one of similar import passed by Henry VII. At its
expiry another was passed in 1535-6, the preamble of
which shows that the defences of the town had fallen

into great decay and weakness. Corruption was rife, and the merchants were inevitably niggardly in their expenditure on them, for they trusted that in case of danger the whole power of the country would be put forth to save them. The system of farming the duties was continued, but in course of time the bargain ceased to be profitable to the Staplers, owing to the decrease in the shipments of wool. In 1551 a petition on the subject complained of the great burdens imposed on the merchants and of the increasing competition of wool sent from Spain to the Netherlands.[1] The payments due to the king, it was represented, amounted to more than the receipts from the customs. The remedy suggested for Spanish competition was to allow only low-priced wools to be shipped to Calais, to prohibit absolutely any export to other places, and to be content with a reduced custom, so that the clothmakers who had been draping Spanish wool might get ' as good pennyworth ' at Calais as they had been getting from the Spaniards.[2] The customs were not reduced, but the suggested restriction of non-staple export was carried out, and in the reign of Mary the Italian merchants were on the point of quitting London in despair of obtaining leave to buy wools.

The monopoly which had endured for so long was gradually breaking up under the stress of changing conditions ; and the loss of Calais in 1558 dealt it a blow from which it never recovered. The amount of wool exported was in any case bound to decrease with the growth of home manufactures,[3] so that the decay of the

[1] The Spaniards established a wool dépôt at Bruges : Kervyn de Lettenhove, i, p. 152.   [2] *R. O., S. P. Dom., Edw. VI*, vol. xiii, No. 81.

[3] Under Henry VIII the wool export decreased by 50 per cent. as estimated on the average number of sacks exported in the first five and last five years of the reign.

CALAIS IN THE FIRST HALF OF THE SIXTEENTH CENTURY.

From Cott. MS. Aug. I. ii. 70.

Staplers' business must not be regarded as a commercial loss to England : it was simply a diversion of the channels of wealth into a new direction. Long-rooted organizations die hard, and the Staplers survived precariously for many decades after the fall of Calais, holding their marts at various places in the Low Countries ; but in course of time England, far from continuing to export wool, became a wool-importing country, the native output being insufficient to keep pace with the growth of manufacture. The completion of the change is marked by an Act of 1660, prohibiting all export of wool, and containing no mention whatever of the once mighty Staple.

CHAPTER IX

FRANCE, SPAIN, AND THE MEDITERRANEAN

THE trade between England and France during the first half of the sixteenth century falls into two divisions : the local cross-channel traffic between Normandy and Brittany and the southern ports of England, and the wine trade with Bordeaux. There was at that time no regular commerce between England and the Mediterranean coast of France. Of the two sections above mentioned the second was by far the more important, since Bordeaux was the outlet for the merchandise of southern France, which could not be obtained elsewhere, while the northern seaboard of that country, similar in climate to the south of England, differed little from it in agricultural products, and had, if the weaving of sail-cloth in Brittany be excepted, no surplus manufactures to dispose of. Hence the elements of an important commerce with it were wanting.

The Bordeaux trade was one of the oldest channels of English enterprise beyond the seas. The town itself, coming under the authority of English kings with the accession of Henry II, in 1154, had survived all the vicissitudes of war until 1453, when the defeat of Talbot at Chatillon involved its permanent transference to the Crown of France. During the three centuries of English rule continual commerce was maintained with Bristol, London, and the intervening ports on the English coast, and the taste for Bordeaux wines became a national habit. As the cloth manufacture increased in England, another valuable commodity, used in dyeing and known as Toulouse woad, was also in demand, and was obtained exclusively from Bordeaux. The loss of the town at the disastrous close of the Hundred Years' War did not, like that of Calais in 1558, involve any diversion of trade, since it did not coincide with any industrial or economic changes such as those which exterminated the wool export. The Bordeaux trade, therefore, was continued, but seems largely to have passed out of English hands during the Wars of the Roses, which, or the rumours of which, recurred sporadically from 1455 until the accession of Henry VII.

It was natural that in a period of unrest and anarchy commercial interests should be neglected by governments engaged in a struggle for bare existence; and thus we find the preamble of Henry VII's Navigation Act of 1489 lamenting the great decay of English shipping engaged in the wine trade. It has been said that preambles to Acts of Parliament invariably exaggerate the grievances which they design to amend, but this one at least must have had some foundation in fact, as is evidenced by the diminished volume of Bristol trade at the beginning of Henry's reign and the rapid recovery of English shipping which resulted from his policy. The Act itself, which extended and rendered permanent a temporary measure of 1485, provided that Gascony wines and Toulouse woad should only be imported into England in English, Irish, or Welsh bottoms manned by crews of the same nationalities. Its importance cannot be over-estimated. It remained in full operation for more than sixty years, and, besides producing a mercantile revival, it provided a training-ground for the seamen

and navigators whose services were so essential to the
defence of the realm in the stormy times of the sixteenth
century. It must be remembered that, in the days when
the Mediterranean trade was in its infancy, the voyages
to Bordeaux and Spain were the only ones habitually
made by the English outside the North Sea, and that
they demanded the use of larger ships than were commonly employed by traders from east-coast ports. In
addition, such a policy had its moral significance ; it
was a blow to foreigners, and it gave Englishmen a sense
of privilege which was gratifying to their pride ; it
supplied at once a cause and a testimony of the relations
of enthusiastic admiration which undoubtedly existed
between the Tudor sovereigns and their seafaring
subjects.

The traffic thus re-established flourished continuously
under Henry VII and his son. The French wars of the
latter produced interruptions, but their actual duration
was not of great extent, and the merchants on either
side were only too eager to resume business as soon as
politics allowed. Every autumn, as soon as the vintage
was complete, the wine ships set out from all English
ports between London and Bristol, together with a few
from Wales and Ireland, and, uniting into fleets for
protection from the voracious rovers who infested the
havens of the French coast, sailed across the tempestuous
Bay to the mouth of the Gironde. There they were
obliged to anchor and send ashore the chambers of their
cannon so that no surprise attempt might be made on
the richest port of France, some of whose citizens looked
back with regret on the golden days of English rule, when
business was brisk and taxes few. The last stage of the
journey then commenced with the toilsome seventy miles'

struggle with the swift yellow stream before anchor
could be dropped in front of the embattled walls of the
wine city.

In a busy year, when the whole wine fleet had arrived,
there were as many as seven or eight thousand Englishmen in the town at one time—merchants, factors, clerks,
and seamen—and no doubt they made the place exceedingly lively; it must have been a depressing winter for
the Bordelais when war prevented their coming. After
two or three months spent in completing cargoes by the
leisurely business methods of the time, the homeward
voyage was begun in January or February.[1] The sailor
of early Tudor times probably differed little from the
type described by Chaucer a century before :

A schipman was ther, woning fer by weste :
For ought I woot, he was of Dertemouthe.
He rood upon a rouncy as he couthe,
In a gowne of faldyng to the kne.
A dagger hanging on a laas hadde he
Aboute his nekke under his arm adoun.
The hoote somer had maad his hew al broun ;
And certainly he was a good felawe.
Ful many a draught of wyn had he y-drawe
From Burdeuxward, while that the chapman sleep.
Of nyce conscience took he no keep.
If that he foughte, and hadde the heigher hand,
By water he sente hem hoom to every land.
But of his craft to reckon well his tydes,
His stremes, and his dangers him besides,
His herbergh, and his mone, his lodemenage,
Ther was non such from Hulle to Cartage.
Hardy he was and wys to undertake ;
With many a tempest hadde his berd ben shake.

[1] *Add. MSS.*, 11716 (*Letters and Papers*, ii, No. 3521) contains a contrast between the treatment of merchants in France and in England,
embodying many of the above details.

He knew wel al the havenes, as they were,
From Scotland to the Cape of Fynestere,
And every cryk in Bretayne and in Spayne;
His barge y-clepud was the *Maudelayne*.

It had been in accordance with Henry VII's indirect
methods of taxation to grant licences to foreigners to
infringe the navigation laws, for which licences they
were obliged to pay sums of ready money. The expenses
of the first war with France, coupled with the temporary
restraint of English trade to Bordeaux which it involved,
tempted his successor to do the same to such an extent
that serious discontent was aroused among the mercantile
community, and a discontinuance of the practice was
demanded. Accordingly, Parliament passed an Act in
1515 revoking all licences granted to foreigners to import
French wines and woad in foreign ships. Thenceforward
the grant of such licences became much less frequent,
and the English monopoly was more firmly established.
It is indicative of the inertness with regard to commercial
matters which prevailed in France that such an arrangement should have continued so long unchallenged. For
French merchants were included in the scope of the
law; they could not send their own wines to England
save in English ships. They were also subjected, in
common with other foreigners, to irritating restrictions
in England, of which the most irksome was the prohibition of taking more than ten crowns in money out of
the realm. In pursuance of this law, they complained,
they were searched to their shirts on departure.

In 1531 the Navigation Act of Henry VII was amended
by a new Act providing that all existing regulations
should be maintained, and with the addition that no
wine was to be imported from France between Michael-

mas and Candlemas (February 2). The reason for this
was apparently to discourage navigation at the dangerous
season of the year by preventing the too early return of
keenly competing merchants. The French took offence
at the interference with trade, and detained several
English ships by way of reprisal. Henry VIII explained
that his action was due to the numerous losses of ships
on the voyage, but promised to remove the offending
regulation, as he was empowered to do by a later Act
of 1534.[1] An international crisis due to religious changes
was impending, and he was obliged to conciliate the
French. He even spoke of abrogating the Navigation
Act altogether, although it is not likely that he really
intended to do anything of the kind. There is evidence,
however, that the administration of the laws was relaxed
and infractions connived at. The new Navigation Act
of 1540 expressly referred to those of 1489 and 1531 and
stated that, although they had been neglected, they were
now to be fully confirmed and regulations as to prices
and freights enforced. For every tun of wine from
Bordeaux the freight was fixed at 18s., and no one was
allowed to retail French wine in England at more than
8d. per gallon. A tun contained 252 gallons and might
thus be sold for more than £8, so that the freight was
not excessive as compared with the value of the goods.
The import duty, or tonnage, was also comparatively
slight, being but 3s. per tun.

In September 1542 the third French war of Henry VIII
was in sight, and was heralded by acts of commercial
hostility. The French, who had hitherto not protested
against the last Navigation Act, suddenly discovered that
they were injured by it, and a proclamation was issued

[1] Various references in *Letters and Papers*, ix and x.

that no goods were to be brought from England to France except in French ships.[1] This was copying English methods with a vengeance. The French proclamation, if enforced, would have involved the stoppage of the wine fleet, as, Englishmen being forbidden to export money, they could not pay for French wines if they were not allowed to do so with English goods. Nevertheless, the situation became more easy for a time, and the wine fleet sailed as usual. On their return in January 1543 sixteen of the laden vessels were taken by four Scottish privateers who waited for them in the neighbourhood of Brest. Orders were sent for those which had not yet left the Gironde to wait until an escort could be provided.[2]   In April 1543 war with France had become a certainty, and Henry refused to allow twenty French ships with wine and woad to proceed up the Channel to the Netherlands, as it would put such a large sum of money into the enemy's pockets. The Netherlands Government had requested a safe-conduct for the wine, as it was for the use of the army which was to act against France, but the king maintained that he personally would rather drink beer, or even water, than permit his own subjects to have wine from the French, to say nothing of allowing it to pass to oblige foreigners.[3]

In 1551–2 the first breach in the Tudor navigation policy was made by the selfish and improvident Council-government of which Northumberland was becoming the moving spirit. An Act of that year effected a partial repeal of previous laws by allowing the importation of wine and woad in the ships of any friendly nation between

---

[1] *Letters and Papers*, xvii, No. 555.
[2] Ibid., xviii, part i, No. 33.
[3] *Letters and Papers*, xviii, part i, No. 416.

February 1 and October 1. Of course the English still
had the privilege of selling, without competition, the
first cargoes of the season which were brought home in
December and January, but it was nevertheless very
injudicious to remove any measure of protection from
English shipping at a time when the naval defences of
the country were being allowed to deteriorate. The
reason alleged for taking this step was the dearness of
wine and woad ; the probable explanation being that the
London retailers brought pressure or bribery to bear upon
the Council, while the seamen and merchants engaged
in the Bordeaux trade had no such corporation to stand
up for their interests as had those who did business with
the Low Countries. An Act of 1563 restored the full
navigation law of Henry VII, and thenceforward there
is no record of any subsequent legislation with regard to
this traffic, from which it would appear that the English
monopoly was allowed gradually to die out. As other
liquors obtained a greater hold upon public favour, French
wines lost their relatively important position ; while
changes in the methods of dyeing rendered obsolete the
use of Toulouse woad in the cloth industry.

The commercial intercourse between England and
Spain, of ancient origin and the subject of careful
negotiations on the part of Henry VII, continued to
expand under his successor until religious cleavage
arising between the two nations threatened it with
extinction. It was advantageous to both countries,
although the Spaniards complained that all the gold
which changed hands went from Spain to England and
nothing but cloth came in return. The reign of
Henry VIII opened with the Anglo-Spanish Alliance

against France, in which the sea power of both England and Spain was utilized to blockade the French coast. Although Henry was bitterly mortified at his desertion by his ally in 1514, he smothered his resentment so far as to conclude a commercial treaty in the following year, which repeated the agreement made by his father in 1489. Commerce in each country was to be free, without necessity for licence or safe-conduct.[1] ' Freedom ' of trade meant, of course, not the abolition of duties, but a guarantee of fair treatment.

Casual and isolated traders visited the northern ports of Spain, more especially during the period of the English expedition to the north-east corner of that country in 1512, but internal communication in the Peninsula was so bad that the products of the south were only accessible to ships reaching the ports of Andalusia. Accordingly, the majority of English merchantmen sailed to Cadiz, to San Lucar at the mouth of the Guadalquivir, and to Seville higher up the same river. The hereditary lords of San Lucar were the Dukes of Medina Sidonia, who, before the centralization of government had been effected, exercised an almost regal authority. English trade became sufficiently important to justify the merchants in asking for extensive privileges, which were granted by the then duke, Don Alonzo Perez de Guzman, on March 14, 1517. The charter set forth that, in accordance with the petition of the English trading to his town of San Lucar de Barrameda, the duke granted them a piece of ground on which to build a Church of St. George; protection from the customs officials of Seville, Cadiz, and Xerez, who oppressed them because they preferred to land goods at San Lucar ; restriction of the duties to

[1] *Foedera*, xiii. 520.

amounts agreed upon in previous privileges ; a promise
to enforce payment of debts by Spaniards to Englishmen,
the latter having suffered losses through the partiality
of the law courts ; protection to the English so that
they might not be killed or molested, nor their goods
sequestered ; permission to the English to carry weapons
by night and day ; and several other minor concessions.[1]
Some expressions in the document indicate that the
English had already a governor and council, although
the original charter of incorporation, if one ever existed,
is not to be traced. Henceforward, San Lucar became
the English head-quarters in Spain, being suitably situated
for tapping the wealth of the southern part of the
country, for the collection of merchandise from the
Canaries and the West Indies, and for the transhipment
of Mediterranean produce to English bottoms.

Matters proceeded smoothly until the divorce of
Henry from Katherine of Aragon and the political
reformation in England sounded the death-knell of the
old friendship between the two countries. During this
period Englishmen made fortunes in the Spanish trade,
as may be judged from the example of Robert Thorne,
who left £17,000, although he died comparatively young.
Some of them even maintained factors in the jealously
guarded Spanish colonies in the west. But ere long
religious hatred was permanently to affect their position
in the country. As early as 1528 a rupture was thought
to be imminent between England and Spain, and the
English were advised to withdraw their goods.[2] The
expected struggle was avoided, but the merchants took
steps to strengthen their position by a closer union

---

[1] *Letters and Papers,* iv, part iii, No. 6686.
[2] *Venetian Cal.* vi, App. 78.

among themselves and by obtaining renewed promises from the Spanish Government. On September 1, 1530, Henry VIII granted a licence to his subjects trading in Spain and Andalusia, who desired to associate for mutual relief and redress of grievances, to assemble once a year, or oftener if need were, and to elect one or more councillors with twelve ' ancient and expert persons ' to be their assistants. The meeting might be held at Seville, Cadiz, or San Lucar, and the merchants of London, Bristol, and Southampton were to be represented. The councillor or governor (only one was actually elected at a time) was to be paid for his services and to be removable at the pleasure of his constituents. He and the twelve assistants were empowered to levy imposts and make ordinances for the welfare of the Company.[1] It will be seen that, in its general outlines, the constitution of the Spanish Company resembled that of the Merchant Adventurers. There was no hint of monopoly ; any Englishman might engage in the trade so long as he paid the prescribed fees to the governor.

Confirmation of the above licence was obtained from Charles V, and the next step was to demand a renewal of the Duke of Medina Sidonia's privileges of 1517, which had apparently not been maintained. On October 15, 1530, Richard Cooper, the newly-elected governor of the English, appeared before the justice of San Lucar and demanded fulfilment of the grant, which the judge ordered to be publicly proclaimed on two successive days.[2] The Church of St. George had already been built.

In the years following the incorporation of the Company the position of the English in Spain was not a happy one. They became unpopular with the people and still

---

[1] *Letters and Papers*, iv, part iii, No. 6654.   [2] Ibid., No. 6686.

more with the Church. According to Spanish complaints
the quality of English cloth fell off considerably, while
an English letter of 1538 confesses that, owing to the use
of many devices to defraud the customs, English credit
was not so good as it had formerly been. Reference
has been made, in the chapter devoted to Henry VII's
commercial policy, to a Spanish Navigation Act prohibiting the lading of foreign ships while native ones
were lying idle in Spanish ports. Originally, the English
were exempted from the operation of this law, but
their privilege seems to have lapsed after the death of
Henry VII. The law was not continuously enforced,
but was revived from time to time after lying dormant,
much to the hindrance of English trade. Another law,
the enforcement of which was continuously held as
a threat over English heads, forbade the import of ' false '
cloths into Spain. The Spaniards frequently asserted
that all the English cloth of this period was ' false ' in
the sense of the statute. It was not to the interest of
Spain to put either of these laws into constant operation,
but they served nevertheless as excellent pretexts for
a sudden embargo on English trade. Such stoppages
became increasingly frequent as time went on.

In spite of all disadvantages the volume of traffic was
considerable. The Andalusian trade resembled that to
Bordeaux, in that the bulk of the English vessels made
their outward voyage in the autumn, arriving about the
middle of October. The trading season was determined
by the nature of the commodities obtained, the chief of
which were wines, raisins, figs, oil, and salted meats.
In one month sixty English ships were expected to arrive
on the Andalusian coast.[1]

---

[1] *Letters and Papers*, xvi, No. 1126.

On April 24, 1539, the merchants at San Lucar
assembled in the Church of St. George and confirmed
the election of William Ostrigge or Ostrich, chosen as
governor in the previous December. In accordance
with the charter of Henry VIII they invested him with
full powers of administration, and fixed a scale of dues
to be paid to the Company by all English and Irish
traders.[1] It was not long before Ostrich, who proved
himself a capable governor, had matters of the utmost
importance to deal with. Already, as early as 1534,
Englishmen in Spain had been troubled by the Inquisition. In 1539 and 1540, the former of which years
had been a time of the utmost tension between England
and the Empire, there was a regular epidemic of persecution. Henry VIII had now finally repudiated the
authority of the Pope, had abolished the smaller monasteries, had put down the Catholic rising known as the
Pilgrimage of Grace with the utmost barbarity, and was
in process of exterminating the remaining religious houses.
His minister, Thomas Cromwell, was a known supporter
of the Protestants, and was negotiating a matrimonial
alliance intended to link England with the cause of the
Protestant princes of Germany. Spanish bigotry had
therefore every incentive to a savage persecution of such
Englishmen as it could lay hands upon ; and Charles V,
who alone had the power to prevent it, held his hand
and allowed matters to take their course.

In March 1539 it was reported, although the story

[1] *Harl. MSS.*, 297, f. 249. There is in the Record Office (*S. P. Misc.*,
No. 107) a manuscript volume containing transcripts of the proceedings
on April 24, 1539, the Letters Patent of Henry VIII in 1530, the privileges
granted by the Duke of Medina Sidonia, the complaint of the merchants
on March 15, 1548, and of certain negotiations with Spain at the end
of Elizabeth's reign.

lacks confirmation, that three English merchants were burnt in Spain, and that the Pope had granted remission of sins to any one who should kill an English heretic.[1] A letter from Henry VIII to Wyatt, who had been sent as ambassador to Spain in 1537,[2] explained that Flemish and Spanish ships had been arrested in England because ' in sundry parts of the sea coast of Spain, English subjects are much molested at the instigation of slanderous preachers suborned thereto by the Bishop of Rome's adherents '.[3] Relations were temporarily ameliorated by the inauguration, in April 1539, of the free trade policy by which foreign merchants had their duties reduced to the same amounts as those paid by Englishmen. But in January of the next year Wyatt wrote from Spain that the king should warn all English merchants that they traded to Spain at their own risk, for that there was a power there which depended upon their adversary the Pope. The Emperor refused to modify the action of the Inquisition.[4] Wyatt went so far as to threaten that if the Inquisition did not cease from troubling Englishmen commerce with Spain must cease.

The usual method of entrapping an Englishman was to engage him in conversation with regard to the Pope's authority over Christendom. If he admitted it he was infringing the Act of Supremacy, which declared Henry to be the supreme head of the Church in England ; if he denied it he was haled before the inquisitors, a heretic confessed. It speaks much for the loyalty and patriotism of Englishmen that they held firm on what was to most of them a purely political quibble, even when the

---

[1] *Letters and Papers*, xiv, part i, No. 466.
[2] G. F. Nott, *Works of Howard and Wyatt*, ii, p. xxxiv.
[3] *Letters and Papers*, xiv, part i, No. 487.   [4] Ibid. xv, No. 38.

shores of England were far away, and the dungeons of
the Holy Office gaped close at hand.

The case of Thomas Pery furnishes a good illustration
of inquisitorial methods. Writing from a Spanish prison
to one of Cromwell's servants, he describes how a priest
got him into argument as to whether the king were
a good Christian or no. On his maintaining that he was,
he was arrested and taken to the Castle of Triana in
Seville. He underwent numerous examinations, with
and without torture, on the matter of the king's orthodoxy, and was also pressed to say whether he thought
the suppression of the monasteries was good or bad.
Finally he, with four other Englishmen whom the Holy
Office had seized for the same cause, were forced to do
public penance, and sentenced to six months' imprisonment with forfeiture of all their goods. At the time of
writing, he says, he was in prison without a blanket or
garment to his back.[1] Ultimately, however, he was
released, and came home to England to lay his complaint
before the Council. The latter communicated with the
Emperor, but it does not appear that any compensation
was ever recovered.

·William Ostrich convened a meeting of the merchants
at San Lucar to protest against the treatment they were
receiving, and a detailed complaint was transmitted to
England. Thomas Pery and his companions had by this
time been released, and had related their sufferings in
person at San Lucar :

'The said Thomas doth allege and say that by force
of torment he was compelled to declare and say as the
judge would he should say. . . . Divers merchants of
England, prisoners with the said Thomas, have declared

---

[1] *Letters and Papers*, xv, No. 281.

before divers of us that they were present when the said Thomas was so tormented. . . . Furthermore it shall please you to understand here, that of long time past and unto this day, all we that hereunder have firmed our names have lived and do live in great peril and fear of our persons and goods, and not only we but all others of our nation trading these parts of Andalusia, for fear of the extreme punishment and cruel intreating of the fathers of the Inquisition and their deputies, which be in all places where our trade doth lie.' [1]

Matters were not improved by the passing of the English Navigation Act of 1540, limiting the free trade privilege granted to foreigners in the previous year to those who shipped in English vessels. However, after a prolonged diplomatic struggle, in which either side fired off all its heavy guns, consisting of embargoes, restrictions, and revivals of obsolete statutes, Henry agreed to exempt both Spaniards and Flemings from the Act. A new alliance against France was shortly afterwards concluded between England and the Empire, and the Inquisition relaxed its activities against the heretic islanders. This early persecution in Spain was undoubtedly the germ of much that bore great fruit in the next generation. The sons of the men of 1540 were the sailors and merchant adventurers of Elizabeth's reign ; and their contemptuous hatred of the Spaniard did not arise exclusively from the events of their own day. The seafarers also became, on the whole, the most staunchly Protestant section of the community, which may be accounted for, on the principle of contrariety, by the torments inflicted on those who, while not themselves Protestants, denied the Pope's supremacy. It cannot be pretended that any man in Henry's reign experienced

[1] *R. O., S. P. Hen. VIII*, § 161, ff. 76–82.

any religious fervour in asserting that his king was supreme head of the Church. Thomas Pery and his friends upheld the royal supremacy because they were loyal Englishmen who were commanded so to do; but their sufferings at the hands of the Papists engendered a hatred of the Catholic form of priestcraft, and inclined them to a corresponding sympathy with Protestantism.

The new alliance between Henry and the emperor was not of long duration. After making war in concert with the English in 1544, and failing to achieve any very decisive results, the emperor unexpectedly made peace with France at Crespi on September 18. England was left to carry on the struggle alone. In 1545 and 1546 the war was largely naval, the privateers of both countries ravaging the Channel and the Atlantic coasts of Europe, to the great annoyance of neutrals. Relations with Spain again became bad, particularly after the capture by an English privateer of an enormously rich Spanish ship from the West Indies, an act which, although justified by specious excuses, was nothing but rank piracy. As a result, orders were given in March 1545 for the arrest of all English merchants and ships in Spain. The arrest was of long duration, extending over more than eighteen months; in fact the affair was not satisfactorily cleared up before Henry's death. The Inquisition again began to arrest Englishmen, who were refused a hearing in the civil courts on the ground that they were heretics. In June an Englishman was sentenced to be burnt at Seville, and a ship's captain who was driven by stress of weather into San Sebastian was promptly seized by the Holy Office.[1]

[1] *Letters and Papers*, xx, part i, Nos. 459, 494, 981, 1003; part ii, No. 874; xxi, part ii, Nos. 371, 509.

When Henry VIII died the Council, under the control
of the Protector Somerset, effected a settlement of the
quarrel with Spain, and trade was resumed. The English
at San Lucar obtained a restoration of their privileges
after lodging a complaint in 1548 to the effect that
the functions of their governor had been usurped by a
Spaniard, who was collecting the dues rightfully belonging to their Company.[1] The troubles with France during
the reigns of Edward VI and Mary rendered the Spanish
voyage very unsafe. In 1552 the Council ordered that
the ships should return from Spain in companies of not
less than ten or twelve at a time.[2] Privateering, once
set on foot by the French war of 1544–6, was not stamped
out until the close of the century ; and the privateers
never hesitated to become pirates if the stakes were
sufficiently large.

Under Mary and a restored Catholic régime in England
there was naturally a period of better relations ; and,
surprising as it may seem, throughout the long period
of veiled hostilities prior to the dispatch of the Armada,
English merchantmen continued to resort to Spanish
ports. John Hawkins, in 1568, actually put into Vigo to
refit on his return from his disastrous third voyage, when
his fleet was scattered by the Spaniards at St. Juan de
Ulloa. In spite of the war to the death which was
carried on in American waters, trade was maintained in
Europe until 1585, when a treacherous attempt to seize
English ships at Bilbao at length precipitated an official
declaration of war.

Some light is thrown on the conditions of English
residence in Spain and the Indies by a relation in Hakluyt

---

[1] *Cotton MSS.*, Vesp. C viii, f. 56.   [2] *A. P. C.*, iv, p. 138.

of the adventures of one Robert Tomson, a merchant who went to Seville in the year 1553. He was possessed with a desire to wander and see the world, but first determined to make himself master of the Spanish tongue. For this purpose he resided for a year at the house of John Field, an Englishman, who had lived at Seville for close on twenty years, and who had a wife and family in that city. Seeing the ships arrive with rich cargoes from the Indies, Tomson determined to make his way thither, and persuaded Field to share in the enterprise. Field purchased a licence for himself, his family, and his friend to sail in the next fleet for New Spain. They made all preparations for departure, providing their own victuals and necessaries for the voyage. Before sailing, however, the fleet was stayed by the king's command, and the two Englishmen, unwilling to wait, shipped themselves in February 1555 in a caravel going from San Lucar to the Canaries, where they knew the Indies fleet would touch for water.

At Grand Canary they found some Englishmen, factors of Anthony Hickman and Edward Castlyn, merchants of London, who gave them good entertainment. After they had waited nearly eight months the Indies fleet at last appeared. Tomson and Field went aboard a ship of Cadiz, belonging to an Englishman named John Sweeting, residing in that city, and commanded by another Englishman, Leonard Chilton, son-in-law of Sweeting. One of the other passengers in the same ship was also an English merchant. The fleet touched at San Domingo and then proceeded to San Juan de Ulloa, the principal port of Mexico. Before reaching that place, however, the ship in which the Englishmen had taken passage sprang a leak and foundered in a gale at sea, all her people being rescued by one of her consorts.

On April 16, 1556, Tomson and his friends landed in Mexico, much distressed by the loss of all their goods in the shipwreck. They were very generously treated by a Spaniard, an old friend of John Field's, who lent them clothes, horses, and money for their journey to the city of Mexico. Disaster still dogged their footsteps. On the road Tomson fell sick with an ague, from which he did not recover for six months; while John Field and three of his family died of the same disease soon after reaching the capital. On his recovery Tomson fell in with a Scotsman, Thomas Blake, more than twenty years resident in the country, and by his assistance obtained employment with a rich Spaniard, who had been one of Cortes's original *conquistadores*. After twelve months' prosperity Tomson was foolish enough to give vent at a dinner-table to some Protestant opinions. An ill-wisher reported his words to the Bishop of Mexico. He was arrested and kept seven months in prison, and then, together with an Italian also charged with heresy, was forced to do open penance in the great church at Mexico. The Italian was sentenced to imprisonment for life, and Tomson for three years. They were sent down to the coast and put aboard a ship bound for Spain, but the Italian contrived to escape at one of the islands of the Azores by swimming ashore. He ultimately made his way to England and died in London. Tomson served his sentence in the Inquisition at Seville, and, on his release, was fortunate enough to marry the heiress of a rich Spaniard who had died on the homeward voyage from Mexico. He says: 'The marriage was worth to me 2500 pounds in bars of gold and silver, besides jewels

P 2

of great price. This I thought good to speak of, to shew the goodness of God to all that put their trust in him, that I . . . should be provided at God's hand in one moment, of more than in all my life before I could attain unto by mine own labour.' And here, to the chink of the precious metal, his story ends.

What is particularly striking in this account is the number of Englishmen encountered by this one traveller in the Spanish seas and colonies. When the Indies were first discovered Castilians alone were permitted to resort to them. After the death of Isabella they were thrown open to all Spaniards; and it would appear that in later days Englishmen had little difficulty in making their way unobtrusively wherever they wished so long as they sailed under the Spanish flag, and were sound on religious matters. Other Englishmen, known to have been early voyagers to Spanish America, will be referred to in the next chapter.

Throughout the Middle Ages Englishmen had inter-mittently engaged in mercantile adventures to the Mediterranean, although it was not until the end of the fifteenth century that any regularly frequented trade was begun.[1] The stirrings of the Renaissance in England and the accompanying social changes developed a growth

---

[1] In the Parliament of 1514-15 an amendment was passed to an Act of Richard III which rendered it obligatory on all merchants bringing goods from the Mediterranean to import therewith a proportionate number of bowstaves. Certain Englishmen had been proceeded against for failing to comply with this law, and the amendment made it plain that it was henceforth only to apply to aliens. This seems to indicate that in the time of Richard III there were few or no Englishmen engaged in the Mediterranean trade, since no discrimination was thought neces-sary in the original Act. If Richard III's Act had been intended to apply to both Englishmen and aliens it would most probably have been expressly so stated.

of the demand for luxuries such as only the East could supply. Prior to 1498, the year of Vasco da Gama's epoch-making voyage to Calicut, the only avenue of approach to the marts of eastern merchandise lay through the Straits of Gibraltar. The discovery of the sea voyage to Asia was destined to revolutionize utterly the conditions of the trade, but the change was slow to accomplish itself, and for half a century to come the Mediterranean route was able to hold its place in competition with the long, dangerous navigation round half the circumference of the globe. Consequently it seemed well worth while to contemporary Englishmen in the days of the early Tudors, ignorant as they were of the vast significance of the discoveries of their time, to make strong efforts to capture a share of the traffic of the Levant.

Hitherto the galleys of Venice and the carracks of Genoa had supplied practically all the eastern goods which England could pay for with surplus wools and cloth, but early in the reign of Henry VII we find evidence, in his tariff dispute with Venice, of a regular voyage of English ships to Candia, Chios, and possibly other Venetian dependencies, to load cargoes of the sweet malmsey wines which were becoming popular in England. The proposal, at the same period, to establish an English wool staple at Pisa has already been described. If carried out, it would have caused an immense disturbance to trade and would probably have ruined the whole Italian colony in London, with diplomatic consequences which Henry must have had little desire to face; but the project was no chimaera, and was sufficiently within the scope of practicabilities to cause intense alarm to the Venetian Government, who concluded the quarrel with Henry on his own terms.

Once established and diplomatically supported, English commerce throve exceedingly in the Levant. Many of the most prominent commercial families—the Gonsons, the Lockes, and the Greshams—took part in it. Hakluyt, speaking on the authority of the old ledgers of the merchants concerned, relates that, as early as 1511, ' divers tall ships of London . . . with certain other ships of Southampton and Bristol, had an ordinary and usual trade to Sicily, Candia, Chios, and somewhiles to Cyprus, as also to Tripoli and Beyrout in Syria '. The goods which they took out with them were hides and various kinds of cloth, while the homeward cargoes consisted of silks, chamlets, rhubarb, malmseys, muscadels and other wines, sweet oils, cotton wool, Turkey carpets, galls, pepper, cinnamon and other spices, everything in fact which advancing material civilization, spurred on by the quickened imagination of the time, could demand.[1] An extensive use was also made of local Mediterranean shipping, which seems to imply the presence of numerous resident English merchants or their factors in those regions.[2]

Concomitantly with the advance of English trade in the Mediterranean, the mercantile marine of Venice declined under stress of wars with the Turk and the Italian powers who were jealous of her success. The Flanders galleys came less and less frequently to England, ceasing altogether before the end of the reign of Henry VIII. The commerce of Genoa had already

---

[1] Hakluyt, vol. v, p. 62.

[2] In Hakluyt's pages some of these factors are mentioned by name : William Heith, factor of John Gresham at Candia ; John Ratcliffe, factor of the same in Portugal ; William Eyms, factor of Sir William Bowyer, the Duke of Norfolk and others at Chios ; Robert Bye and Oliver Lesson, also factors at Chios.

fallen before the attacks of her great rival, and the trend
of events rendered impossible any revival of Italian sea-
borne trade. Consequently the English vessels not only
bore the goods of their own merchants, but also developed
a carrying traffic on behalf of the Italian factors and
agents in London, who had to forward in some way the
wools and rough fabrics which provided employment for
the population of the great cities, indispensable now that
their commerce was deserting them.[1] When the Mediterranean trade became well established, consuls were
appointed at Chios and Candia with full authority over
English merchants while in port,[2] but otherwise the
trade was absolutely free, and there was never anything
resembling an incorporation of the merchants interested
until the granting of a Charter to the Turkey Company
by Queen Elizabeth in 1581. By that date the conditions had entirely changed ; the trade had languished
and had then been revived, while the hostility of Spain
and the necessity of negotiating with the Turks had
rendered co-operative working and mutual support with
capital and armed force essential to success.

In the first half of the century, on the other hand,
Turkish sea power was not yet at its height in the
Mediterranean, while the length of the voyage and the
diversity of the places visited made it difficult for the
merchantmen to sail in fleets. At that period the ships
generally proceeded alone or, at most, in pairs, and the
immense risks were no doubt compensated by corresponding profits. The freedom of trade did not, of
course, extend to raw wool and the other articles con-

[1] Various references to this trade : *Letters and Papers*, i, pp. 46 and
120 ; xiv, part i, No. 538, &c.
[2] *Foedera*, xiii, 353 ; xiv. 424, 703.

stituting the Staplers' monopoly, for which special licences had to be obtained. So lucrative was the trade that these licences were sought after by the most prominent men in the land, and maritime adventure must have received a great stimulus from their participation. In 1510 a syndicate composed of Sir Edward Howard, son of the Earl of Surrey, Sir Thomas Knyvet, Charles Brandon (afterwards Duke of Suffolk and brother-in-law of the king), and Sir Edward Guldeford obtained permission to export wool, leather, lead, tin, &c., for three years in a ship called the *Mary and John* of London.[1] Sir Edward Howard was killed in the attack on Brest in 1513, but we find his brother, Thomas Howard, Lord Admiral and Duke of Norfolk, engaging in the same trade about 1540, when he had a factor at Chios.

Voyages such as these, which occupied on an average a full year from departure to return, necessitated the use of larger ships than were customary in the older and more local trades. It was obviously more economical to employ one well-armed and capacious vessel with a large crew than to send two or three smaller ones which would be liable to part company on a long trip, and would be much more open to peril from storms and pirates. The same considerations had caused the Venetians to build merchantmen of 1,000 tons burden, and they undoubtedly assisted in the development of naval architecture in England which was so remarkable between the accession of Henry VII and the defeat of the Armada. There was more essential difference between the unwieldy basin-shaped 'cog' of the fifteenth century and the vessels with which Drake outmanœuvred the Spaniards, than there was between Drake's ships and those of Nelson at Trafalgar.

---

[1] *Letters and Papers*, i, p. 186.

In times of peace the ships of the navy, heavily armed
and stoutly built, were sometimes employed on Mediterranean voyages. The *Regent,* afterwards lost in the fight
off Brest in 1512, was sent with wool to Italy in 1510 ;
and as late as 1552 two king's ships, the *Jesus of Lubeck,*
of 800 tons, and the *Mary Gonson,* of 600, were chartered
by merchants for £1,000 for a voyage to ' Levants-end '.[1]
In 1515 the *Christ,* a ship which had served against the
French in the war just concluded, made a most unfortunate voyage to the Mediterranean. She was chartered
by three London merchants and laden with wools and
other merchandise for Italy. After leaving London she
was driven by a storm on the coast of Zealand, arrested
for tolls by the authorities, and released after much
delay on security being given. Proceeding on the voyage,
she was captured by the Moors off the Barbary coast.
The ship and cargo were of course hopelessly lost, and
the crew were held to ransom, for the payment of which
a certain John Hopton received a licence to gather alms
for three years in England.[2]

This begging to raise the ransom of captive friends
was a common custom. In 1510 two Provençal merchants
were licensed to ask alms for the ransom of nineteen of
their comrades who still survived out of twenty-eight
taken by the Turks two years previously ; and indulgences
were granted by the Pope to all who should aid them.
Another instance was that of Isabella Lascarina, ' a gentle-
woman of Greece ' who was trying to raise 1,300 ducats
for the ransom of her four children, taken by the Turks
ten years before. As long as the Turkish power flourished

---

[1] *Journal of Edward VI,* p. 61. The tonnage is given as there stated,
but is probably exaggerated.
[2] *Letters and Papers,* ii, Nos. 738, 811.

in the Mediterranean the aid of the charitable continued to be invoked for such cases.

Hakluyt, writing at the end of the century, was able to get into touch with a veteran survivor of these early voyages, and obtained from him many interesting particulars.[1] This man, John Williamson by name, was living in 1592 in the parish of St. Dunstan's in the East, and had sailed as cooper in one of Gonson's ships. In 1534, he says, a voyage to Candia and Chios was made by two ships named the *Holy Cross*, of 160 tons, and the *Matthew Gonson*, of 300 tons. The latter was commanded by Richard Gonson, a son of William Gonson, the paymaster of Henry VIII's navy. Richard Gonson died at Chios in the course of this, his first voyage. The two vessels brought home cargoes consisting of the usual Levant goods, together with some ' very excellent muscatels and red malmesey, the like whereof was seldom seen before in England '. The double journey occupied a full year, and was the last made by the *Holy Cross*, ' which was so shaken in this voyage, and so weakened, that she was laid up in dock, and never made voyage after '. In 1535 the *Matthew Gonson* made another voyage alone, commanded this time by Captain Richard Gray, who afterwards died in Russia. William Holstocke, who in later days rose to be Controller of Elizabeth's navy, sailed as purser, having been the captain's page in the previous voyage. The ship was evidently well armed, for the crew numbered 100 and included six gunners. There were also four trumpeters who all deserted at Messina, ' and gat them into the galleys that lay near unto us, and in them went to Rome '. The voyage was finished in eleven months, and in that

[1] Hakluyt, v. 67–8.

time only one man died of sickness. The *Matthew Gonson* was still trading to the Mediterranean in 1553.

Another narration,[1] that of Roger Bodenham, captain of the *Barke Aucher*, goes more into detail, and gives a vivid picture of the perils of Mediterranean trading. Leaving Tilbury on January 6, 1551, after long delay by reason of contrary winds, they proceeded in charge of a pilot to Dover, whither Sir Anthony Aucher, the owner, had journeyed to bid them farewell. On the 11th they arrived at Plymouth, whence they departed two days later and sighted Cape Finisterre on the 16th. On January 30 they entered the harbour of Cadiz, discharged part of their cargo, and took in fresh goods, not leaving that port until February 20. After being delayed five days by contrary winds among the Balearic Islands, they passed in sight of Sardinia and arrived at Messina on March 5, discharging ' much goods ' there. Thenceforward the dangerous part of the voyage was entered upon as ' there was no going into Levant, especially to Chios, without a safe-conduct from the Turk '. The principal owner of the cargo, a foreigner named Anselm Salvago, had promised to obtain such a safe-conduct and have it ready for the ship at Messina, but it was not forthcoming, and Bodenham was obliged to go on to Candia without one. There he was assured he would find a safe-conduct to continue the voyage to Chios, the destination of most of the merchandise. Reaching Candia without mishap he was again disappointed, and on sending a messenger to Chios to ask for a safe-conduct, received answer that the Turks would give none. As a fleet of Turkish galleys was then at sea he announced

[1] Hakluyt, v. 71.

his determination not to proceed any further, in spite of the urging of the merchants who owned the cargo.

Certain small Turkish vessels which were in the port made sail that day for Turkey, carrying the news that a rich English ship was in Candia and intended to remain there. Perceiving that this might afford a chance of slipping through to Chios, Bodenham changed his plan and made sail the same evening, trusting that the Turks would not be on the look-out for him. He had some trouble to induce the crew to set out on such a risky enterprise, but finally won them all over except three, whom he sent ashore. At the last moment they also begged so hard to be received on board again that he was constrained to take them with him. When in the midst of the Archipelago the wind failed and he was obliged to anchor for ten or twelve days at an island called Micone, where he picked up a Greek pilot who undertook to bring the ship to Chios. The voyage was resumed, and Chios was sighted in the afternoon, but Bodenham decided to stand off for the night as he preferred to enter the port in the morning. A number of small Greek vessels, however, which had accompanied him from Chios, decided to make for the harbour that night. Shortly after they had parted company three ' foysts ' full of Turks were seen preparing to attack them. The Greek pilot, who had a son in one of them, entreated Bodenham to go to the rescue. This he did, and the pirates were driven off by a single effective shot from one of his guns.

Next morning the *Barke Aucher* was lying off the mole of Chios, and Bodenham sent in his boat with word to the merchants that if they wanted their goods they must come out and fetch them, as otherwise he would take

them back to Candia. Finally he allowed himself to be
persuaded, and entered the harbour on receiving a bond
from the city for 12,000 ducats as a guarantee of his
safety for twenty days. He was making haste to get his
business done, fearing the approach of the Turkish fleet,
when some of the citizens informed him privately that
he was in great danger, and that they had no means nor
intention to defend him, living as they did entirely at
the mercy of the Turk. Bodenham, realizing the condition of affairs, determined to make off at once, but the
merchants, who had not completed their cargoes, tried
to prevent him by instigating the crew to demand
payment of their wages and an opportunity to spend
the same ashore. The men, who had before been so
backward in face of danger, were now in a reckless
mood, and there was fresh trouble before the ship could
depart.

To continue in the captain's own words :

' But God provided so for me, that I paid them their
money that night, and then charged them, that if they
would not set the ship forth, I would make them to
answer the same in England, with danger of their heads.
Many were married in England and had somewhat to
lose, those did stick to me. I had twelve gunners : the
master gunner, who was a mad-brained fellow, and the
owner's servant had a parliament between themselves,
and he upon the same came up to me with his sword
drawn, swearing that he had promised the owner, Sir
Anthony Aucher, to live and die in the said ship against
all who should offer any harm to the ship, and that he
would fight with the whole army of the Turks and never
yield. With this fellow I had much to do, but at the
last I made him confess his fault and follow mine advice.
Thus with much labour I got out of the mole of Chios
into the sea by warping forth, with the help of Genoese

boats and a French boat that was in the Mole ; and
being out, God sent me a special gale of wind to go my
way.   Then I caused a piece to be shot off for some of
my men that were in the town, and with much ado they
came aboard, and then I set sail a little before one of
the clock.'

He was only just in time, for, not two hours afterwards,
seven Turkish galleys arrived to capture the ship, and
next day a hundred more.   A great fleet in fact, consisting of 250 sail, was at sea with the intention of
proceeding against Malta.   Three days afterwards Bodenham got into Candia, which proved to be a safe refuge.
The Turkish fleet sailed past in sight of the town, but
the inhabitants had made good preparations for defence,
and they were left undisturbed.   After loading with
wines and other goods the *Barke Aucher* set sail for
Messina, rescuing by the way some Venetian vessels
which were being attacked by Turkish galleys.   From
Messina she sailed in safety through the Straits to Cadiz
and thence home to London.   Richard Chancellor, afterwards the first Englishman to reach Moscow, was one
of the crew, as was also Matthew Baker, who became
chief shipwright to Queen Elizabeth.

Anthony Jenkinson, another pioneer of Russian and
Asiatic travel, was also engaged in the Mediterranean
trade in his earlier years.   In 1553 he obtained a patent
from the Sultan Solyman, granting him full liberty
to travel and trade throughout the Turkish dominions,
with protection for his factors and goods.   But, notwithstanding the Sultan's goodwill, from this time onwards the traffic declined, probably owing to the lawless
state of the Levant waters ;   and Hakluyt relates that
it was ' utterly discontinued, and in manner quite for-

gotten, as if it had never been, for the space of twenty years and more '. But about the year 1575 some London merchants sent two representatives overland through Poland to Constantinople to obtain a fresh safe-conduct, whereupon trade was resumed and the Turkey Company received its letters of incorporation from the queen in 1581.

CHAPTER X

VOYAGES AND PROJECTS OF DISCOVERY UNDER HENRY VIII

DURING the reign of Henry VIII, although English prestige increased and commerce became firmly established, it must be confessed that commensurate progress was not made in discovery and oceanic enterprise. The king himself was intermittently anxious to promote such undertakings, but the preoccupations arising from Continental politics proved too strong for him. His hostility to France involved the maintenance of the old alliance with the Netherlands and Spain ; and while that alliance endured England was barred from all the more profitable parts of the New World.

Also, there was as yet no real public interest in discovery ; England was not *awake* to matters that were common knowledge and subjects of eager discussion in the Peninsula, in France, Italy, and even in inland Germany. Although diligent chroniclers and accomplished men of letters existed in Henry's England, we look in vain for a Hakluyt, or even a Richard Eden, to record for us the details of such minor adventures as were actually attempted. Hakluyt himself in after years lamented ' the great negligence of the writers of those times, who should have used more care in preserving of the memories of the worthy acts of our nation '. Closely connected, either as cause or result, with this indifference was a deplorable want of the knowledge necessary to success. As seamen the Englishmen of the time were unsurpassed, but with a few honourable exceptions, such as Robert Thorne and William Hawkins, they took no interest in the advance of navigation and cosmography. Thorne is the only Englishman in the reigns of the first two Tudors who is known to have written on such matters. Consequently the lack of an enthusiastic, well-informed leader was even more detrimental to the accomplishment of important discoveries than was the want of public support. The adventures of the reign of Henry VIII illustrate the truth that expansion must be national and spontaneous if it is to produce permanent results; the early attempts of the Cabots and their Bristol contemporaries had been allowed to die of neglect, and it was not until the revival of oceanic enterprise, first by William Hawkins and afterwards by the merchant companies who sent fleets to West Africa and the White Sea, that world-wide interests became a regular factor in English life and history.

The first recorded project of the reign is an alleged voyage to the North-West by Sebastian Cabot and Sir Thomas Pert or Spert in 1516. Its actual occurrence is doubtful, and rests primarily on the authority of Richard Eden, who, in the dedication to his *Treatise of the Newe India*, published in 1553,[1] says : ' Our Sovereign Lord King Henry VIII, about the same year of his reign (i. e. 1516 or 1517), furnished and sent forth certain ships under the governance of Sebastian Cabot, yet living, and one Sir Thomas Perte, whose faint heart was the cause that voyage took none effect.' This is the sole definite and express statement that such a voyage took

---

[1] Reprinted, 1885, by Dr. E. Arber, p. 6.

place. Purchas, it is true, refers to it, but he evidently copied Eden and had no independent knowledge. It has been suggested that Ramusio's note in the preface to his third volume (see Chap. IV, pp. 89–90), and also the lines in the *New Interlude* (Chap. V, pp. 111-13), refer to this expedition, but it must be allowed that they apply equally well to other voyages. The doubt as to their intention thus destroys any value they might have as evidence of the occurrence of a voyage in 1516.[1]   In favour of Eden's statement it must be remembered that Sebastian Cabot was in England in 1553 and was personally known to the author, who probably derived his information from him direct. But Cabot, as is evidenced by other incidents in his career, had no scruple in distorting the truth when it suited his purpose, and it was certainly to his interest to magnify his services to England at a time when he was living on the bounty of the English Crown, and was engaged in promoting fresh northern explorations.

The ascertained record of the doings of Cabot throws little light on the matter. He was in England in May 1512, when he was paid twenty shillings for making a map of Gascony and Guienne for the use of the expedition sent to Biscay under the Marquis of Dorset for the invasion of those provinces. This is his first reappearance in history after the voyages at the end of the fifteenth century. Whether or not he had lived in England during the interval is unknown. He accompanied Dorset's expedition to Spain, and transferred himself to the service of King Ferdinand, by whom, on October 20,

---

[1] To make Ramusio, iii, Preface, apply to 1516, it is further necessary to assume a misprint in his work, as he distinctly says that the voyage he describes took place under Henry VII.

1512, he was appointed a naval captain. He then took
up his abode at Seville. His residence in Spain can be
continuously traced until November 13, 1515, after which
date no further mention of him occurs until February 5,
1518, when he was appointed Pilot Major of Spain by
the Government of Charles V, Ferdinand having died
in January 1516. He is thus quite unaccounted for
during the years 1516 and 1517. It is possible that,
thinking his prospects in Spain unpromising, he returned
to England on the death of Ferdinand.[1]

The movements and employments of Thomas Spert
can be much more satisfactorily traced. As a mariner
in the service of Henry VII he had carried dispatches
between England and Spain.[2] He served, evidently with
credit, in the navy during the war of 1512–14. In
1512–13 he was master of the *Mary Rose*, one of the
most important fighting ships in the fleet. On the
approaching completion, towards the end of the latter
year, of the *Henry Grace à Dieu*, the largest vessel then
constructed in England, he was transferred to her as
master. On November 10, 1514, he was granted an
annuity of £20, which was confirmed in January 1516.[3]
Again, on July 10, 1517, he was granted the office of
ballasting ships in the Thames, which office he was to
hold during pleasure at a rent of £10 a year.[4] This
militates strongly against one part of Eden's story,
namely, that it was Spert's misconduct which spoiled
the success of the voyage of discovery. The office was

[1] For Sebastian Cabot's career in Spain see Harrisse, *John and Sebastian
Cabot* (1896), which contains a syllabus of documents relating to him.
[2] R. O., *Book of King's Payments* (T. R. Misc., Bk. 214): 'Ann.
21 Hen. VII Aug. 7th. Item to Thoms Perte maryner in rewarde that
come from the king of Castill, x sh.'
[3] *Letters and Papers*, ii, No. 1462, and p. 875.
[4] Ibid., No. 3459.

evidently one of profit, and would hardly have been granted to one who had recently disgraced himself. But indeed the whole theory of Spert's connexion with a voyage of discovery at this time is effectively killed by a document in the Record Office which has not hitherto been quoted in this connexion. It is a manuscript book [1] showing the issues of various stores to the masters of the king's ships, and it proves beyond doubt that between 1515 and 1521 Thomas Spert never vacated his post as master of the *Henry Grace à Dieu*. There are entries showing his presence in that ship on April 7 and July 3, 1516, and on April 28 and September 17, 1517, which, together with the grant on July 10 of the last-mentioned year, are conclusive evidence that he could not have made a voyage to America at the period in question.

What is known of the remainder of Spert's career shows that he continued in high favour. He served in the war of 1522–5 and was consulted by the admiral as to the best way of cutting out some Scottish privateers in Boulogne harbour. He remained master of the *Great Harry* until 1530. His next promotion was to be 'Clerk Controller' of the king's ships. By the year 1533 he had been knighted.[2] In 1542 he was granted lands in Essex, and he is last heard of in 1544 as the owner of a ship

---

[1] *Exchequer T. R. Misc. Bks.*, vol. x. The entries relating to Spert all resemble the following : ' The herry gce diew. Delyv'de the xxvij daye of september anno dicto [7th year of Henry VIII] to thoms spte for the herry gce diew iiij cabulls. . . .'

' The herry gce diew, the katryn fortune and the gabryell riall. Delyv'de to thoms spte [and the other two masters] the vijth. daye of ap'll anno dicto [7th year of the reign] vj barells tarre.' In no case is any other person but Spert designated as the master of the *Henry Grace à Dieu*.

[2] His knighthood has been disputed, but two official documents speak of him as Sir Thomas Spert (*Letters and Papers*, vi, No. 196; xvii, No. 1258).

called the *Mary Spert*, which was serving with the fleet against the French.[1] It is probable that he died soon afterwards; it may be deduced from Eden's remarks that he was not living in 1553.

On the whole this voyage of 1516 must be ranked as of extremely doubtful authenticity. Spert certainly had nothing to do with it, but there is nothing in the known evidence to render it impossible that Sebastian Cabot had. On the other hand, it has left no contemporary record in official papers, and the chroniclers of the reign are absolutely silent with regard to it. The most feasible conclusion is that the story was the combined product of the credulity of Richard Eden and the senile romantic tendencies of Sebastian Cabot.

Whatever may have happened in 1516, there is no doubt that Henry's mind was running on schemes of western discovery; and in 1521 a new design was mooted whose details rest upon much surer authority.[2] Early in that year two members of the Privy Council, Sir Robert Wingfield and Sir Wolston Brown, were deputed to lay the king's proposals before the Livery Companies of London. The plan was as follows : the Companies were to furnish five ships of not more than 120 tons each for a voyage to ' the Newefound Iland ', and to be responsible for the victualling and wages; the king was to find the tackle and ordnance and ' bear the adventure of the said ships ', whatever that may mean; the City of London should have control of the whole enterprise, although other towns might participate—Bristol had already promised two ships; ten years' exclusive monopoly of

---

[1] *Letters and Papers*, many references.
[2] *Wardens' Manuscript Accounts of the Drapers' Company*, vol. vii, 86–7. Printed *in extenso* in Harrisse, *Discovery of North America*, iii. 747.

the new trade was offered, with exemption from customs for the first thirty months. As will be seen from what follows, the expedition was evidently to be placed under the command of Sebastian Cabot, although his surname is nowhere mentioned.

The germ of the enterprise was most probably the departure in 1519 of Magellan's squadron for the discovery of a south-west passage into the Pacific. The actual existence of that passage was not yet known, for Magellan's *Victoria* did not return until 1522 with the news of the discovery of the Strait of Todos Sanctos and the circumnavigation of the globe. All that Henry knew was that the Spaniards were challenging the Portuguese monopoly of trade with eastern Asia ; and he doubtless felt at liberty to do the same if he could find a north-west passage past the new-found lands which English enterprise had explored in his father's reign. Most probably King Henry knew of Sebastian Cabot's former attempt in this direction—we may fairly assume that a man of his learning would be acquainted with Peter Martyr's *Decades of the New World*, published in 1516, even if he had as yet no personal knowledge of Cabot himself—and it was natural that he should wish to entrust the command of the new expedition to a man with previous experience of the task.

The cautious merchants of the Livery Companies, however, showed little eagerness to adventure their ships and money in a scheme which had already proved financially unsound within the memory of many of them. Moreover, any success which might be obtained would inevitably be more to the profit of Bristol than of London. The seamen and merchants of the former port were more accustomed to distant enterprises, and their geographical position would give them as much advantage in a north-western trade as it did in the traffic with Bordeaux and Spain. Accordingly, the Companies hung back and advanced objections. The wardens of the Drapers said that they had no authority to bind their fellowship to any outlay ; also that there were in their Company ' but few adventurers, saving only into Flanders, whereunto requireth no great ships '. If the king would supply the vessels they would do their best to find a cargo, but they feared trouble with Spain, which would entail perilous consequences to their legitimate trade.

The Drapers seem to have taken the lead in opposing the design. In a communication to the Mercers they suggested that it would be advisable to have more information from English mariners with respect to the route proposed, ' although it be further hence than few English mariners can tell. And we think it be too sore adventure to jeopard five ships with men and goods unto the said Island upon the singular trust of one man called, as we understand, Sebastian, which Sebastian, as we hear say, was never in that land himself, all if he makes report of many things as he hath heard his father and other men speak in times past.' [1] Also, they continued, even

---

[1] This passage has been regarded as fatal to the connexion of Sebastian Cabot with a voyage in 1516, and even to his claims to have made discoveries under Henry VII. As regards the former, it is quite compatible with an expedition which returned without discovering land, which is precisely what Eden hints at. On the latter point it is to be remarked that the third Cabot voyage (that of Sebastian in search of the North-West Passage) ended in failure and obscurity and was overshadowed by the expeditions of the Bristol syndicates ; thus it is not surprising that the London Drapers were able to profess a very convenient ignorance of it. They could hardly do the same about John Cabot in view of the notoriety of his discovery in 1497, and the brilliance of his reception in London in that year.

if Sebastian had been there, and were the most cunning
navigator imaginable, it would be a great risk to venture
five ships in the event of his death or of a separation of
the fleet, in which case four ships at least would be in
peril by lacking a pilot. They concluded by objecting
that it was impossible to victual the ships for a whole
year. The other eleven Companies gave a partial and
grudging acquiescence. They were willing to find two
ships and ' they supposed to furnish the third ', but they
desired a longer respite. The king and the Cardinal,
however, would be content with no half measures. The
Lord Mayor was sent for to speak with the king. ' His
Grace would have no nay therein, but spake sharply to
the Mayor to see it put in execution to the best of his
power.' But passive hostility triumphed ; a few niggardly
subscriptions were collected and then the whole matter
was allowed to drop. As far as is known, not a single
vessel put to sea.

It is plain that the ' Sebastian ' of the Drapers' protest
was Sebastian Cabot. The reference to his father is
sufficiently conclusive, and the contention is borne out
by two other circumstances. In 1524 Sir Thomas Lovell
died, and among the debts paid after his death occurs
the following item : ' 18 Feb. (year not stated), to John
Goderyk, of Foly, Cornwall, draper, for conducting
Sebastian Cabot, master of the pilots in Spain, to
London, at our testator's request, 43s. 4d.' [1] This of
course might possibly relate to the dubious voyage of
1516, especially as, in that event, his coming to England
in February would tally very well with the death of
King Ferdinand on January 23. But the supposition is
rather far-fetched, and is further vitiated by the fact

[1] *Letters and Papers*, iv, part i, p. 154.

that Cabot was not Pilot Major until 1518. It seems more likely that Cabot's visit to England was in connexion with the 1521 project. Again, when he was plotting to betray his geographical secrets to the Venetian Government, Cabot made the following statement to their envoy Contarini at Valladolid in December 1522 : 'Now it so happened that when in England three years ago, if I mistake not, Cardinal Wolsey offered me high terms if I would sail with an armada of his on a voyage of discovery. The vessels were almost ready, and they had got together 30,000 ducats for their outfit. I answered him that, being in the service of the King of Spain, I could not go without his leave, but if free permission were granted me from hence, I would serve him.' [1] Allowing for Sebastian's constitutional inaccuracy in the matter of dates, which in this case expands twenty-one months to ' about three years ', there is here fairly trustworthy evidence on the question. We are not, of course, obliged to believe that Sebastian failed to take the command from the motive of high principle which he describes. Henceforward he had no further concern with English enterprises until his final reappearance in England in 1548.

In 1525 Henry was in treaty with another foreign navigator, Paolo Centurioni the Genoese, to whom he promised the leadership of an expedition for the discovery of new countries. Centurioni came to London, but died there before the plan took practical shape ; and the affair was again in abeyance for lack of a skilled leader.[2] Centurioni's idea was apparently to open up

[1] *Venetian Cal.*, iii, No. 607.
[2] Agostino Giustiniani, *Castigatissimi Annali*, Genova, 1537, lib. vi, f. cclxxviii. Quoted by Harrisse in *John and Sebastian Cabot* (1896), pp. 337-8.

communication with Asia by way of Muscovy and the North-East—a foreshadowing of Willoughby's expedition of 1553.

The idea of a northern passage to the Pacific was again revived in 1527. In that year Robert Thorne, a Bristol merchant then residing at Seville, addressed to King Henry a *Declaration of the Indies*,[1] in which he exhorted him again to take in hand the promotion of northern exploration, not only because the Spaniards and the Portuguese had already monopolized the western and eastern routes, but also ' because the situation of this your realm is thereunto nearest and aptest of all other : and also for that you have already taken it in hand . . . though heretofore Your Grace hath made thereof a proof and found not the commodity thereby as you trusted, at this time it shall be no impediment. For there may be now provided remedies for things then lacked, and the inconveniences and lets removed that then were cause Your Grace's desire took no full effect, which is, the courses to be changed, and followed the foresaid new courses.' Thorne appealed to the honour of the king and the nation not to be left behind in the race. He minimized the danger of Arctic voyages, and enlarged on the advantages to mariners of the perpetual daylight of the Arctic summer. He argued that the Arctic seas were everywhere navigable, and suggested a route to eastern lands right over the Pole itself. ' For they, being past this little way which they named so dangerous, which may be two or three leagues before they come to the pole, and as much more after they pass the pole, it is clear that from thenceforth the seas and lands are as temperate as in these parts.' After

[1] Hakluyt, ii. 159-63.

passing over the Pole, he continued, three routes lay
open to navigators : they might turn towards eastern
Asia, reaching Tartary, China, Cathay, the Moluccas,
and so home by the Cape of Good Hope ; or they might
decline to the west and go down by ' the back side of
the new found land, which of late was discovered by
Your Grace's subjects, until they come to the back side
and south seas of the Indies occidentals ', and then
through the Straits of Magellan to England ; but if
they should take a middle course between these two,
' and then decline towards the lands and Islands situated
between the Tropics and under the Equinoctial, without
doubt they shall find the richest lands and islands of the
world of gold, precious stones, balms, spices, and other
things that we here esteem most, which come out of
strange countries ; and may return the same way. By
this it appeareth Your Grace hath not only a great
advantage of the riches, but also your subjects shall not
travel half of the way that other do, which go round
about as aforesaid.'

Thorne also expressed his ideas in greater detail to
Doctor Lee, Henry's ambassador at that time in Spain.[1]
He enclosed a map, which Hakluyt has preserved, and
entered into elaborate calculations to show that the
northern route to the Pacific was much shorter than
those used by either the Spaniards or the Portuguese.
He referred to the Spanish expedition which had sailed
from Seville in the previous year for the Spice Islands,
and mentioned that he and his partner had invested
1,400 ducats so as to have an excuse for sending two
Englishmen to accompany it and report on those regions.[2]

---

[1] *The Book made by Master Robert Thorne*, Hakluyt, ii. 164-81.
[2] This was Sebastian Cabot's expedition, which never passed the

He claimed that his father and Hugh Elyot were the original discoverers of Newfoundland, and that they would have reached the Indies but for a mutiny.

That the book to Dr. Lee was written in the first quarter of 1527 is evidenced by a reference to Cabot's squadron of 1526 as having sailed ' in April last past ', but there is no clue to the month of the letter to the king. Hence it cannot be stated with certainty that the expedition which we have next to consider was a consequence of that letter.

Whether it was or not, the fact remains that two ships were commissioned in 1527 and placed under the command of John Rut, a master mariner who, like Spert, had served in the navy during the French wars. Grafton's *Chronicle* has a brief entry relative to their departure : ' This same month (May, 1527) the king sent two fair ships, well manned and victualled, having in them divers cunning men, to seek strange regions ; and so forth they set out of the Thames the 20th day of May ; if they sped well you shall hear at their return.' In spite of which promise, the *Chronicle* makes no further mention of them. Hakluyt attempted to glean some further information about this voyage, with very little success. Martin Frobisher and Richard Allen told him that one of the ships was called the *Dominus Vobiscum*, and that a canon of St. Paul's, whose name they did not know, but who was a great mathematician, was a promoter of the enterprise and went with it in person : and that, ' sailing very far north westward, one of the ships was

Straits of Magellan, but turned instead into the River Plate. The two Englishmen were Roger Barlow and Henry Latimer. There is no record of their personal adventures, although the details of the voyage are well known. See Harrisse, *John and Sebastian Cabot* (1896).

cast away as it entered into a dangerous gulf, about the
great opening between the north parts of Newfoundland
and the country lately called by Her Majesty Meta
Incognita. Whereupon the other ship, shaping her course
towards Cape Breton and the coasts of Arambec, and
oftentimes putting their men on land to search the state
of those unknown regions, returned home about the
beginning of October of the year aforesaid.'

Although Hakluyt was ignorant of the fact, however,
two letters from members of the expedition were in
existence, and Purchas printed one of them in his
Pilgrims.[1] This, the first letter on record from America
to England, is worth quoting in full for the quaintness
of its style and the unconscious picture which it affords
of the mind of an early Tudor seaman. Purchas remarks :
' John Rut writ this letter to King Henry in bad English
and worse writing, Over it was this superscription :

" Master Grube's two ships departed from Plymouth
the 10 day of June, and arrived in the Newfoundland
in a good harbour, called Cape de Bas, the 21 day of July :
and after we had left the sight of Selle (Scilly), we had
never sight of any land, till we had sight of Cape de Bas." '

The letter itself runs thus :

' Pleasing your honourable Grace to hear of your
servant John Rut, with all his company here, in good
health, thanks be to God, and your Grace's ship the
Mary Gilford, with all her . . . thanks be to God : And
if it please your honourable Grace, we ran in our course
to the northward, till we came into 53 degrees, and
there we found many great islands of ice and deep water,
we found no sounding, and then we durst not go further
to the northward for fear of more ice ; and then we
cast about to the southward, and within four days after

[1] Maclehose edition, 1905, xiv. 304.

we had one hundred and sixty fathom, and then we came into 52 degrees and fell with the mainland. We met with a great island of ice, and came hard by her, for it was standing in deep water; and so went with Cape de Bas, a good harbour and many small islands, and a great fresh river going far up into the main land, and the main land all wilderness and mountains and woods, and no natural ground but all moss, and no inhabitation nor no people in these parts: and in the woods we found footing of divers great beasts, but we saw none, not in ten leagues. And please your Grace, the *Samson* and we kept company all the way till within two days before we met with all the islands of ice, that was the first day of July at night, and there rose a great and a marvellous great storm, and much foul weather; I trust in Almighty Jesu to hear good news of her. And please your Grace, we were considering and a writing of all our order, how we would wash us and what course we would draw, and when God do send foul weather, that with the Cape de Sper she should go, and he that came first should tarry the space of six weeks one for another, and watered at Cape de Bas ten days, ordering of your Grace's ship and fishing, and so departed toward the southward to seek our fellow: the third day of August we entered into a good haven, called St. John, and there we found eleven sail of Normans, and one Brittaine, and two Portugall barks, and all a fishing, and so we are ready to depart toward Cape de Bas, and that is twenty five leagues, as shortly as we have fished, and so along the coast till we may meet with our fellow, and so with all diligence that lies in me toward parts to that islands that we are commanded by the Grace of God, as we were commanded at our departing: And thus Jesu save and keep your honourable Grace, and all your honourable Rever(ences), in the Haven of Saint John, the third day of August, written in haste, 1527.

'By your servant John Rut to his uttermost of his power.'

Purchas continues : ' I have by me also Albert de Prato's original letter, in Latin style, almost as harsh as the former English, and bearing the same date, and was indorsed : Reverend. in Christo Patri Domino Domino Cardinali & Domino Legato Angliae: and began Reverendissime in Christo Pater salutem. Reverendissime Pater, placeat Reverendissimae paternitati Vestrae scire, Deo favente postquam exivimus a Plemut quae fuit x Junii,'&c. (the substance is the same with the former and therefore omitted). Datum apud le Baya Saint Johan in Terris Novis, die x Augusti, 1527. Rever. Patr. vest. humilis servus, Albertus de Prato. (The name written in the lowest corner of the sheet.)'

How were these letters dispatched to England ? Probably by one of the fishing vessels which was on the point of returning to Europe. It was evident that Rut had no immediate intention of turning back. The ' Master Grube ' of the endorsement must certainly be a perversion of Rut's name. It is impossible that there should have been two independent pairs of ships both departing from Plymouth on the same day and both making the same landfall in Newfoundland at the same time. Unfortunately Purchas's editing was very careless, as witness his remark that Rut's and de Prato's letters were of the same date ; and, in spite of his assurance of their identity in substance, one cannot help suspecting that important details may have been contained in de Prato's letter.

From quite a different source we hear of the further adventures of Rut and his vessel. Herrera in his *Historia General*,[1] under the erroneous date of 1519, says that a Spanish caravel encountered an English ship off the

---

[1] *Historia General*, Madrid, 1601, Dec. II, lib. v, cap. iii, pp. 144-5.

island of Porto Rico—a ship of three masts and about
250 tons. Gines Navarro, the Spanish captain, thinking
it was a Spanish ship, was going aboard when he was
met by a pinnace with twenty-five armed men and two
guns. They said they were English, and had set sail
with another large ship to find the land of the Grand
Cham, and that a storm had separated them. They had
been in a high latitude and had encountered great icebergs, and turning further south they had come into
a hot sea, and lest it should melt their pitch they had
made for the Baccalaos, where they found fifty ships
fishing—Spanish, French, and Portuguese. They landed
there to make inquiries of the Indians, who killed the
pilot, a Piedmontese. Navarro asked them what they
were doing in those islands, to which they replied that
they wished to make a report to their king, and to
trade. They asked him to show them the course for
San Domingo. When they arrived at that island they
were fired upon, and so did not land. They went back
to Porto Rico and traded with the inhabitants, and then
disappeared. The ship had sixty men with plenty of
guns and merchandise. Oviedo's *Historia General das
Indias* gives a corroborating account under the correct
date, 1527, and adds that, as nothing more was heard of
this ship, she was supposed to have been lost.[1]

Such, however, was not the case, for, in the autumn
of 1528, John Rut, still in the *Mary Gilford*, was engaged
in bringing wine from Bordeaux to England.[2] There is
no further trace of the *Samson*, and it is probable that
she was lost, although Frobisher's story that she foundered
in Hudson's Strait does not agree with John Rut's

[1] 1852 ed., Bk. 19, chap. xiii, p. 611.
[2] *Letters and Papers*, iv, No. 5082.

northernmost latitude of 53°.[1] Before setting out on his voyage John Rut received, on May 24, 1527, a grant of an annuity of £10.[2] This is two days later than the sailing date from London given in the *Chronicles*, but the discrepancy is not serious, for England was not finally lost sight of until June 10.

In reviewing the evidence above set out, it is evident at once that here was another quest of the North-West Passage. John Rut's letter, describing the attempt to force a way northwards through the icebergs of Davis Strait, and its reference to the islands which he had received instructions to make for—evidently not the islands of the new-found land, but far beyond them— point to that conclusion; and the story told to the Spanish captain, as to seeking the land of the Grand Cham, is conclusive. We may therefore set this down as the third authenticated English expedition for the discovery of the northern route to Asia, those of Sebastian Cabot and the Anglo-Portuguese syndicate being the first and second.

On closely comparing the above accounts with Robert Thorne's letter to the king, it is evident that the voyage of John Rut was *not* an attempt to put Thorne's theories into practice, but rather a revival of Sebastian Cabot's old plan of finding a passage by closely hugging the supposed northern shore of America. Thorne, on the other hand, wished to send his expedition over the Pole itself, and such a course would have taken it well to

---

[1] The author of an article in the *English Historical Review* (vol. xx, p. 115) suggests that it was the *Samson* and not the *Mary Gilford* which visited the West Indies, but there seems to be no satisfactory proof of this. The balance of evidence certainly points to the loss of the *Samson* in the North-West.

[2] *Letters and Papers*, iv, No. 3213 (20).

the east of Iceland and Greenland, and would, in fact, have lain almost at right angles to that actually followed by Rut. Hence it becomes certain, either that Thorne's ideas were modified by the king's advisers in London, possibly by Albert de Prato, who seems to have been a man of learning, or that Thorne's letter was written after the unsuccessful return of the surviving vessel. It must be remembered that, although the *Book to Dr. Lee* is dated by internal evidence early in 1527, there is no such clue to the date of the letter to the king. Also, certain expressions quoted from the letter as to the advisability of following new courses, if literally construed, are consonant with the recent return of an expedition which had failed on the old course. On the whole, then, it must be left in doubt whether Thorne may claim the honour of being the author of the voyage of 1527.

Yet another mystery is the identity of the Italian pilot who, according to the Spanish captain's account, was killed by Indians. There is absolutely no confirmatory evidence that such a man accompanied the expedition. It is more probable that, apart from Rut, there was no pilot in the ordinary sense of the word as then used, and that Albert de Prato was the man referred to. There is no proof of his return from the voyage, and it is quite possible that, in the conversation between the English and the Spaniards, with an imperfect command of each other's languages, a man with a knowledge of geography and astronomy might have been described as a ' pilot '.

A brief account of the Thorne family may be of interest, especially as an incomplete article on them appears in a recent authority on the subject, the *Dic-*

tionary of National Biography. The father of the Robert
Thorne who wrote the treatises above considered was
another Robert Thorne, who, at the opening of the
sixteenth century, was a prosperous merchant of Bristol.
According to his son he accompanied Hugh Elyot on
a voyage of discovery to the North-West about the year
1502, although his name does not appear in the charters
granted for that purpose by Henry VII. In 1510 he
was one of a group of Bristol men who were appointed
to act as commissioners for the office of admiral in their
town.[1] In 1514 he was mayor of Bristol,[2] and in 1523
was returned as Member of Parliament for that city,[3]
dying in London shortly afterwards. He was evidently
dead at the time his son was writing, in 1527. A Bristol
historian, however, states that he died in 1519, in which
case the M.P. of 1523 must have been Robert Thorne
the younger (J. Latimer, *Sixteenth Century Bristol*, 1908 ;
authorities not given). He was buried in London in
the Temple Church, and his epitaph runs as follows :

Epitaphium M. Roberti Thorni, sepulti in Ecclesia
Templariorum Londini.
Robertus jacet hîc Thorne, quem Bristolia quondam
   Praetoris merito legit ad officium.
Huic etenim semper magnae Respublica curae
   Charior & cunctis patria divitiis.
Ferre inopi auxilium, tristes componere lites
   Dulce huic consilio quosque juvare fuit.
Qui pius exaudis miserorum vota precesque
   Christe huic coeli des regione locum.[4]

Barrett, writing in 1789, speaks of this epitaph as still
existing in his time.

[1] *Letters and Papers*, i, No. 1050.
[2] See his epitaph and Barrett, *Antiquities of Bristol* (1789), p. 683.
[3] Archives of Bristol, quoted by Fox Bourne, *English Merchant*
(London, 1866), i. 155.   [4] Hakluyt, ii. 181.

Robert Thorne the younger was born in 1492 [1] and was four years senior to his brother Nicholas Thorne.[2] They were both merchants, and carried on their father's business, which seems to have been principally with the ports of Andalusia. Robert had a house in Seville and resided there for some years. The Thornes and other English merchants traded with the Canary Islands and even with the West Indies, sending their goods by way of Spain. Hakluyt, who was in possession of some of their ledger books and letters, mentions that in 1526 they dispatched two English agents in a Spanish ship to Santa Cruz in Teneriffe with a cargo of cloth and soap, with instructions to sell the goods in the Canaries.[3] From the same source we learn that an Englishman named Thomas Tison acted as a kind of secret factor for them in one of the West Indian islands, and distributed the goods which they shipped in Spanish vessels. Tison, the first recorded Englishman to reside in the West Indies, was a Bristol man who served as a mariner against the French in 1514. He is mentioned in Robert Thorne's will, and returned in safety from the Indies, as we find him doing business at Cadiz in 1534.[4]

Robert Thorne the younger was held in great estimation in Seville. Dr. Lee, writing to Wolsey in 1526, mentions that the emperor had spoken to ' a right toward young man as any lightly belongeth to England, called Thorne '. His geographical writings show him to have been a man of learning and originality of mind, while his distant enterprises, and especially his investment of a large sum in Cabot's fleet of 1526 so that Englishmen might accompany it, indicate a breadth of

---

[1] See his epitaph, p. 261.   [2] Barrett, p. 483.   [3] Hakluyt, vi. 124.
[4] *Letters and Papers*, i, No. 5026 ; vii, No. 938.

view and a generous willingness to take risks for great results, in keeping with the best traditions of English commercial enterprise. In 1532 he was again in England, and, with his brother and others, set about the founding and endowing of a grammar school in Bristol. Before the completion of this purpose, however, he died unmarried on Whit-Sunday of the same year. The inventory of his goods, drawn up by his brother Nicholas, shows that his fortune amounted to nearly £17,000, a large sum for those days.[1] In his will,[2] made shortly before his death, he made numerous bequests to his sisters, his business friends and servants, and his brother. He left £400 towards ' the making of a free school of St. Bartholomew in Bristol '. A reference to ' Pawle Withipole, my master ' suggests that he belonged to the Company of Merchant Adventurers, of which body Withipole was then a prominent member. Barrett (p. 650) says that Thorne was buried in the Church of St. Christopher, London, with the following epitaph, for which he does not mention his authority :

Robertus cubat hic Thornus, mercator honestus,
    Qui sibi legitimas arte paravit opes :
Huic vitam dederat puero Bristollia quondam,
    Londinum hoc tumulo clauserat atque diem,
Ornavit studiis patriam, virtutibus auxit,
    Gymnasium erexit sumptibus ipse suis.
Lector quisquis ades requiem cineri precor optes,
    Supplex et precibus numina flecte tuis.
        Obiit 1532, aetatis vero suae anno 40.[3]

[1] Ibid., iv, No. 2814.

[2] Robert Thorne's will is copied in an Elizabethan hand on the back of folio 209 of *Cotton MS.*, Vitellius A xvi, a city chronicle which was printed by C. L. Kingsford in 1905. The will is not included in the printed edition.

[3] *The Dictionary of National Biography* states : (1) that Nicholas Thorne was the father of Robert, and the participator in Hugh Elyot's

Nicholas Thorne outlived his brother several years, taking a prominent part in the affairs of his native city. He was a friend of Thomas Cromwell's, and engaged in business transactions on his behalf. In 1536–7 he built a merchant vessel for Cromwell, which was named the *Saviour* and made her first voyage to Andalusia.[1] He was evidently of the Catholic party in Bristol, to judge from some very insulting and disparaging references to him in a Protestant letter of 1539.[2] In 1544 he became mayor of Bristol, and in the following year we find him appealing on behalf of some English merchants who had suffered ill-treatment at San Sebastian.[3] He died in 1546 at the age of fifty,[4] leaving two sons, of whom one was named Nicholas.

One other voyage to the North-West remains to be chronicled under Henry VIII. In the year 1536 a certain Master Hore of London, a man learned in cosmography, and apparently of good position and fortune, was possessed with the desire to make a voyage to North America. He

voyage; and (2) that Robert Thorne junior died in 1527 at Seville. The latter statement is evidently due to the fact that the inventory of Thorne's goods, drawn up by his brother, is calendared in the *Letters and Papers* under the date 1527. There is nothing in the document itself (*R. O., S. P. Hen. VIII*, § 40, f. 219) to indicate its date. On the other hand, the will (Vitellius A xvi, f. 209b) distinctly says, 'Anno 1532 on whitsonday dyed Robart Thorn'. The grant in connexion with the Grammar School on March 2, 1532 (*Letters and Papers*, v, No. 909), shows that Robert Thorne junior was living at that date, and also speaks of Robert Thorne deceased. The possibility that the Robert Thorne of Seville and the Robert Thorne who died in 1532 were two different men is negatived by a comparison of the inventory with a signed letter (*R. O., S. P. Hen. VIII*, § 81, f. 151) by Nicholas Thorne. The hand-writing of both is identical, showing that the inventory was written by Nicholas, and therefore that it referred to the goods of his brother who, as the will shows, died in 1532.

[1] *Letters and Papers*, vi, No. 1696; xii, No. 233; xiv, part ii, No. 172.
[2] Ibid., xiv, part i, No. 184.
[3] Ibid., xx, part ii, No. 874. [4] Barrett, p. 483.

was joined by others of the same mind, including Armigil Wade or Ward, who afterwards held an official position under Henry VIII and Edward VI. With the king's consent and good will two ships, the *Trinity* and the *Minion*, were fitted out, and 120 persons embarked, of whom 30 were gentlemen, many of them being lawyers of London. They departed from Gravesend at the end of April 1536.

Hakluyt,[1] the authority for this voyage, received a personal relation of it from Thomas Butts, one of the participators, who survived until his time; and the editor's cousin, also named Richard Hakluyt, furnished him with an account he had personally received from Oliver Dawbeny, another survivor. After leaving Gravesend the explorers were more than two months at sea before reaching Cape Breton. Thence they coasted north-eastwards along the Newfoundland shore, visiting an island which they called the Island of Penguins, on account of the numbers of birds they saw there. Black and white bears were also encountered. They failed to get into touch with the natives, who fled at their approach, and soon their stock of food became exhausted. As time went on the agonies of famine became so acute that, when scattered over the country in search of food, some of the members of the party were killed by others and their flesh cooked and eaten. Hore did his best to stop these excesses, gathering the whole company and exhorting them to perish rather than 'be condemned everlastingly both body and soul to the unquenchable fire of hell'. Nevertheless, they were again on the point of casting lots to see who should be killed when a French ship arrived in the bay, well stocked with food. She

---

[1] Hakluyt, viii. 3.

was attacked and captured by the starving Englishmen, who victualled themselves and set sail immediately for home. Meeting with much ice on the way, they arrived at St. Ives at the end of October. Butts, as he told Hakluyt, who made a journey of 200 miles to obtain his narrative, was so changed by hunger and misery that his parents failed to recognize him.

Some months afterwards the Frenchmen who had been relieved of their victuals arrived in England and complained to King Henry ; but he, after inquiring into the matter, ' was so moved with pity that he punished not his subjects, but of his own purse made full and royal recompense unto the French '.

This expedition can hardly claim to rank as a serious voyage of discovery ; it was rather of the nature of a tourist's cruise under very incompetent guidance. It was not promoted by sailors but by landsmen, who, whatever their book-knowledge, had very little practical experience of voyaging. The necessity for cannibalism in a country swarming with game and a sea teeming with fish could hardly have arisen in an expedition organized by other than amateurs. There is no mention of any purpose of trading or searching for a passage to the North-West. Hore's associates, as Hakluyt says, were mainly ' gentlemen of the Inns of Court and of the Chancery, and divers others of good worship, desirous to see the strange things of the world '. It was not from such a party that any useful results could be expected, lacking, as it did, the essentials of success : clearly defined purpose, strong leadership, and knowledge tempered by experience.

As far as is now known, no other English ship set out to solve the problem of the north until 1553, the date of Willoughby's departure in search of Cathay by the north-east. That the matter was not entirely forgotten we are reminded by a passage in Chapuys's correspondence with the Queen of Hungary. Writing on May 26, 1541, he says :

'About two months ago there was a deliberation in the Privy Council as to the expediency of sending two ships to the northern seas for the purpose of discovering a passage between Iceland and Engronland (Greenland) for the northern regions, where it was thought that, owing to the extreme cold, English woollen cloths would be very acceptable and sell for a good price. To this end the King has retained here for some time a pilot from Seville well versed in the affairs of the sea, though in the end the undertaking has been abandoned, all owing to the King not choosing to agree to the pilot's terms, so that for the present at least, the city of Antwerp is sure of not losing the commerce of woollen cloth of English manufacture.' [1]

There is no reason to suppose that the pilot of Seville was Sebastian Cabot, as has been suggested. The professional training which the Spanish pilots received before being granted their certificates produced numerous competent navigators, many of whom would have been superior in theoretical knowledge to the master mariners of England, and therefore able to render good service in Arctic exploration.

The majority of the North Atlantic voyages already considered were for discovery with an ultimate view to trade ; but towards the end of Henry VIII's reign certain adventurers undertook purely trading expeditions to regions already explored and partially occupied by the Portuguese. Hakluyt relates that William Hawkins, of

[1] *Spanish Cal.* vi, No. 163.

Plymouth, father of Admiral Sir John Hawkins, and one
of the principal sea captains of the west of England,
made three voyages to the coast of Brazil in 1530 and
the years following.[1] Details are given of only two of
the voyages, which were made in a vessel of 250 tons
called the *Paul*, of Plymouth. Of the first, no information is forthcoming, unless it was on this occasion that
Hawkins touched at the coast of Guinea on his way out,
buying ivory and the other produce of the country.
This circumstance is so vaguely described as to be applic-
able to any or all of the expeditions. On the second
occasion such good relations were established with the
natives of Brazil that they consented to allow Hawkins
to take one of their chiefs to England, leaving as a hostage
one of the crew, Martin Cockeram by name. This is
the man whom Kingsley introduces in *Westward Ho !*
as conversing, in extreme old age, with the captains
assembled on Plymouth Hoe when news was brought of
the approach of the Armada. There was nothing impossible in such a situation, since Hakluyt, writing in 1599,
says : ' Martin Cockeram, by the witness of Sir John
Hawkins, being an officer of the town of Plymouth, was
living within these few years.'

The Brazilian chief was brought to England and presented to Henry VIII at Whitehall. The whole court
was astonished at his appearance, ' for in his cheeks were
small holes made according to their savage manner, and
therein small bones were planted, standing an inch out
from the said holes, which in his own country was
reputed for a great bravery. He had also another hole
in his nether lip, wherein was set a precious stone about
the bigness of a pease. All his apparel, behaviour and

[1] Hakluyt, xi. 23.

gesture were very strange to the beholders.' After nearly
a year in England, Hawkins, according to his promise,
set sail to Brazil once more to take him back. But he
was destined never to see his native shores again, for,
'by change of air and alteration of diet', he died at sea.
Nevertheless the natives were so impressed with the
honourable dealings of the English that they accepted
their explanations without demur and restored the hostage unharmed.

From his third voyage Hawkins returned with his ship
freighted with the commodities of the country, which
are not further specified. The exact locality, also, to
which his journeys were made, is unknown. Hakluyt
tells no more of William Hawkins, but he has brief
notices of other adventurers to Brazil at about the same
period. He was informed that ' this commodious and
gainful voyage' was frequently made by numerous
Southampton merchants, and, in particular, by Robert
Reneger and Thomas Borey in 1540; also that one
Pudsey, of Southampton, made a voyage to Baya de Todos
Santos in 1542, and built a fort not far from it.

The details of another Brazil voyage have recently
come to light among the Admiralty papers at the Record
Office.[1] On March 7, 1540, the *Barbara* of London set
sail from Portsmouth under the command of John
Phillips. She captured a Spanish bark off Cape St. Vincent, and later on a caravel also. Arriving at the coast
of Brazil on May 3, Phillips first traded and afterwards
fought with the natives, losing many of his crew. After
this unsatisfactory experience he sailed homewards by
way of the West Indies. At San Domingo he fought

---

[1] See the *English Historical Review*, xxiv. 96, article by R. G.
Marsden.

with two Spanish vessels, one of which he captured. On his return to Dartmouth, in August of the same year, he and the surviving members of his company were arrested for piracy at the instance of Chapuys. The result of their trial is unknown. Fuller evidence on these transactions is believed to exist in Spain, and it is to be hoped that it will soon be made public.

With regard to Hawkins's further operations, a letter exists from him to Thomas Cromwell in 1536, to the following effect :

'Most honourable and my singular good lord : so it is that I durst not put myself in press to sue unto your good lordship for any help or succour to be obtained at your hands in my poor affairs, until such time (as) I had first put my ship and goods in adventure to search for the commodities of unknown countries, and seen the return thereof in safety ; as, I thank God, hath metely well happened unto me, albeit by four parts not so well as I suppose it should if one of my pilots had not miscarried by the way. Wherefore, my singular good lord, I now, being somewhat bold by the reason aforesaid, but chiefly for the great hope and trust I have in your accustomed goodness, I most humbly beseech your good lordship to be mean for me to the King's highness, to have of His Grace's love four pieces of brass ordnance and a last of powder, upon good sureties to restore the same at a day. And furthermore, that it may please His Grace, upon the surety of an hundred pound lands, to lend me £2000 for the space of seven years towards the setting forth of three or four ships. And I doubt me not but in the mean time to do such feats of merchandise that it shall be to the King's great advantage in His Grace's custom, and to your good lordship's honour for your help and furtherance herein. . . .

Your most bounden orator,
William Hawkyns of Plymouth.' [1]

[1] *R. O., S. P. Hen. VIII*, § 113, f. 180.

If the above refers to trading voyages to Guinea and Brazil, as seems reasonably probable, it would appear that Hawkins had given up going in person with a single ship, and was acting as manager of a fleet of vessels which were sent out under employed captains in the manner of a modern shipping company. The trade was evidently thought worthy of cultivation.

Another sidelight on the Brazil trade is thrown by a letter of Chapuys to Charles V.[1] Writing on January 2, 1541, he says that to obviate piracy he will try to get it enacted that no armed ship shall sail from the ports of England for Brazil and such countries without giving security not to attack the emperor's ships. This supports the theory of the regular traffic which Hakluyt described as being carried on from Southampton at the time. It is significant also of the growing interest in strange lands that in 1541 a request was made by the Privy Council that Englishmen might be allowed to accompany the next Portuguese navigation to Calicut to buy spices for English consumption. Needless to say, it was not granted. During this period French adventurers were also making voyages to Brazil. Francis I forbade the enterprise to his subjects in December 1538, but withdrew his prohibition in 1540. Early in the next year the English envoy in France reported that the Portuguese ambassadors were daily suing for the stay of the ships that were being permitted to sail to Brazil. If they persisted in going, he added, they were likely to suffer, as the Portuguese had sent many armed vessels thither. It is strange that we have no record of similar protests being made in England, especially as a Portuguese ambassador was in the country at the time. Whether

[1] *Spanish Cal.* vi, part i, No. 148.

they were or not, it would seem that the Brazil voyages were discontinued during the 'forties' of the sixteenth century. The reason was probably to be found in the renewal of war with France and the unsettled state of the narrow seas quite as much as in Portuguese remonstrances or warships. On the outbreak of war the large vessels suitable for transatlantic voyages would be requisitioned for the fleet ; and thenceforward for many years Hawkins and the others found piracy, thinly disguised under letters of marque, more profitable than trade.

A few facts relating to Hawkins and Reneger may be of interest. The former was a supporter of Cromwell, and acted as one of his numberless correspondents—to use no harsher word—on the affairs of his part of the country. There was a bitter feud, for reasons now unknown, between Hawkins and a faction headed by Thomas Bolle, who was mayor of Plymouth in 1537. In the previous year the parties had been summoned before Sir Piers Edgecumbe, and had agreed to waive their differences and live together in peace according to the old customs of the town. Bolle, however, wrote to Cromwell, in 1537, protesting against Hawkins's conduct and accusing him and his friends of disturbing the peace of the place. He further asked that the Hawkins faction might be expelled from the town council. Hawkins evidently triumphed in this affair, for he was chosen mayor in 1538-9, at which time he and his friend James Horswell, who had previously been banished, were engaged in taking over Church property for the Government.

The war of 1544 brought him to the front in a new capacity. In September of that year a commission was made out for Hawkins, Horswell, and John Elyot, empowering them to proceed to sea and annoy the French with four, six, or eight barks at their own charges, and also to impress such mariners, gunners, victuals, and artillery as they needed. In May 1545 Hawkins was denounced by a Spaniard for 'colouring' French goods. He was also charged, jointly with Thomas Wyndham, with capturing a ship belonging to the Spaniards. He apparently paid little attention to the charge, for, two months later, he was committed to prison by the Council for selling the Spaniards' goods. Next year another privateer of which he was part owner—the *Mary Figge*— took some goods illegally. The owners of the *Mary Figge* were slow to disgorge, and the personal authority of the king had to be called in to coerce them. Henry, in spite of his tigerish fierceness towards any others who withstood him, could always find a soft place in his heart for his sailors who erred from over-boldness ; and he ordered that they should be given another chance to make amends before being punished. As Hakluyt relates, Hawkins was ' for his wisdom, valour, experience and skill in sea causes, much esteemed and beloved of King Henry '. He gradually attained a kind of official position, being entrusted with the construction of a fort at Plymouth and with the supply of victuals for the fleet. He was Member of Parliament for his town in 1539, 1547, and 1553. He died at the end of the latter year or at the beginning of 1554. Energetic, versatile, able to turn his hand to politics, trade, discovery, or war, headstrong and quarrelsome, defiant of the law in an age of dreadful penalties, and yet withal patriotic and humane to the weak, it is a pity that our knowledge is so scanty of a career which was so typical of the new, progressive Englishmen of the Renaissance.

Robert Reneger at Southampton was something of a counterpart to William Hawkins of Plymouth. Like him, he was not content with petty coasting voyages and European trade hampered by the surviving shackles of mediaevalism. Like him also, he abandoned the lucrative Brazil trade for still more lucrative privateering when the renewal of the wars rendered the western seas of Europe a treasure-ground for the brave. In 1543 he obtained letters of marque against the French, after entering into a recognisance not to attack the Emperor's subjects. Nevertheless, in March 1545, he and his son John Reneger, with four ships and a pinnace, captured off Cape St. Vincent a Spanish treasure-ship homeward bound from Hispaniola with gold, pearls, and sugar, and worth the dazzling sum of 29,315 ducats. Such a prize, foreshadowing the exploits of the Elizabethans, must have furnished an object-lesson on the wealth of the Spanish Indies which was never forgotten by the seamen of the southern shores of England.

The immediate consequence was almost a war with Spain. All English merchants and ships in that country were arrested and were not released for many months. Reneger asserted that he had only made just reprisal for the confiscation of a prize of his in Spain ; and the Spaniards complained that he, although a known pirate, was swaggering at court as though he had done a meritorious deed. No doubt his merit consisted in a judicious distribution of shares of the plunder, after the manner of Drake in later times. Henry, who loved success and the man that gained it, and who was angry at the conduct of the Emperor in other matters, did not make any real attempt at enforcing reparation. It was only after his death that the Council compelled a partial restitu-

ENGLISH WARSHIP, TEMP. HEN. VIII.
From Cott. MS. Aug. I. ii. 70.

tion, and the affair was patched up. The richness of
the prize may be gauged from the fact that the bribe
of bullion offered to the king alone was worth at least
£5,000 in modern currency. It was this sum (13 lb. 3 oz.
of gold and 131 lb. 5 oz. of silver) which the Council
ordered Reneger to restore. He is last heard of as
Controller of the Port of Southampton in 1556.[1]

[1] The above notes on Hawkins and Reneger are drawn from numerous
references in the later volumes of *Letters and Papers*, and from the *Acts
of the Privy Council*.

CHAPTER XI

THE AFRICAN VOYAGES

IN the days of Queen Elizabeth, when Michael Locke and Martin Frobisher were contemplating the revival of the search for the North-West Passage, a certain James Alday wrote to the former, asking to be employed in the project.[1] As a recommendation he put forward the claim to have 'invented' the trade to the coast of Barbary in the reign of Edward VI. Sir John Lutterell and other merchants, he said, appointed him to command the first expedition to that land in the year 1551. But a great epidemic of the sweating sickness broke out; most of the promoters of the voyage died, and Alday himself was struck down. The ship, called the *Lion* of London, a vessel of 150 tons, was then at Portsmouth. Thomas Wyndham assumed the command and, leaving Alday behind, took her out to the Atlantic coast of Morocco to a port named Santa Cruz. There he traded, presumably with success, and returned, bringing with him two Moors of noble blood to England. Such is all that is now known of the opening voyage of the African trade, which assumed great importance in the decade which followed.

Thomas Wyndham was the son of a Norfolk knight who had served at sea against the French, and who became a councillor and vice-admiral under Henry VIII. He himself also served in the navy, taking part in the

[1] Hakluyt, vi. 136.

fighting against the French and Scots in 1544–5, and filling spare moments with piracy as did William Hawkins and others of Henry's officers. In 1547 he was vice-admiral in the fleet which accompanied Somerset's army up the east coast to the Battle of Pinkie. His next exploit was the Barbary voyage above described. By all accounts he was a fierce, masterful man, making more enemies than friends among his equals, but always able to command the loyalty of his crews ; just the type of character of which the service and personality of King Henry bred such numerous examples, and whose traditions were handed on to the golden age of Elizabeth's sea captains.

A second voyage to the Barbary coast was set forth in 1552, on a larger scale, and its history was written by Hakluyt [1] from the relation of James Thomas, Wyndham's page on the expedition. Three vessels, the *Lion*, 150 tons, the *Botolph*, 80 tons, and a Portuguese caravel of 60 tons purchased at Newport in Wales, the whole fleet manned by 120 persons, sailed from Bristol at the beginning of May 1552 with Wyndham in chief command. Sir John Yorke, Sir William Gerard, Sir Thomas Wroth, Francis Lambert, and other London merchants, were the promoters or ' adventurers ', as the investors were then called. After a prosperous passage, which occupied only a fortnight, the fleet arrived at Zafia on the coast of Barbary, in 32° latitude. Some goods were there set on shore to be conveyed to the city of Morocco, and they then proceeded to Santa Cruz, where the *Lion* had been in the previous year. A French ship was already in the port on their arrival, and hastened to take refuge under the walls of the town, a precaution which was not

[1] vi. 138.

unjustifiable in view of the reputation for piracy which the English had by this time established at sea. The townspeople, mistaking their intentions, at first fired on them, but on recognizing them as having been there before, received them amicably. Three months were spent at this place before cargoes were completed, consisting of sugar, dates, almonds, and molasses.

On the return voyage the ships stood well out into the ocean in order to get a west wind for England. The *Lion* sprang a leak, and it was decided to make for Lancerota in the Canary Islands to effect repairs. Part of the *Lion's* cargo was unloaded on the island, some of the men being set to guard it. The inhabitants took note of these proceedings and, seeing that the caravel was not of English build and supposing that she had been unlawfully acquired, made a sudden attack on the shore party. Some of the latter were captured and seventy chests of sugar were carried off. Seeing this, Wyndham sent three boats full of men to the rescue and put the Spaniards to flight, killing many and making prisoner the governor of the island, an old gentleman of seventy. After this, both sides having suffered losses, a parley ensued and a mutual restoration of prisoners was agreed upon. In addition, the Spaniards gave an acknowledgement of the damage inflicted which, it was decided, was to be recovered from the Spanish merchants residing in London.

The leak being mended the voyage was resumed. As the English were leaving the roadstead a Portuguese armed fleet sailed in, but did not give chase. The Portuguese had already taken great offence at the English trading on the African coast, and threatened to treat as belligerents any Englishmen found there. When it

came to fighting, however, they were generally very
faint-hearted, and they never succeeded in capturing
an English ship.

After seven or eight weeks' sailing Wyndham and his
fleet reached Plymouth, and thence proceeded to London,
arriving at the end of October 1552.

The experience gained in these voyages emboldened
those interested to attempt a much more distant adventure, having for its object the acquisition of cargoes
more valuable than dates and sugar. There was in
London at that time a Portuguese refugee named Antonio
Anes Pinteado. He is described as a skilled pilot and
captain, who had formerly served on the coasts of Brazil
and Guinea, and who was therefore well acquainted with
the intricacies of the navigation in the latter region.
The cause of his quarrel with his own country is not
known, but he was so much in dread of his compatriots
that he would not venture unaccompanied into their
society even in London ; neither was he to be deceived
by the fair promises made him by the Portuguese Government, which doubtless was eager to stop the mouth of
one who knew so much. This man placed his services
at the disposal of the African adventurers, and was
engaged by them to guide an expedition to the coasts
of Guinea and Benin, where gold, ivory, and other rare
commodities were obtainable. With him went Thomas
Wyndham, who assumed the chief command. It does
not plainly appear whether Pinteado was intended to
have any share of the control of the expedition beyond
what his duty as pilot entitled him to ; if such was the
intention of the promoters it was soon overruled by
Wyndham, who kept the Portuguese in a strictly subordinate position.

The sole existing account of the voyage is not very
satisfactory. It was written by Richard Eden and published by him in his *Decades of the New World* in 1555.[1]
It is marred by the deep prejudice against Wyndham
and a corresponding bias in favour of Pinteado displayed
by the writer. Eden, although he did his contemporaries
good service by arousing their interest in travel and
geography, was one of those unhappy people who can
discover nothing good in their own country and have
nothing but censure for the acts of their own countrymen. His temperament can best be illustrated by a
quotation of his own words. In the preface to the work
above mentioned, after a general eulogy of the Spaniards
and King Philip and a severe condemnation of those
Englishmen who resented that monarch's intrusion into
the affairs of England, he proceeds : ' Stoop, England,
stoop, and learn to know thy lord and master, as horses
and other brute beasts are taught to do. Be not indocible
like tigers and dragons, and such other monsters noyous
to mankind. . . . But oh, unthankfull England and void
of honest shame ! Who hath given the face of a whore
and the tongue of a serpent without shame to speak
venomous words in secret against the anointed of
God . . .', with a great deal more to the same effect.
To such a man Wyndham, asserting his authority, was
an insane tyrant, ' a terrible Hydra, with virtues few or
none adorned ' ; while Pinteado, a renegade and traitor
to his own country, selling that country's most cherished
secrets to its rivals, was ' a wise, discreet and sober
man, . . . a man worthy to serve any prince, and most
vilely used '. A realization of Eden's infirmity is necessary to a just appreciation of his account of the voyage.

[1] Reprinted in Hakluyt, vi. 141–52.

On August 12, 1553, not quite a month after Mary's accession, the little squadron consisting of two ships and a pinnace set sail from Portsmouth. The ships were the *Lion*, which had made the two Barbary voyages, and of which Wyndham was part owner, and the *Primrose*, the pinnace being named the *Moon*. The two last-mentioned belonged to the navy and were lent for the expedition.[1] The three vessels were manned by 140 men, including several of the merchants who had ' adventured ' the voyage. Most of them were destined never to return. They touched first at Madeira, where wines were bought and duly paid for. Here they encountered a great Portuguese galleon, full of men and guns, expressly sent to prohibit their voyage ; but, on a closer view, she refrained from interfering with them, and they proceeded unmolested. At this point the disagreements between Wyndham and Pinteado began. Eden implies that hitherto they had had equal authority, the fleet ' having two captains ', an improbable arrangement. However that may have been, Wyndham was henceforth supreme, and was evidently backed by the officers and crews, while the merchants, if we are to believe Eden, sided with Pinteado. Voyaging in leisurely fashion so as not to arrive on the coast before the end of the hot season, and touching at various islands on the way, they at length reached the River of Sestos in the westernmost part of Guinea, known as the Grain Coast (the modern Liberia). They did not tarry to load the ' grains ' of the district, although cargoes of them were frequently brought to Europe by the Portuguese ;[2] but, ' by the persuasion or

[1] Strype, *Memorials*, ii. 504. Strype says the two ships were lent to Wyndham and his associates in 1552, and were intended for the voyage in search of the North-East Passage.

[2] Stanford's *Compendium* (1907) says that the ' grains ' of this coast

rather inforcement of this tragical captain ', they pushed
on to the Gold Coast, and there traded on either side
of the Castle of Mina, the head-quarters of the Portuguese.

The position of the latter on the Guinea coast at this
time somewhat resembled that of the English and French
on the coast of Coromandel at the opening of Clive's
career, with the exception, of course, that the Portuguese
officials were the servants of the Government and not
of a trading company.   There was no effective occupation of the hinterland or even of the entire coast, but at
various places along the latter were Portuguese forts and
trading stations, of which Mina, not far from the modern
Cape Coast Castle, was the chief.   Other places on the
coast were ruled over by native chiefs in a state of
vassallage to the Portuguese, whose hold over them was
not sufficiently rigorous to prevent them from trading
with the English and French.   Thus there was no colony
in the sense in which the word was applied to the Spanish
settlements in America, but merely a chain of commercial
' factories '.   Liberty of trade among the Portuguese
themselves was restricted to those who had the royal
licence for that purpose, a fact which redoubled their
annoyance at the invasion of their preserves by others.

Wyndham did not touch at Mina itself, but exchanged
his wares with the native chiefs, obtaining in all about
150 lb. weight of gold, a sum which in itself would have
cleared all the expenses of the expedition and have paid
a handsome profit besides.   Eden asserts that it was
Wyndham's unbalanced brain which then caused him to
leave this lucrative trade and push on to Benin to seek

were pepper. Eden, although he describes them as ' a very hot fruit ',
speaks of pepper as a distinct article further on.

pepper. But, judging from the accounts of later voyages, it is probable that no more gold was then forthcoming, or that the demand for English goods had slackened. Only one other expedition of which we have particulars secured more than 150 lb. of gold, the supply being limited ; and the natives were always very grasping and prone to take offence. The record of Wyndham's career certainly gives no ground for the supposition that he would forsake the certainty of gold for the possibility of pepper.

The decision to make for Benin was the prelude to a series of disasters. Pinteado opposed it owing to the lateness of the season, and a violent scene was the result. ' Wyndham . . . fell into a sudden rage, reviling the said Pinteado, calling him Jew, with other opprobrious words, saying : This whoreson Jew hath promised to bring us to such places as are not, or as he cannot bring us unto : but if he do not, I will cut off his ears and nail them to the mast.' Pinteado submitted, and piloted the fleet to the river of Benin,[1] up which he himself with Nicholas Lambert and other merchants proceeded for some sixty leagues in the pinnace. Having completed this distance, they left the pinnace and travelled thirty miles inland to the town of a native king, by whom they were civilly received. The king could speak Portuguese, and promised to buy all their merchandise in exchange for pepper. In the course of a month eighty tons of pepper were collected, and the merchants were assured that more would be obtained until the fleet should be fully laden.

In the meantime the inaction and the climate were producing dire effects on the crews left at the mouth of the river. The men ate without moderation of the

---

[1] Probably the Niger.

tropical fruits, and drank the liquor exuding from the
trunks of palm trees, ' and in such extreme heat running
continually into the water, . . . than which nothing is
more dangerous, were thereby brought into swellings
and agues ', so that they sickened and died at a terrible
rate, sometimes four or five in a day. This could not
go on for long without entailing utter extermination to
an expedition which numbered only 140 men to begin
with. Therefore, a month having elapsed, Wyndham
sent word to Pinteado and the others to return immediately, contenting themselves with such cargo as the
pinnace could bring down. But they failed to comply,
and wrote instead, telling of the quantity of pepper
which they hoped to secure. Wyndham replied with
a peremptory order to come back at once, under threat
of being left behind ; then, in desperation at their
callous disregard of the sufferings of the crews, he lost
control of himself and ' all raging, brake up Pinteado's
cabin, brake open his chests, spoiled such provision of
cold stilled waters and suckets as he had provided for his
health, and left him nothing, neither of his instruments
to sail by, nor yet of his apparel ; and in the meantime
falling sick, himself died also.'

On receipt of the second summons Pinteado had
started for the coast to expostulate, the other merchants
still remaining up the river. Before his arrival Wyndham was dead. The surviving officers and men were
thoroughly exasperated, and gave him a very bad time
with copious abuse and threats of violence. In vain he
asked to be allowed to fetch his companions from the
interior. They would stay for nothing, and refused even
to let him remain behind with the ship's boat and an
old sail, with which he promised to bring Lambert and

the others back to England. Eden's account is very confused, and there is no mention of the pinnace having come down the river again, the messages having evidently been conveyed by smaller boats, possibly by natives. If the merchants still had the pinnace their case would not be altogether desperate. There is no information as to their ultimate fate.

Before commencing the homeward voyage one of the ships was abandoned and sunk for lack of men.[1] A week afterwards Pinteado, who had been degraded to a menial position, fell sick and died 'from very pensiveness and thought, that struck him to the heart'; and when the remaining vessel at length reached Plymouth scarcely forty men were left of all those who had set forth.

The lessons enforced by the disasters of this voyage were taken well to heart by subsequent adventurers. The succeeding expeditions confined themselves to the Guinea coasts, and left Benin severely alone. They were also careful not to remain on the coast after the beginning of the season of extreme heat, and, as they probably took greater personal precautions against disease, we hear of very little mortality thenceforward. The importance of the information supplied by Pinteado cannot be over-estimated. The arrival without a hitch on the Grain Coast, the successful trading in the neighbourhood of Mina, the finding of the native town 150 miles up the Benin river which none of the English had ever seen before, all point to the fact that the expedition was availing itself of the experience that the Portuguese had taken a century to gather. It is no wonder that Pinteado, lending himself to such a purpose, went in fear of his

---

[1] Eden speaks of having seen the *Primrose* after her return, hence it must have been the *Lion* which was abandoned.

life, as his admirer tells us, from his own countrymen. No provocation can justify a man in betraying his country's interests, and we cannot feel much commiseration for his melancholy end ; he was a traitor receiving a traitor's wages. Eden's denunciations of Wyndham's character as a commander are largely discounted by the fact that he was in command at all. He was a tried man, and his record was known ; no company of merchants would have entrusted him with their lives and goods if he had been the irresponsible maniac whom Eden depicts. No doubt he was jealous of his authority, and rightly so, for a hazardous adventure cannot be conducted on republican lines. In the days when success at sea depended primarily on the captain's personal powers of discipline, harshness was often the only justifiable course, as Drake and many another were to prove.

Terrible as had been the personal sufferings in Wyndham's last voyage, the commercial possibilities of the Guinea coast had been proved to be most encouraging. A strong syndicate was therefore formed to send out another expedition in 1554, including among others the names of Sir George Barnes, Sir John Yorke, Thomas Locke, Anthony Hickman, and Edward Castlyn. Five vessels were prepared—the *Trinity*, 140 tons, the *John Evangelist*, 140, the *Bartholomew*, 90, and two pinnaces, one of which foundered before getting clear of the English coast—the whole being placed under the command of John Locke. Locke was a merchant rather than a sailor, and the arrangement was thus analogous to that which obtained then and long afterwards in the navy, when the captain of a ship was commonly a soldier, the master being responsible for the handling of the vessel. This was the same John Locke who had made a pilgrimage

to Jerusalem in the previous year, of which Hakluyt
prints a very entertaining account. Eden again supplies
the story of this voyage and, having no quarrel with any
individual concerned, gives a much more intelligible
description of what occurred.[1]

The squadron sailed from the Thames on October 11,
1554, was detained for a fortnight at Dover by adverse
winds, and again for three or four days at Rye. After
touching once more at Dartmouth the English coast was
finally lost sight of on the night of November 1. Thence
a fair passage was made to Guinea, the first point of
which, Cape Mensurado, was sighted on December 21.
Next day they entered the River of Sestos, the principal
haven on the Grain Coast, and remained there for a week,
trading for grains. Five more days were spent at the
mouth of another stream, the Rio Dulce, 75 miles to
the south-eastward, and altogether 630 butts of grains
were obtained. On January 3, 1555, the expedition made
sail along the coast to the eastward, passing Cape Palmas
which marks the division between the Grain Coast and
the Ivory Coast. Apparently no stay was made at the
latter on the outward passage, for by the 11th they had
reached Cape Tres Puntas, which similarly divides the
Ivory Coast from the Gold Coast. Fifteen miles to the
west of Cape Tres Puntas there was a Portuguese fort
named Arra. Their head-quarters, the Castle of El
Mina, lay about 90 miles to the eastward of the same
cape, and well in the middle of the Gold Coast.

Very successful trading was done at the native settlements on either side of El Mina, and altogether 400 lb.
of gold was secured—the greatest haul recorded by any
single expedition. In particular, they were well received

[1] Reprinted by Hakluyt, vi. 154–77.

at a town called Cape Corea (probably Cape Corso, the present Cape Coast Castle), where a native chief named Don John maintained his independence against the Portuguese. At another place, called Samma, however, the negroes were in possession of two or three cannon, with which they fired at the English after taking a hostage. The hostage was detained, and the ships had to go on without him. During this time the *Trinity* had proceeded still further east to the limits of the Gold Coast, and, the others having overtaken her, the homeward voyage was begun from Perecow Grande, otherwise called Egrand, the easternmost port of all. Although it is not specifically mentioned, considerable trading must have been done on the Ivory Coast while the ships were slowly beating westwards against wind and current ; for Eden relates that there were 250 tusks among the cargo brought home, and there was no time for these to have been obtained on the outward passage. Also, at some town not named, Robert Gainsh, master of the *John Evangelist*, kidnapped five natives, who were brought home as slaves.[1] This had an unfavourable effect on the attitude of the natives towards succeeding expeditions.

Up to this point Eden follows closely the log of the pilot who gave him the account of the voyage, but here he diverges into a dissertation on elephants, and gives only very meagre details of the homeward passage. Although the latter was begun in the middle of February, it was April 22 before the latitude of 9° was reached, but this was a common experience. Wind and current made it extremely difficult for ships rigged in the fashion of the time to get away from the Guinea coast, and

---

[1] See Towerson's first voyage, and marginal note to Eden's account of the present voyage.

even when that had been accomplished, the course had to be laid well out into the ocean, and contrary winds were met with until the Azores were passed. The expedition arrived in England at some time in July or August 1555. Eden does not give the date, but says the passage took twenty weeks and that twenty-four men died on the way home. Financially, it must have been a dazzling success ; the value of the grains and ivory is difficult to estimate, but the gold alone was easily worth £20,000 in the currency of the time, and none of the large ships had been lost.

When these transactions became known in Portugal intense indignation was aroused ; already, before the return of John Locke, a protest had been lodged, and on July 18, 1555, the Privy Council sent instructions to the authorities of London and Bristol to stop all voyages to Guinea until further orders.[1] This did not mean that the Portuguese view was already accepted, but simply that no decision on the matter had yet been arrived at. The chief factors in the situation were these : King Philip, still remaining in England since his marriage in the previous year, was a supporter of the Portuguese monopoly, based as it was on the papal bull which divided all extra-European lands between Spain and Portugal ; it was clear to him that if English merchants carried their point in this affair, a challenge of his own monopoly in the west was certain, sooner or later, to arise. The Council, next in importance so far as effective influence went, were naturally desirous of encouraging the efforts of their fellow countrymen, but at the same time stood in considerable awe of Philip and would not go to the length of defying his clearly expressed com-

[1] *Acts of the Privy Council*, v. 162.

mands. Finally, the queen, priest-ridden, harassed, and miserable, but yet at bottom a patriot, was torn between reverence to the decree of Rodrigo Borgia and a consciousness that, in obeying that decree, she was betraying the nation whose crown she wore. While the decision was still in suspense Philip sailed, early in September, for the Netherlands, whence he still continued to exercise his authority over the affairs of England. The Portuguese ambassador, Lopez de Sousa, continued to urge his suit, and the queen committed the negotiations to the Council, which had arrived at no conclusion as late as October 21.[1] A week later they transmitted a copy of his allegations to Philip, together with their own opinion thereupon.[2]

The Portuguese statement was to the following effect : [3] News had been received that in January of this same year, 1555, three large English merchant ships (evidently John Locke's squadron) had visited the coasts of Guinea, which were either in the possession of the King of Portugal or under his protection, and had forcibly exchanged their merchandise with the natives for huge quantities of gold and ivory, of which commodities they had wellnigh stripped the whole country ; in which process they had stirred up the resentment of the natives against the Portuguese. This trade was only permitted under restrictions to the King of Portugal's own subjects, those who infringed the regulations being severely punished. The ambassador was therefore to demand the punishment of the Englishmen concerned, the handing over of any Portuguese who should have assisted them, the

---

[1] *Venetian Cal.* vi, No. 251.

[2] *R. O., S. P. Dom., Mary*, vol. xiv, Nos. 4 and 5 (erroneously calendared under date 1558).

[3] *R. O., S. P. For., Mary*, vol. vii, No. 448.

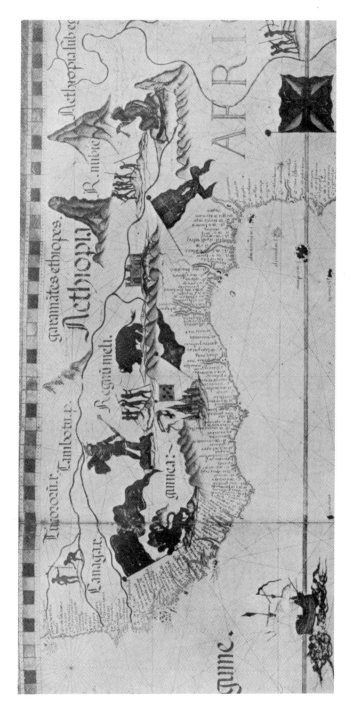

MAP OF GUINEA AND BENIN, 1558.

From Add. MS. 5415. A. 7.

restitution of the treasure, and a proclamation forbidding such enterprises in future under the severest penalties.

Such was the position, based on the world-dividing bull of Alexander VI, taken up by the two nations of the Peninsula, and now for the first time flaunted in all its arrogance in the face of an English Government. The Government, already discredited in the eyes of the country, and entangled in the net of the Counter-Reformation, lacked the insight and the courage to take up the challenge. For many a year to come it was to be left to private men, with the fear of the gallows before them, to assert the right of Englishmen to sail all seas and do business in all lands, the prohibitions of popes and emperors notwithstanding. The reply of the merchants opens with words which might serve as the title-deed of a commercial empire.

' First we say we be merchants who, by common usage of the world, do use traffique in all places of the world, as well Asia and Africa and Europa, and have never been restrained from resort to any places. . . . And following this our accustomed usage we have of late resorted to sundry places both towards the south and north parts of the world, in both which we find the governors and the people of the places well willing to receive us friendly and gently. Amongst other places, our factors did about two years past resort to sundry places where we found several princes or governors, and with them traffiqued, exchanging merchandises for merchandises, and from them returned quietly, thinking that without any offence we might use there (where we found no resistance) the same liberty that we use and do find in all other places of the world.'

After their return, they continued, they prepared to set forth another expedition to the same place, but were

stayed by the Council and commanded not to enter any
dominion of the King of Portugal or any other prince
without his permission ; which command their factors
punctually obeyed, not landing in any place where the
said king had a town, fortress, or officers or other persons
that forbade them. Their factors did not land in any
force, but awaited in their ships the resort of the people
to them, and even then did not trade with them until
the people assured them that they were no subjects of
the King of Portugal. The inhabitants offered them
ground to build upon if they wished to land and fortify
the country, and the assistance of slaves in the work
without any charge.[1] Their factors were also with a king
of those parts, ' a prince of power ', whom they call the
King of Bynne, in whose country they traded after
obtaining his licence ; and they left behind them there
three English merchants to further view the country,
bringing with them also certain men of that country to
England, and promising to return in a short time.[2]
Accordingly, they made preparations for another voyage
at the beginning of this last summer, but were again stayed
by command of the king and queen, the King of Portugal
saying that his subjects were wronged by these navigations, and promising to show proofs in six weeks or two
months at latest. They obeyed this second command,
and in the meantime had heard that three ships had sailed
from France to those countries, and that two others
were preparing to sail. Upon which they continued

[1] This evidently refers to John Locke's voyage, and tallies with Eden's
account, except that the latter does not mention the offer of land for
a settlement.

[2] This would seem to relate to Wyndham's visit to Benin. No other
place-name is mentioned in any of the voyages which bears any resem-
blance to ' Bynne '. If such is the case, it throws a fresh complexion
on Eden's story of the abandonment of the merchants.

their preparations, and, if the voyage were now stayed, they would be ruined. They concluded by begging to be allowed to continue the voyage, and offered to bind themselves not to visit or do violence to any of the possessions or merchants of the Portuguese, nor to trade with any country without its ruler's consent.[1]

The Council, as has been said, forwarded to King Philip a copy of the ambassador's statement, and put before him at the same time their own advice as to the course to be pursued, namely, that the merchants were within their rights in making these voyages, and ought not to be debarred from the same, especially as they were also being made by the French. Their opinion was, then, that the merchants should be allowed to proceed at their own risk, after giving the sureties which they themselves had offered for their good behaviour.

The intercession of the Council, and also that of the queen, was unavailing : Philip, seeing the great principle involved, was obdurate, and commanded that the voyage should be stayed. In a later communication (December 17, 1555),[2] he expressed a wish to have the merchants compensated, but took no active steps to secure that end. A memorandum of the Council's affairs, however, suggests that the queen herself paid them the costs of the goods which they had provided for the trade.[3] On December 30 Edward Castlyn, Jeffrey Allen, Rowland Fox, and Richard Stockbridge were summoned before the Council to hear its reluctant decision. By the queen's command they and all other merchants concerned were to bring their ships to such places as were

[1] R. O., S. P. For., Mary, vii, No. 449.
[2] Cal. For. S. P., Mary, p. 198.
[3] R. O., S. P. Dom., Mary, vi, No. 83.

convenient, and there to discharge all the wares they had provided for the Guinea trade, such as were not vendible in any other place ; receipts should be given and compensation paid. As to their other expenses, the matter of compensation should be considered.[1]

The queen at the same time wrote a letter to the King of Portugal acquainting him with the above decision.[2] The Venetian envoy, in a dispatch to his Government, states that the queen interceded with the ambassador of Portugal to consent to the Guinea voyage being made ' this once only ', but that he would not agree. He adds that two or three ships had nevertheless gone secretly.[3]

The official prohibition of the Guinea trade was more ostensible than real. The Council had no intention of stopping it—possibly some of its members were financially interested—and was not prepared to go further than a purely paper submission to the demands of Philip and the Portuguese. Even the steps taken to prevent the individual voyage of Castlyn and his associates were not effectual ; for although metal basins and sham jewellery formed part of the cargoes taken to Guinea, there was also generally a considerable quantity of cloth, which would not come under the description of goods not vendible elsewhere, and which would therefore not be surrendered. Such being the attitude of the Council, that of the customers and port authorities throughout the country may well be imagined. When large armed vessels were being manned and provisioned for long voyages and laden with goods which would find a market in no European port, they shut their eyes, or looked another way. And so, besides the three remaining Guinea

---

[1] *A. P. C.*, v, p. 214.   [2] *R. O., S. P. For., Mary,* vii, No. 450.
[3] *Venetian Cal.* vi, No. 327.

expeditions of Mary's reign of which Hakluyt has preserved the particulars, there are traces of several others,
doubtless quite as successful, which King Philip, with all
his influence over the queen, was quite unable to prevent.
While the official decision had been still under consideration, and while the ships of the syndicate already
mentioned had been under a provisional arrest pending
a final prohibition, another expedition had slipped off
to Guinea on September 30, 1555, sailing from Newport
in the Isle of Wight. It was under the command of
William Towerson, a merchant of London, and was
probably unconnected with the venture of Castlyn and
his friends, of whom no mention is made. Towerson,
who is himself the narrator of the voyage,[1] refers to the
presence of other merchants in the ships, but it is very
likely that he himself was the principal adventurer. This
time there were only two ships, the *Hart*, of 60 tons, commanded by John Ralph, who had sailed with Locke in
the previous year, and the *Hind*, commanded by William
Carter, and probably not much larger, since Towerson
himself sailed in the *Hart*. After finally clearing from
Dartmouth on October 20 they made a fair run down
to the Canary Islands, which were sighted on November 6.
Thence standing in to the main land they fished in
14 fathoms and caught a quantity of sea bream. A day
or two later they saw six Portuguese caravels fishing in
the neighbourhood of the Rio del Oro in the present
Spanish territory to the south of Morocco, and over-
hauling one of them they took various stores out of her
which they liberally paid for.

On December 12 they sighted the Guinea coast, and
on the 15th entered the River St. Vincent, eight leagues

[1] Hakluyt, vi. 177–211.

to the eastward of the River of Sestos. They found it impossible to beat back to the latter river on account of the winds and currents which set always to the eastward. In the River St. Vincent they obtained a small quantity of grains and ivory, but found the inhabitants very greedy and no profitable trading to be done. After coming very nearly to blows they departed and sailed on towards the Ivory Coast, doubling Cape Palmas on the 23rd. During the ensuing week they bought ivory in a river lying about 40 miles to the east of the cape, and on January 3, 1556, they sighted Cape Tres Puntas, the westernmost boundary of the Gold Coast. Arriving at the town of Samma, where last year a man had been kidnapped and the ships fired upon, they went in cautiously and were able to do little trading at first, but afterwards obtained a fair quantity of gold there. They next proceeded to Don John's town, beyond the Mina, and after some bartering the sons of that chief attempted to betray them to the Portuguese. Some of the *Hart's* men narrowly escaped an ambush, whereupon cannon were mounted in the ships' boats, which sailed in close to the shore and engaged in an artillery duel with the Portuguese upon a hill. The English suffered no damage. At another place they found the negroes distrustful because some of them had been carried off by the master of the *John Evangelist* in the previous voyage.

From January 14 to February 4, however, they did excellent business on the more easterly portion of the coast, taking several pounds of gold daily. On the latter date, having taken stock of the provisions, and finding them running low, and finding also that the beer, without which no sailor at that time considered himself

properly fed, was turning sour, they decided to begin
the return voyage. One entry in Towerson's log is
significant as pointing to the existence of other clandestine expeditions at this time : 'The fifth day we
continued sailing and thought to have met with some
English ships, but found none.' He had evidently
received information of their presence on the coast.
Towerson made a better homeward passage than did
his predecessors. By February 13 he was clear of Cape
Palmas, having passed the whole of the Gold and Ivory
Coasts in nine days. He had found by experience, he
says, that from two hours after midnight until eight in
the morning the wind blew off the shore from the north-
north-east, although all the rest of the time it was at
south-west. On March 22 he had reached the latitude
of Cape Verde, and a month later that of the Azores.
On May 14, 1556, both his vessels dropped anchor at
Bristol after a most prosperous voyage. Apparently not
one man died in either crew. He does not give the total
amount of the treasure secured, but a reckoning up of
the various daily takings mentioned shows a total of
about fifty tusks and 130 lb. of gold. Considering the
small size of the two ships employed, and consequently
of the general working expenses, this must have yielded
an excellent return on the outlay.

The successful return of the *Hart* and the *Hind* was
the signal for renewed preparations for further Guinea
adventures, and for a fresh outburst of activity on the
part of the Council, ostensibly intended to frustrate
the same. On July 7, 1556, orders were sent to all
customers, &c., not to permit any one to ship goods for
' Mina, Guynye, Bynney or any other place thereabouts
within the King of Portingales dominions ' ; and on the

28th the command was repeated with instructions for warning to be given to all merchants. Again on August 8 the Council addressed a letter to Anthony Hussey, Governor of the Merchant Adventurers in the Low Countries, to the effect that they had heard that Miles Mordeyne, a London merchant, had prepared a cargo in Flanders to be sent to Bristol and thence to Guinea. Hussey was to make search for the wares and sequester them until further orders, sending particulars as to their condition and value. On the same date they also sent word to the Mayor and Customers of Bristol to arrest and unload two ships which certain merchants contemplated setting forth for Guinea. The cargoes had been secretly conveyed to the Welsh coast to be loaded. Miles Mordeyne, who was apparently at Bristol, was to be sent before the Council. On September 22 Giles White and Thomas Chester were held to bail in £500 as a guarantee of their appearance when called upon in the matter of sending two ships from Bristol to Guinea.[1]

These measures give the impression that the Council was actually in earnest ; but the fact remains that, in spite of them, Towerson and others were able to sail once more for Guinea in this same autumn. If there had been any genuine desire to put a stop to these enterprises nothing would have been easier than to imprison the adventurers on their return and to confiscate their spoils. The fact that this was never done leads to the conclusion that the Council was merely making a show of zeal to deprecate Philip's anger.

Towerson, on his second expedition,[2] had to use more precaution than formerly in order to get safely away.

---

[1] *A. P. C.*, v. 305, 315, 322, 358, 384.
[2] Hakluyt, vi. 212–31.

The *Tiger*, of 120 tons, his principal ship, was equipped at Harwich, and sailed from thence to Scilly on September 14, 1556. At Scilly he was to meet the *Hart* and a pinnace of 16 tons which had been prepared at Bristol. These may have been the two vessels which the Council professed itself so anxious to arrest. The *Hart* and the pinnace failed to appear at the rendezvous, at which the *Tiger* arrived on the 28th. After waiting for some time Towerson in the *Tiger* put back to Plymouth, being joined there by his consorts shortly before the middle of November, and on the 15th of that month the whole squadron set sail for Africa nearly two months after the intended time of departure. The nature of the intrigue which finally set them at liberty can only be imagined, as no clue has survived, but it is difficult to suppose that they departed otherwise than with the knowledge and connivance of the Council.

As was usual, a fairly quick outward passage was made, the Guinea coast being sighted on December 30. The inaccuracy of the prevailing methods of calculating longitude is illustrated by the fact that the River of Sestos, the intended landfall, was overshot by some 150 miles. Shortly after reaching the coast the sails of three ships and two pinnaces were seen to windward. The English prepared for action, manœuvred to recover the wind, and then gave chase. The strangers likewise cleared for action and, when ready, offered battle ' very finely appointed with their streamers and pendants and ensigns, and the noise of trumpets very bravely '. When within hailing distance, however, it was discovered that the opposing fleet was manned, not by Portuguese, but by Frenchmen, bound upon the same errand as the English ; and, instead of fighting, an alliance was struck up, both sides agreeing to trade without cutting prices and to support each other against the Portuguese. The French ships were from Havre, Rouen, and Honfleur, under the chief command of Denis Blondel. He informed Towerson that they had been six weeks upon the Grain Coast with very little result, apparently fearing to push on to the Gold Coast on account of reports of a Portuguese armed fleet at Mina. They had fallen upon a single Portuguese vessel of 200 tons in the River of Sestos, and had burned her, only three or four of the crew being saved. Blondel seemed extremely glad of the presence of the English, and offered to share his victuals with them and act under their orders in all things.

For the first fortnight of January 1557 they all proceeded slowly along the Ivory Coast, arriving at Cape Tres Puntas on the 14th. A small quantity of ivory was picked up on the way, but for the most part the negroes were shy of trading. At one point they attempted elephant hunting on their own account, without success. Their methods certainly read as if they were designed rather for the assault of a city than of an elephant : thirty men were landed, ' all well armed with harquebusses, pikes, long-bows, cross-bows, partizans, long swords, and swords and bucklers : we found two elephants, which we stroke divers times with harquebusses and long-bows, but they went away from us and hurt one of our men '.

At a native town where they were well received the negroes told them that they had witnessed a fight of two ships against one a month before ; and further on they received definite intelligence of the presence of another English ship on the coast, which had brought back one of the negroes kidnapped by Robert Gainsh two years previously. The Frenchmen also asserted that they knew of five other French vessels making the same voyage. The combined squadrons were now past Cape Tres Puntas and doing daily business with the inhabitants of the Gold Coast, who seem at this time to have been in a state of hostility towards the Portuguese. On January 25, while they were anchored off Samma with most of the ships' boats and merchants ashore, five Portuguese ships suddenly appeared. Guns were fired, the crews hastily embarked, and anchors were weighed; but by this time night had fallen and nothing could be done but prepare for action on the following day. In the morning it was seen that the Portuguese had anchored near the shore; the English and French did likewise, 'within demiculverin shot of them'. It was not for them, in their rôle of peaceful traders, to commence hostilities, but the challenge was sufficiently obvious. Night again came on without further developments taking place.

Next day both sides made sail, but the allies gained the wind of the Portuguese and gradually bored them in towards the shore until they were forced to tack and make for them. The allies tacked also and stood out to sea ahead of the enemy ; then, when they had sufficient room to fight, they took in their topsails and waited. The Portuguese came up one by one, the first being a small bark well armed and very fast, which exchanged broadsides and then passed on ahead. Next came a caravel, which did some damage to the French admiral's ship. After her came the Portuguese admiral in a large ship, whose fire was ineffective owing to the guns being carried too high, followed by two caravels more. Towerson says that the *Tiger* 'was so weak in the side, that she laid all her ordinance in the sea', which seems to

mean that the wind laid her over so much that sufficient
elevation could not be given to the guns. The Portuguese, being to leeward, were just as badly off, since they
could only fire over their enemies' heads. Accordingly
the *Tiger* and the *Espoir*, Denis Blondel's ship, made an
attempt to board the Portuguese admiral. The *Espoir*
missed her and fell astern, missing also the two caravels
which followed. The other two Frenchmen stood aloof,
and the *Hart* was far behind. Nevertheless, the Portuguese made no offer to stop and fight Towerson, but
stood on out to sea. He chased them for two hours,
and they then turned shorewards again, hoping to catch
the French admiral, who for some unexplained reason
was close to the land. He was caught under the lee of
the whole Portuguese squadron, received all their broadsides, and would have been boarded but that the *Tiger*
stood in to his assistance. The *Hart* and the other two
French ships meanwhile looked on and did nothing.
The French admiral was still full of fight and, with the
Tiger, regained the wind of the enemy and chased them
till nightfall.

Next day the whole fleet reunited, with the exception
of one Frenchman who had fled. The master of the
Hart excused himself, saying that his ship ' would neither
rear nor steer '. The French admiral had half his crew
sick or dead, and the other Frenchmen said they could
do no more fighting. The English pinnace had to be
burnt owing to her bad state of repair. However, the
Portuguese had likewise had enough of it, and troubled
them no more.

Trade was now resumed, and the allies sailed slowly
down to the eastern part of the Gold Coast, where the
natives were more amenable and the greater part of the

profits of the voyage were obtained. Business went on
throughout the month of February, entirely undisturbed
by the Portuguese. The English kept to the leeward
or eastward of the French, doubtless skimming the cream
off the trade ; and when one of the Frenchmen attempted
to push on ahead of them he was fired on and reduced
to obedience. After this incident Towerson makes no
further mention of the French, and it is evident that
the allies parted company here or soon afterwards. At
the end of February a native chief called King Abaan
sent friendly messages, inviting them to make a settlement and build a fort. His town was said to be as large
in circuit as London, and with 1,000 ricks of corn outside the walls. After doing business at this place they
began to retrace their course along the coast, passing
a fort where they saw the five Portuguese ships at anchor.
Next day they were surprised at anchor by a new fleet
just out from Portugal, consisting of a ship of 500 tons,
another of 200, and a pinnace ; but they were able to
escape without fighting. The *Hart* was badly handled,
and her captain was reproved by Towerson.

The new arrivals brought the enemy up to a strength
of seven fighting ships against the English two, and it
was folly to expect that any more undisturbed trading
could be done. Towerson therefore sailed for England
on March 4. On the 18th the *Hart* parted company,
intentionally as was thought, her master having taken
offence at his reproof. The *Tiger's* perils were not yet
past ; on April 23, when nearing English waters, they
were set upon by a Frenchman of 90 tons, who, judging
them weak from a long voyage, laid them aboard and
commanded them to strike sail. ' Whereupon ', to quote
Towerson's words, ' we sent them some of our stuff,

crossbars and chain shot and arrows, so thick that it
made the upper work of their ship to fly about their
ears, and we spoiled him with all his men, and tore his
ship miserably with our great ordinance, and then he
began to fall astern of us, and to pack on his sails and
get away : and we, seeing that, gave him four or five
good pieces more for his farewell ; and thus we were
rid of this Frenchman who did us no harm at all.' On
April 29, 1557, having failed to double the Land's End
for Bristol, they arrived instead at Plymouth after an
exceptionally quick passage. The daily takings of gold
on the coast for this voyage amounted to 76 lb., but the
figures for some of the trading are not given, so the total
must have been actually greater.

There is no record of any official notice being taken
of Towerson's return, nor of further proclamations being
issued against African voyages. The Government was
preoccupied with other things ; a war was beginning
with France (formal declaration, June 7), and Philip's
influence and pretensions were becoming more and more
unpopular in the country. It was therefore not a fitting
time to punish Englishmen for distant trading adventures.
The difficulty in obtaining large ships, caused by the war,
may have been the reason that Towerson did not begin
his third voyage until January 30, 1558 [1], instead of
setting out in the autumn as was usual. In the winter
most of the vessels of the fleet were put out of commission, a piece of economy which resulted in the loss
of Calais ; and Towerson sailed for Guinea with the
Minion, the *Christopher*, the *Tiger*, and the *Unicorn*,

[1] The date of this voyage is given, by a misprint, in the 1598-9 editions
of Hakluyt as 1577. Modern reprints have perpetuated the mistake.
The date is correctly given in the 1589 Hakluyt as 1557, that is 1558
by our present style of beginning the year on January 1.

a pinnace. The Count of Feria, Philip's representative
in England, wrote to his master that two of the above
were queen's ships and among the best she had, and
that they sailed with the knowledge and approval of
William Howard, the Lord Admiral. He added that the
adventurers gave out that they were going to Barbary,
and distributed 3,000 ducats in bribes, being in reality
bound for Guinea.[1]

The day after leaving England they fell in with two
Danzig ships coming from Bordeaux with wines. They
examined them strictly on suspicion of carrying French-
owned cargo, and, in spite of denials, convicted them.
But considering the lateness of the season they did not
think well to take them back as prizes to an English port,
and, having despoiled them of such goods as they needed,
including eight guns, they let them go. On February 12
they entered the roadstead of Grand Canary to repair
the pinnace, which had broken her rudder. While they
were there a Spanish fleet of nineteen sail, bound for
the Indies, came in. Compliments were exchanged, but
afterwards a misunderstanding arose owing to the English
refusing to strike their flag. The Spaniards fired upon
them, but the Admiral apologized, declaring that it had
been done without his orders.

On March 10 they arrived at Rio das Palmas on the
Grain Coast. Going on from thence to the River of
Sestos they heard news of six French ships on the coast,
and decided at once to make for the Mina region lest
the French should spoil their trade. Picking up some
ivory on the way, they reached Hanta on the Gold Coast
on March 31. Next day five Portuguese ships were

[1] Kervyn de Lettenhove, *Les Pays-Bas et l'Angleterre*, i. 152 : ' Los
navios . . . eran dos de la Reyna y los mejores que Su Majestad tenian.'

sighted, but no action took place till after dark, each
side cautiously manœuvring to get to windward of the
other. In the night Towerson in the *Minion*, having
got the wind of the Portuguese admiral, fought with
him for about two hours, shooting him several times
through the hull, while the Portuguese were only able
to fire into the *Minion's* rigging. After this the Portuguese sheered off and attacked the *Christopher* without
doing much damage. Next morning the enemy were
nowhere to be seen ; it was decided to seek for and fight
them before continuing to trade, but after two days'
fruitless search the plan was given up and the squadron
returned to the coast.

Here they heard that some French ships were in the
vicinity, and, England and France being now at war,
decided to attack them. On April 5 they saw three
Frenchmen and gave chase. They were successful in
capturing one of 120 tons, the *Mulet de Batuille*, and
in her 50 lb. 5 oz. of gold. Arriving at Egrand, the
easternmost place on the Gold Coast, they found the
French prize to be leaky, and were obliged to spoil and
sink her. Towerson now proposed to go on to Benin,
but the majority of the company refused. The fleet
then separated to trade at various places on the coast,
agreeing to rally on the *Minion* if attacked. At this
time the men began to be sickly, and six died. Having
sold all her cloth at Egrand the *Minion* sailed westwards
on May 10, picking up the *Christopher* and the *Tiger*
on the way. Both reported little trade, and the negroes
in general seemed hostile and suspicious. For another
six weeks they continued on the coast, trading at some
places and being repulsed at others, until victuals began
to run short. The crews of the *Tiger* and the *Christopher*

were willing to attack the Portuguese ships at Mina and
so supply themselves, but the *Minion's* men would not
consent for fear of hanging when they should reach home.
At Samma the natives refused to supply either gold or
food, having made an agreement with the Portuguese,
and the English therefore burned the town. Next day,
June 25, they set sail for England.

Great difficulty was experienced in getting away from
the coast. Six days after sailing they again sighted land
and found themselves 18 leagues to leeward of the place
they had started from, owing to the extraordinary
strength of the current. It was now decided to head
southwards as far as the equator before attempting to
beat to the westwards, and on July 7 they arrived at
the Island of St. Thomé. A stay of nearly a month was
made at this island before, on August 3, a fresh start
was made and the homeward passage was begun in
earnest. The shortage of victuals became more serious,
and on the advice of a Scot, taken prisoner in the French
ship, they called at the Isle of Salt, one of the Cape
Verde group. They obtained a few goats and a quantity
of fish and sea-birds. The Scot went ashore on the island
and was not seen again : it was supposed that the
inhabitants found him asleep and carried him off. On
August 24 the master of the *Tiger* reported his ship
leaky and his men too weak to keep her afloat. There
were now only thirty sound men in the whole fleet.
A fortnight later the *Tiger* had to be abandoned in mid-
ocean, in latitude 25° N. Still the long voyage was
protracted, and the latitude of Cape St. Vincent was not
reached until October 6. The *Christopher* being now
very weak, it was agreed to put into Vigo and send for
more men from England. But a fair wind sprang up,

and Towerson decided to make one more effort to reach home, fearing that, once in Vigo, the treasure would never be allowed to go out again. Two guns were fired to warn the *Christopher*, and the *Minion* sailed on. The *Christopher* appeared to be following, but, the next morning being foggy, they lost sight of her. Towerson mentions that he concluded at the time that she had either outsailed· them or gone back to Vigo, but he strangely omits to state which supposition turned out to be correct, and we are left quite in the dark as to the *Christopher's* fate. At the time they parted company there were only twelve men in health in the two ships. After losing most of her sails in a great south-westerly gale, the men being too weak to handle them, the *Minion* arrived at the Isle of Wight on October 20, 1558.

The total amount of gold and ivory obtained on this voyage cannot be stated owing to want of clearness in the account, but it would appear that it was not nearly such a successful venture as the previous ones, although more capital was involved. The truth was that, between the French and the English, the Guinea trade had been somewhat overdone, and the huge profits of the first adventurers could not be expected to continue. The Portuguese had hitherto restricted their own trade on the coast for this very reason, but now the negroes were becoming spoiled and inclined to play off one competitor against the other. One new thing was certainly revealed by these voyages, and that was that the Portuguese were impotent to make good their boasted monopoly. A simple process of reasoning led Englishmen to ask if the Spaniards were in the same case ; and it was not long before an affirmative answer was to be supplied by Hawkins and Drake.

CHAPTER XII

THE NORTH-EAST PASSAGE AND THE WHITE SEA

SHORTLY after the death of Henry VIII there reappeared in England that mysterious and elusive figure which has so often flitted across the page of this history—Sebastian Cabot. Although he had passed thirty-five years in the service of Spain, had received high pay and honour, had been appointed to the command of an important expedition, and had been forgiven for his mistakes and incapacity on his return, he was never really content, and was for ever ready to plot and intrigue that he might skip from the service of one master to that of another. But Sebastian Cabot was not the subtle and calculating villain that he has often been painted. The key to his unending restlessness was nothing more nor less than an egregious vanity, a never-satisfied desire to be praised, looked up to, consulted, a morbid fear that he was falling in the esteem of his fellows. Hence his offers to betray secrets which he never possessed, his boasts of exclusive knowledge in astronomy and navigation which he never revealed, and his tacit acquiescence in the attribution to him by contemporary historians of the honour of being the original discoverer of North America. Yet with all his hollowness he was a useful man : he probably knew as much of the scientific side of navigation and geography as any man living, although he professed to know much more ; and in the course of his long career he could not have failed to acquire a very perfect knowledge of the details of Spanish methods of exploration and discovery.

For some ten years at least he had been contemplating the re-transference of his services to England. In November 1538 he approached Sir Thomas Wyatt, Henry VIII's envoy in Spain, with a request to be recommended to the king. Wyatt's memorandum runs : ' To remember Sebastian Cabote. He hath here but 300 ducats a year, and he is desirous, if he might not serve the King, at least to see him, as his old master.' This touching manifestation of affection failed of its effect. Henry showed no inclination to outbid the emperor for Cabot's expensive talents, and no more is heard of the intrigue until 1547. On October 9 of that year, some eight months after the accession of Edward VI, the Council made out a warrant for £100 ' for transporting one Shabot a pilot to come out of Hispain to serve and inhabit in England '.[1] The sum was far too large for the expense of the journey alone ; possibly some bribery was needed to get Cabot out of the country. The affair was still not cleared up nearly two years later when an entry occurs relative to this same sum of £100, the warrant for which was to be ' taken up by exchange ' by Henry Ostrich, a member of a business house which had dealings in Spain.

The date of Cabot's flight can only be approximately stated. It almost certainly took place in the summer or autumn of 1548. On the 6th of January of the following year King Edward, or rather the Protector Somerset, granted him an annual pension of £166 13s. 4d., payable quarterly, the first instalment to date from Michaelmas, 1548 ; which date was doubtless near the

[1] *Acts of the Privy Council*, ii. 137.

commencement of his service in England.[1] Cabot had probably given out that he had travelled to England on private business. He certainly made no resignation of his office of Pilot Major of Spain. Consequently more than a year elapsed before the emperor troubled to ask for his return. In November 1549 Sir Philip Hoby wrote from Brussels that the emperor had expressed a desire for Cabot to be sent back. Five months later the Council replied that they were not detaining him in England, but that he refused of his own accord to leave; and that as he was an English subject they could not compel him. With this the matter dropped. Cabot was frequently described by writers of the latter half of the sixteenth century as an Englishman by birth, although there is little doubt that he first saw the light in Venice. He himself lied freely on the point as occasion demanded, and at this period it was obviously to his interest to pose as an Englishman.

His position and occupations in England at this time are obscure. Hakluyt states that he was 'Grand Pilot' of England, but there is no other evidence that such an office then officially existed. The adventurers of the Council doubtless entertained schemes of diverting some of the wealth of the new worlds into the coffers of their own State. The long stagnation of the English mind on such subjects was at last breaking up, as many contemporary events indicate; and mid-century England was virgin ground for the boastings and mystifications of the old intriguer, who revelled in the impression he

[1] Hakluyt, vii. 156–7. Some confusion has arisen as to the year of this patent, but it is perfectly clear. 'The sixt day of Januarie, in the second yeere of his raigne. The yeere of our Lord 1548' is January 6, 1549, by the present style. Edward VI succeeded to the throne on January 28, 1547.

produced on the unsophisticated islanders. The esteem
in which he was held is proved by several passages in
Eden and Hakluyt. But the only project, prior to that
of the north-east voyage to Cathay, of which even a hint
survives, is that referred to in a letter from Cabot to
Charles V, informing him of a design of the Duke of
Northumberland to fit out an expedition to Peru in
co-operation with the French.[1] Needless to say, the
scheme was never put into execution. Cabot was simply
amusing his credulous hosts while at the same time
ingratiating himself with the emperor by betraying them.
It almost looks as if he had in view at this time yet
another change of employers. His one real achievement
during his declining years did not take shape until the
last year of Edward's reign.

The general progress of discovery and the growth of
English manufactures led to the project of finding a
passage to Cathay by the north-east. Theoretically there
were four ways of reaching from Europe the shores of
eastern Asia, which were still regarded as the most
desirable mercantile goal in the world. The most
practicable route, via the Cape of Good Hope, had been
discovered and monopolized by the Portuguese, and no
ship of any other nationality had yet traversed it. The
Spaniards had opened up the corresponding western
voyage through the Straits of Magellan or South-West
Passage, although they did not use it to anything like
the same extent, preferring to reach the Pacific by
transhipment across the isthmus of Panama. Frequent
attempts, English for the most part, had ended in nothing

---

[1] Navarette, *Colección de Documentos inéditos para la historia de la
España*, iii. 512. The letter is here dated November 15, 1554, but was
probably written at least two years earlier. Northumberland was executed
on August 22, 1553.

but discouragement for those who dreamed of a North-West Passage through the ice-strewn gate of Davis Straits. The fourth method only then, through ' the north east frostie seas ', remained to be tried. Few practical men could at this stage have put any trust in the facile theory of Robert Thorne that it was possible to sail due north over the Pole itself. But the coast-line of northern Russia and Siberia was entirely unexplored, and, on the principle of *omne ignotum pro magnifico*, it seemed to offer a glorious solution of the great problem. Some expansion of the field of England's commerce was imperatively needed, for the old European markets were now being exploited to the fullest possible extent, and the increasing luxury of living, coupled with the industrial unrest due to the transformation of the land system, rendered an extension of oversea trade essential to the salvation of the country. The new England of the Renaissance, seething with restless energies which waited to take shape and direction, was incapable of living in a state of economic isolation from the rest of the world.[1]

In the months preceding the spring of 1553 a strong combination of capitalists, courtiers, and merchants was formed for the prosecution of the Cathay enterprise. It included the Marquis of Winchester, the Earls of Arundel, Bedford, and Pembroke, Lord William Howard, Sir William Cecil, Sir John Gresham, Thomas Gresham, Sir George Barnes, and about two hundred others.[1] None of the documents relating to the Company prior to the first voyage are now known to exist with the exception of Sebastian Cabot's ordinances for the

[1] Charter of Philip and Mary, February 6, 1555, and *Cal. S. P. Dom. Addenda, Mary*, p. 439. The latter is a list of the members in May 1555. It includes the names of three women among the adventurers.

guidance of the commanders. From a reference in the
latter, however, it is evident that a charter of incorporation was granted by Edward VI, and that the government
of the Company was regularly constituted. Article 20
of the ordinances, relating to the disposal of merchandise,
provides that an inventory shall be 'presented to the
Governor, Consuls and Assistants in London, in good
order, to the intent the King's Majesty may be truly
answered of that which to his Grace by his grant of
incorporation is limited'. It would appear by this that
in return for granting a monopoly the king was to have
a share of the profits. Sebastian Cabot acted as chief
expert adviser to the new company, and, in consideration
of his services, he was appointed its first Governor, in
which position he was confirmed by the subsequent
charter granted by Philip and Mary in 1555. His dimly
reported adventures in search of the North-West Passage
under Henry VII were no doubt supposed to give weight
to his opinions on the North-East, although in reality he
was as ignorant as was every one else on the subject.
The Company raised, for the setting out of the first
voyage, a capital of £6,000 divided into £25 shares.
The subscribing of a single share entitled an investor to
membership.

It is important to emphasize the fact that this new
company of 'Merchants Adventurers of England for
the discovery of lands, territories, isles, dominions and
seignories unknown' was an organization quite distinct
from and independent of the old Merchant Adventurers
who exported cloth to the Low Countries. The term
'merchant adventurers' was of general and not particular
application, although, during the time when there was
only one such society in London, it had naturally tended

to be used as a proper noun. The fact that by force of circumstances the name of the new combination was soon changed, and that it came to be called the Russia or Muscovy Company, has perpetuated the error as to its origin, from which serious misconceptions have arisen. One of these is the story that Sebastian Cabot was Governor of the Low Countries Merchant Adventurers, and that, in that capacity, he took a leading part in the struggle with the Hansa which ended in the abolition of that society's privileged position in England. This supposition, first advanced in Campbell's *Lives of the British Admirals*, and repeated by subsequent writers, is unsupported by any contemporary evidence, and is manifestly absurd. The Governor of the Low Countries Merchants had to reside at Antwerp, their head-quarters. Antwerp being Imperial territory, Cabot would not have dared to set foot in it after 1548. Moreover, the names of the Governors of the old Merchant Adventurers during Cabot's presidency of the new company are traceable in the State papers of the time : from 1548 to 1558 Thomas Chamberlain, William Dansell, and Anthony Hussey successively filled that office. They were London merchants, intimately acquainted with the cloth trade, and exercising administrative control over the business of their fellows in Antwerp. It is obvious that Cabot lacked the qualifications for such a duty. The whole legend falls to the ground when it is realized that there were now two companies of Merchant Adventurers.

From a crowd of eager applicants Sir Hugh Willoughby was selected to be Captain-General of the first expedition, mainly on account of his good record of war service and his commanding appearance. Richard Chancellor, a protégé of Sir Henry Sidney, was appointed chief pilot

and second in command. Little is known of Willoughby's
previous career, except that he had served on land in
the Scottish wars. Chancellor was a professional seaman
who had been with Roger Bodenham in the adventurous
voyage of the *Bark Aucher* to the Mediterranean in 1551.
At the same meeting at which these appointments were
made it was decided that the voyage must begin before
the end of May in case the way should be barred by ice
before the passage had been effected. It is evident that
both the length of the Arctic winter and the distance to
be traversed before the eastern flank of Asia should be
turned were grossly underestimated ; otherwise the
voyage would certainly have been postponed till the
next year. But none of the geographical factors of the
project were known, and, after a vain attempt to extort
information from the dense stupidity of two Tartar
stableboys who had somehow found their way to London,
and who were interrogated before the assembled adventurers, the issue had to be left to the fates.

The fleet consisted of the *Bona Esperanza*, 120 tons,
the *Edward Bonaventure*, 160 tons, and the *Bona Confidentia*, of 90 tons. Each ship was accompanied by
a pinnace and a boat. Willoughby sailed in the *Esperanza*,
having with him six merchants, including his kinsman
Gabriel Willoughby, and a crew of thirty-one, of whom
three were discharged at Harwich before clearing from
the English coast. Chancellor was captain of the *Edward
Bonaventure*, with Stephen Borough as master and John
Buckland mate. His crew numbered thirty-seven, among
whom were William Borough and Arthur Pet, both in
the forecastle. He had also with him ten landsmen—
merchants, gentlemen adventurers, and a chaplain. The
Confidentia was commanded by Cornelius Durforth, with

three merchants and twenty-four officers and men. The pinnaces were manned by drafts from the ships to which they were attached. Cabot's ordinances[1] contain many interesting details. They embody the experience gained in more than half a century of Spanish exploration, with modifications suitable for the special circumstances of the voyage. Loyalty and goodwill in executing orders are prominently insisted upon. The Admiral is to submit all important matters to the decision of a Council of Twelve in which he is allowed a double vote. The fleet is to be careful to keep together and the commanders are to go on board the Admiral's ship as often as he shall require. Logs are to be kept by every person capable of writing and to be compiled into a common ledger to be preserved for record. The Admiral and Council have power to reduce in rank inefficient officers and to set delinquents on shore in any English port. Morning and evening prayers are to be read daily, and no blasphemy, swearing, lewd talk, dicing, card-playing, or other devilish games to be permitted. The merchants are only to trade with the consent of the captains, councillors, and head merchants, or a committee of four of them. Petty merchants must show their accounts to the head merchants, and all goods must be carefully packed and not opened until the end of the voyage. No person may engage in private trade until the Company's interests are first satisfied. In dealing with strangers all must be careful not to enter into any discussion about religion. Persons may be enticed aboard the ships to give useful information, but no violence must be used, although it is recommended

---

[1] The authorities for these voyages are to be found, unless otherwise indicated, in Hakluyt (Maclehose ed., 1903), vol. ii.

to make them drunk if possible. Strangers must not be offended by arrogance or ridicule. If invited to festivities the landing party should go in force and well armed. News is to be sent home whenever possible, especially in the event of the passage being found. The last article contains an impressive warning against ' conspiracies, partakings, factions, false tales, and untrue reports ', and an exhortation to behave always as loyal and honourable men, ' with daily remembrance of the great importance of the voyage, the honour, glory, praise, and benefit that depend . . . upon the same, toward the common wealth of this noble realm, the advancement of you the travailers therein, your wives and children '.

The twelve councillors were Sir Hugh Willoughby, Richard Chancellor, George Burton, head merchant, Richard Stafford, minister, Thomas Langlie, merchant, James Dalabere, gentleman, and the masters and mates of the three ships.

No better planned and equipped expedition had ever before left an English port on a voyage of discovery. The commander was a man of rank and good repute, while the chief navigator was a practical seaman and no mere book-learned amateur. The crews were of the best that could be found, and acted up to the spirit of their instructions ; there is no hint of insubordination in any accounts of the voyage, although the bitterest hardships were encountered. In addition to Chancellor there were in the *Bonaventure* alone three men who afterwards rose to eminence in their profession and commanded important expeditions. The ships were the largest that could conveniently be used, for, although greater tonnage was common in the navy, big vessels were not yet a success for trade and exploration, being too unhandy for naviga-

tion on uncharted coasts. The Admiral was furnished
with letters of friendship and recommendation from
Edward VI to all princes and potentates inhabiting the
north-east parts of the world as far as the empire of
Cathay. For reasons obvious enough now, the attempt
to force a passage to Asia was foredoomed to inevitable
failure, but that failure was due to no fault in the promotion or execution of the voyage. It resulted from
a want of the knowledge which was only to be obtained
from actual trial and experience.

All preparations being complete, the fleet departed
from Ratcliff on May 10, 1553. The next day, towing
down the river, they passed Greenwich with great pomp,
the mariners all attired in their uniform of sky-blue
cloth, kept for such occasions, and the ships discharging
their ordnance in a salute to the king, who was then
lying sick in the palace. The Privy Councillors looked
out from the windows, ' the courtiers came running out,
and the common people flocked together, standing very
thick upon the shore ... but, alas, the good King Edward,
in respect of whom principally all this was prepared, he
only by reason of his sickness was absent from this show,
and not very long after the departure of these ships the
lamentable and most sorrowful accident of his death
followed '.

Proceeding in leisurely fashion out of the estuary and
along the East Anglian coast, it was not until the 23rd
of June that the voyage fairly commenced with a final
clearance from Orford Ness. After getting well away
from the land, a course was steered due north until the
27th. Then, westerly winds preventing them from
touching at Shetland, after much ' traversing and tracing
the seas by reason of sundry and manifold contrary

winds', they came to the southern end of the Lofoten
Archipelago on the coast of Norway. Touching at
various points they arrived on August 2 at the island
of Senjen in latitude 69½°. A skiff put off from the land
and informed them of their whereabouts, promising also
that a pilot should be furnished next day to conduct
them round the North Cape to Vardo, the Danish
stronghold which marked the furthest outpost of European civilization in the North-East. Beyond Vardo all
was unknown.

Before the promised pilot could come aboard a sudden
and violent storm arose and scattered the fleet far out
to sea. The night came on and the wind so increased
that Willoughby was forced to heave to. In the morning
he was rejoined by the *Confidentia*, but the *Edward
Bonaventure*, Chancellor's ship, was nowhere to be seen.
At this point the story of the expedition forks into two,
for Chancellor and Willoughby never met again. It will
be convenient first to follow to their conclusion the
fortunes of the latter.

As it had been agreed that in case of a separation
Vardo should be the rendezvous, Willoughby, with the
Esperanza and the *Confidentia*, set about finding his way
thither. The gale abating on August 4, he sailed north-
east by north, but soon found that he was quite out of
his reckoning and that his charts were incorrect. With
frequent changes of direction owing to varying winds,
but all the time making headway eastwards, he sailed
on until August 14, when land was discovered in latitude 72°. His course cannot with any certainty be laid
down ; on some days the distance traversed is not stated
in the log, the eccentricities of the compass in northern
latitudes render untrustworthy the bearings given, there

was then no accurate method of calculating longitude, while such factors as currents and leeway caused serious errors in an attempt to estimate the distance by dead reckoning. The one certain datum is the fact that the land discovered lay in 72°. Latitude was then usually ascertainable within a degree of correctitude ; William Borough's chart of these regions, drawn up a few years later, contains no error greater than $\frac{3}{4}$°, and only one in any way approaching that. Therefore it is evident that Willoughby, on August 14, 1553, discovered Novaia Zemlia, probably in the neighbourhood of Moller Bay.[1] Between it and Greenland there is no other land in latitude 72°. Willoughby's error in longitude may be judged from the fact that he thought it to be 480 miles east by north from the island of Senjen on the coast of Norway ; actually it is about 700 miles. The prospect was desolate in the extreme : ' Early in the morning we descried land,' he says, ' which land we bare with all, hoising out our boat to discover what land it might be : but the boat could not come to land, the water was so shoal, where was very much ice also, but there was no similitude of habitation. . . . Then we plyed to the northward the 15, 16 and 17 day.' There was no occasion here for the use of the king's friendly letters to princes and potentates, but the explorers did not lose heart. The last quoted phrase seems to imply that Willoughby took this land to be a promontory of the continent and that he was seeking to find the passage round it to the northward, having by this time given up the idea of

---

[1] Purchas, xiii. 6, thinks that Spitzbergen was the land found. The lowest point of Spitzbergen is in 76½°. It is impossible that Willoughby could have committed such a serious error in latitude Moreover, Spitzbergen is due north of Senjen.

meeting Chancellor at Vardo. However, after three
days' 'plying' or beating to windward, the *Confidentia*
was found to be leaking, and, putting about, they ran
70 leagues before the wind to the south-south-east to
seek a harbour for her repair.

From hence onwards the actual course is altogether
conjectural ; the daily distances are seldom given, and
no more latitudes are mentioned. But the general
direction was now westwards, and it is evident that the
quest for the passage had been given up for that year.
The object was now to return to some safe wintering
place on the coast of Norway. On August 23 land was
sighted on a west-south-westerly course, low-lying and
deserted, and running west-south-west and east-north-
east. This was probably the coast to the west of Cape
Ruskoi and the Petchora River. After coasting westwards for some distance they drew off into the sea, and
seem next to have sailed south-westwards into Cheska
Gulf. Land was again seen on the 28th, barren as before
and running north-eastwards to a point, after which it
turned to the west. This can only be identified with
Kaninska Island, the eastern arm of the entrance to the
White Sea. The explorers landed in a neighbouring
bay and saw signs of human habitation, although no one
appeared. On September 4 they lost touch with the
coast by reason of contrary winds, but regained it on
the 8th. It was probably during this interval that the
entrance to the White Sea, where Chancellor had already
found safety, was passed and missed. From September 8
to the 17th they coasted north-westwards along the
dreary shore of Lapland, and finally, turning back for
a short distance, they entered on the 18th a haven known
as the River Arzina, which they had noted a day or two

before. It was some six miles long by one and a half wide, and was full of seals and large fish, while on the land were seen bears, deer, foxes, and other beasts, but no sign of man. After spending a week in this place they decided to winter there as the weather had become too bad to admit of further exploration. Groups of men were sent out in three directions to search for inhabitants, but all alike returned ' without finding of people or any similitude of habitation '. With these words closes the log of Sir Hugh Willoughby, written by his own hand, and found a year later by Russian fishermen in the cabin of the *Bona Esperanza.*

The details of the sufferings and death of the sixty-three men who formed the crews of the *Esperanza* and the *Confidentia* are unrecorded : not one of them survived the long Arctic winter. The only other document besides the log of which we have any record was a will made in January 1554 by Gabriel Willoughby, from which it was evident that Sir Hugh and most of his crew were still alive in that month. The will came into the possession of Samuel Purchas, by whom it was kept as a relic, but it has long since disappeared. They certainly did not die of starvation, for, when the ships were visited in 1555 by agents of the Company, a considerable quantity of provisions was recovered. Henry Lane, writing from Russia many years afterwards, ascribed their fate to ' want of experience to have made caves and stoves '. At that we must leave it. A wildly imaginative description by Giovanni Michiel, the Venetian agent in London, forwarded to his Government in 1555, says : ' The mariners now returned from the second voyage narrate strange things about the mode in which they (i.e. Willoughby and his men) were frozen, having found some of them seated in the act of writing, pen still in hand, and the paper before them ; others at table, platter in hand, and spoon in mouth ; others opening a locker, and others in various postures, like statues, as if they had been adjusted and placed in those attitudes. They say that some dogs on board the ships displayed the same phenomena.' Other statements in the same letter are demonstrably false, and it need only be said that the above account is extremely unlikely to be true.

Chancellor, in the *Edward Bonaventure*, had better fortune. After losing sight of Willoughby in the storm of August 2, he steered for Vardo as had been pre-arranged. Reaching that place without difficulty he waited a week for the other two ships and then decided to proceed on the voyage without them. The pluck and loyalty of Chancellor and his crew are altogether admir-able. If they had not exhibited those qualities in the highest degree the whole project would have ended in complete failure, and a disastrous check would have been sustained by the exponents of the new movement of maritime expansion just when, for the first time, there was some sign of national interest aroused. After the separation from the rest of the fleet Chancellor's company became, according to Clement Adams, ' very pensive, heavy and sorrowful ', and an incident which took place at Vardo was not calculated to raise their spirits. They encountered there certain Scotsmen who, hearing of their intention to seek the North-East Passage, did their best to dissuade them, magnifying the dangers of the northern seas and omitting no arguments to divert them from their purpose. The Scotsmen, if they had been resident for any length of time at Vardo, must have spoken with good reason, and what they said was believed by the

English to be inspired by pure good will and without
envious intent. Chancellor stood firm, however, and
' holding nothing so ignominious and reproachful as
inconstancy and levity of mind, and persuading himself
that a man of valour could not commit a more dis-
honourable part than, for fear of danger, to avoid and
shun great attempts, he was nothing at all changed or
discouraged with the speeches and words of the Scots,
remaining stedfast and immutable in his first resolution :
determining either to bring that to pass which was first
intended, or else to die the death '.

His men rose to his own height of resolution, and the
most hearty good will prevailed between captain and
crew. Accordingly, about the middle of August they
set forward once more, arriving at length at the entrance
of the White Sea. It does not appear whether or not
he believed this to be the mouth of the passage. In any
case, ignorant as he was of the shape and extent of the
northern coast of Asia, it was his duty to explore it,
especially as it ran southwards at first and then curved
to the east in the Bay of Mezen. Having penetrated far
into this great gulf the explorers sighted a boat full of
fishermen, the first men seen since leaving Vardo. They
fled in terror at the sight of the strange English ship,
of a size and loftiness hitherto undreamed of by their
simple minds. Chancellor manned his boat and overtook them, finding them ' in great fear as men half
dead '. He reassured them by his gentleness and courtesy,
the report of which was spread abroad and caused ' the
barbarous Russes ' to flock round the ship with offers of
food and welcome. At this point the English learned,
somewhat to their surprise, that they had discovered the
dominions of the Czar. There is no hint in Sebastian

Cabot's instructions of any such result being contemplated. A marginal note to a later account of Russian adventures in Hakluyt says that they arrived first at the village of Newnox (Nenoksa), twenty-five miles west of St. Nicholas and somewhat further from St. Michael (Archangel).[1]

News of their coming was at once sent to the Czar Ivan, not yet called the Terrible, whose authority was so respected, even in those remote regions, that the natives dared not buy the Englishmen's goods without his permission. In the meantime Chancellor, who at once realized the commercial possibilities of his discovery, was eager to set out for Moscow to deliver in person to the Czar his king's letters of recommendation. The local authorities were still awaiting instructions, pending the arrival of which they made excuses to defer the journey. At length they yielded on Chancellor's threat to depart forthwith by the way he had come. They provided him with sledges and post-horses with which he and a few companions set forward over the snow-covered plains to the south. On the way he encountered the messenger returning from the Czar with a letter couched in cordial terms and injunctions to the inhabitants to defray all the expenses of the journey. Such was the weight of Ivan's word that the Russians quarrelled and fought for the honour of supplying horses to the travellers.

Twelve days after arriving at Moscow Chancellor was summoned before the Czar. He was conducted through an outer room, wherein sat a hundred courtiers in cloth of gold, into the presence chamber filled with a hundred and fifty more. Ivan sat on a lofty throne, with crown and sceptre and a most regal countenance. Nothing

[1] Hakluyt, iii. 74, 331.

abashed, the sailor strode up to him and saluted after the English fashion, and then presented the letters of Edward VI. The emperor, having read the letters, conversed a little with him and commanded him and his companions to dinner. The meal was served in high state, with impressive ceremonies and massive vessels of gold ; but the English were quick to detect barbarian squalor beneath barbaric display. They were greatly impressed, however, by the hardiness of the people, and by the iron discipline which prevailed throughout the land ; also by the military power of the Czar, concerning which they gave credit to exaggerated reports.

Chancellor made good use of his opportunities. His account of Russia and that of Clement Adams (based entirely on reports of this first voyage) are full of useful and generally correct information on the cities, government, laws, religion, and products of the country, to an extent that is wonderful when one considers that at the outset he was utterly ignorant of its language and almost of its very existence. In his bearing toward the Czar and his ministers he remembered always that he was the representative of England, and that his conduct would mainly determine the attitude which they would take up towards his country. His combined modesty and dignity caused him to be favourably treated from the first, and secured valuable privileges for the Company.

After a stay in Moscow of unknown duration, Chancellor and his comrades returned to the Bay of St. Nicholas, where his ship had been laid up for the winter. He was the bearer of a letter from Ivan to the English sovereign, dated February 1554, in which a cordial invitation was extended to Englishmen who should wish to trade with Russia. The Czar promised

them his protection and complete freedom to buy and
sell in any part of his dominions. As soon as navigation
became possible the *Edward Bonaventure* set sail for
England, arriving in the summer of 1554, after having
been robbed on the way by Flemish pirates.

Chancellor's return with tidings of a promising new
outlet for English trade created a great stir in commercial circles. The quest of the North-East Passage
was for the moment forgotten, and a second expedition
to the White Sea was prepared for 1555. In February
of that year the Company obtained a fresh charter of
incorporation from Philip and Mary, in supersession of
that granted by Edward VI. Sebastian Cabot, as having
been ' the chiefest setter forth of this journey or voyage ',
was confirmed in the office of Governor. Four consuls
and twenty-four assistants to the Governor were to be
elected yearly by the shareholders, meeting in London
or elsewhere. The first list of appointments to these
offices was stated in the charter. Among the four consuls
were Anthony Hussey, Governor of the Low Countries
Merchant Adventurers, and Sir George Barnes, whom
we have already seen as an adventurer in the African
voyages. Sir John Gresham was one of the assistants,
as were also Sir Andrew Judde, Miles Mordeyne, and
others who took an active part in the Guinea trade.
The Governor, consuls, and assistants were to have full
administrative powers over the merchants of the Company. It is interesting to note how naturally the English
tradition of representative government took its place in
the affairs of these mercantile societies. The constitu-
tions of the old Merchant Adventurers, of the Staplers,
and of the various provincial merchant guilds, were very
similar to the one now under consideration. The habits

of thought which they kept alive were undoubtedly a factor in preventing England from becoming an absolute monarchy after the example of her Continental neighbours. The charter proceeded to grant power to the Company to acquire real estate in England, to plead in the courts, to make statutes for its own governance, to impose penalties for the enforcement of the same, to proceed with the discovery of new lands and to conquer them in the name of the English Crown, and finally, to enjoy a monopoly of the newly instituted trade with Russia, in which all other persons were forbidden to engage.

The 1555 expedition consisted of two ships, the *Edward Bonaventure* and the *Philip and Mary*.[1] They sailed from London at the end of May. The instructions were for the former to go to the White Sea while the latter stopped at Vardo, there to collect a cargo of fish and train oil. Richard Chancellor was in chief command, sailing in the *Edward*. With him were Richard Gray and George Killingworth, appointed to be agents for the Company in Russia. John Brooke was to fulfil a similar duty at Vardo. Killingworth must have been a man of striking appearance : Henry Lane records that on one occasion, when dining with the Czar, ' The prince called them to his table to receive each one a cup from his hand to drink, and took into his hand Master George Killingworth's beard, which reached over the table, and pleasantly delivered it to the Metropolitan, who, seeming to bless it, said in Russe : This is God's gift. As indeed

[1] The Venetian agent (*Venetian Cal.* vi, No. 89) says three. The error arose from the name of the *Philip and Mary*, which the Italian doubtless took to be two vessels. The instructions for the voyage leave no doubt that only two ships were sent. See also Henry Lane's letter (Hakluyt, iii. 332).

at that time it was not only thick, broad and yellow coloured, but in length five foot and two inches of a size.' The agents were ordered to go with Chancellor to the Czar, to present the queen's letters, and to obtain from him a grant of privileges. They were also to set up warehouses in Moscow or other towns and sell their goods to the best advantage. They were to use all diligence in inquiring about the route from Russia to Cathay, and in obtaining news as to Willoughby's fate, of which nothing was yet known in England.

All this was duly carried out. The *Edward's* cargo was unladen at St. Nicholas, and the goods transported up the Dwina to Colmogro (Kholmogori), and thence to Vologda, where they were warehoused. Vologda was about half-way between St. Nicholas and Moscow. At the end of September Chancellor, with four others, set out for the capital to perform their errand to the Czar. They were as well received as on the previous occasion, and it was agreed that they should establish factories at Colmogro and Vologda, the one fifty and the other five hundred miles up the Dwina. The Czar made a formal grant of privileges, including freedom from tolls and customs, freedom from arrest, and recognition of the jurisdiction of the Chief Agent of the Company over all Englishmen in Russia.

After the departure of Chancellor in the previous year the bodies of Willoughby and his men had been discovered in their ships at Arzina by Russian fishermen. The vessels were still lying at the same anchorage, and were now visited by some of Killingworth's men, a considerable quantity of the cargoes being recovered. It is possible that Willoughby's body was sent home. His ships, for lack of sufficient seamen, had to be left for another year.[1] Richard Chancellor, with the agents, remained in Russia for the winter, but the *Edward Bonaventure* was sent home before the navigation closed. She picked up the *Philip and Mary* at Vardo, and they arrived together in the Thames at the beginning of November.[2]

Next year (1556) the *Edward* and the *Philip and Mary* were again sent out, in company with a pinnace called the *Serchthrift* under the command of Stephen Borough. The latter was not intended to trade, but to pursue the north-eastern discovery towards the River Obi. The two large ships had surplus crews for the manning of Willoughby's vessels, the *Bona Esperanza* and the *Bona Confidentia*, found in the previous year. They left Ratcliff on April 23. Soon afterwards occurred one of the last recorded incidents in the life of Sebastian Cabot :

' The 27th, being Monday, the right worshipful Sebastian Cabota came aboard our pinnace at Gravesend, accompanied with divers gentlemen and gentlewomen who, after they had viewed our pinnace and tasted of such cheer as we could make them aboard, they went on shore, giving to our mariners right liberal rewards : and the good old gentleman Master Cabota gave to the poor most liberal alms, wishing them to pray for the good fortune and prosperous success of the *Serchthrift* our pinnace. And then at the sign of the Christopher, he and his friends banqucted, and made me (Stephen Borough) and those that were in the company, great cheer : and for very joy that he had to see the towardness of our intended discovery, he entered into the dance himself amongst the rest of the young and lusty company : which being ended, he and his friends departed most gently, commending us to the governance of almighty God.'

[1] The Venetian envoy wrongly states that they were brought home in 1555.   [2] *Venetian Cal.* vi, No. 269.

This was his last personal appearance on the page of history. All that remains thereafter is a document or two relative to his pension, and a reference to his death by his friend Richard Eden. The latter event almost certainly took place towards the end of 1557, when he must have been at least eighty-two years of age.

The *Serchthrift* and the two large vessels made a prosperous voyage to the north. In the mouth of the White Sea Stephen Borough with the *Serchthrift* parted company to go on his own business, whilst the others proceeded to St. Nicholas. Borough's little vessel was excellently suited for exploring the shallow waters and sandy coasts lying to the north-east of the White Sea. Her tonnage is not stated, but she was able to float in five feet of water. Yet her cabin was sufficiently large to admit of the entertainment of several people at once. She was fully rigged with three masts, and carried a skiff upon her deck. Probably she approximated to the type which in Latin countries was called a caravel. Her crew numbered ten, including Stephen's brother William.[1]

Although he bade farewell to the *Edward Bonaventure* on May 31, it was not until June 22 that Borough's voyage was fairly begun. In the interval he explored the southern shore of the Bay of Mezen and anchored in the Kola River. A fleet of Russian ' lodias ' or fishing-boats collected in the estuary, bound for the summer fishing off the Petchora. They were undecked, fitted with oars and sails, and were of even lighter draught than the *Serchthrift*, although they carried twenty-four men each. The skipper of one of them, Gabriel by name, was very friendly and rendered useful services to

---

[1] These details are scattered here and there in Borough's account of the voyage.

the English. On June 22 all sailed in company, rounding Cape St. John, the northern arm of the bay. Two days later the *Serchthrift* was in peril of being wrecked on a lee shore. Gabriel, whose craft had reached shelter, came out in a skiff to render aid. He lent them his own anchor and another which he had borrowed, their own being too heavy, and, these anchors being taken seawards and dropped by the skiff, they were able to warp off the shore.

On July 9 they rounded the cape called Kanin Nos and proceeded to Morgoviets, thence pushing on to the mouth of the Petchora, which was reached on the 15th. At this point Borough observed the variation of the compass to be $3\frac{1}{2}°$ W. Five days were spent in the Petchora. On July 21, the day after leaving, the *Serchthrift* was in great peril from ice, being hemmed in by a monstrous floe only half an hour after first sighting it. After six anxious hours she got clear. An easterly course was followed a little to the north of the seventieth parallel until the 25th, on which date the small islands which lie to the south of Novaia Zemlia were discovered. Borough named them St. James's Islands. The variation was here $7\frac{1}{2}°$ W. A Russian vessel passing by gave them some information as to the River Obi, the intended goal of the voyage, and they plied eastwards against a head wind until July 31. On that date they arrived at the Island of Vaigats, the most easterly point they were destined to reach. In its neighbourhood they remained for more than three weeks, experiencing very bad weather, storms, rain, and fog. They encountered some Samoyedes who lived in deer-skin tents and worshipped idols; and Richard Johnson, one of the crew, wrote a graphic description of their wizardry and 'devilish rites'. He was left behind among these savages for the winter, but the manner of his return to civilization does not appear.

At length, on August 22, Stephen Borough determined to give up the hope of further progress for that year. The winds were continuously unfavourable, the ice was increasing, and the nights were becoming dark. He turned his sails westwards therefore, doubling Kanin Nos on August 30, and reaching Colmogro, where he wintered, on September 11. He intended to pursue his discoveries further in the following year, but was sent instead to look for traces of the ill-fated vessels lost on the Norwegian coast in the autumn of 1556, as will be described below. Nothing further was done towards the solution of the north-eastern problem until the abortive expedition of Pet and Jackman in 1580.

In the meantime the two trading vessels sent out in 1556 had reached St. Nicholas and there discharged their cargoes. The extra hands were sent to take possession of Willoughby's derelict ships, and brought them also into the bay to be loaded for England. When all were ready to sail for home Richard Chancellor came down to St. Nicholas, bringing with him a Russian ambassador for England, Osep Nepea, Governor of Vologda. Both took passage in the *Edward Bonaventure*, which carried also sixteen other Russian passengers and £20,000 worth of goods. The *Bona Esperanza* had a cargo worth £6,000 and ten more members of the ambassador's suite. The ladings of the *Bona Confidentia* and the *Philip and Mary* are not specified. The homeward voyage was disastrous. Violent storms drove the fleet on to the Norwegian coast: the *Philip and Mary* struggled into Trondheim and passed the winter there, not arriving in the Thames until April 18, 1557; the *Bona Confidentia* was seen to split on a rock at the entrance to the same port, and perished with all hands ; while the *Bona Esperanza* was never heard of again. The *Edward Bonaventure* alone continued the voyage, only to meet her fate on the Scottish coast. On November 10, 1556, after a four months' passage, she was driven on a lee shore at Pitsligo in Aberdeenshire in the darkness of a winter's night. Chancellor, intent on saving the ambassador, took to the boat, placing him in it with seven of his compatriots. But it was swamped before reaching the shore ; the ambassador was saved, but the other seven Russians perished, together with Chancellor and several of the crew. It would appear that those who stuck by the ship saved their lives ; for the remaining nine of the ambassador's suite survived, as also did John Buckland, the master of the vessel. The hungry Scots of the coast plundered the wreck, not £500 worth of goods being ever recovered.

The death of Richard Chancellor was a great loss to his country. He had been successful as seaman, explorer, and diplomatist. His courage in face of misfortune on the first voyage and his admirable conduct at the court of the Czar had alone made the success of the new company possible, and entitle him to take a worthy place among the great Englishmen of his age.

As soon as the news of the wreck reached London the Company obtained letters from the queen to the Regent of Scotland, and dispatched Dr. Lawrence Hussey to conduct the ambassador to England and to recover the ship's cargo. Mary of Guise, the Regent, did her best to obtain restitution of the stolen goods, but her efforts were for the most part unavailing ; a few small packages of wax were given up by the poorer sort of Scots, ' but the jewels, rich apparel, presents, gold, silver, costly furs, and such like, were conveyed away, concealed and utterly embezzled'. Finding the business hopeless, Hussey set out with the ambassador, crossing the Border on February 18, 1557, and drawing near London on the 27th. The Czar's representative was accorded a most magnificent reception, entering London like a conquering king. Twelve miles out of the city he was met by eighty merchants in costly apparel and chains of gold, who conducted him to a house in the suburbs. Next day the members of the Russia Company, as it may now be called, to the number of 140, led him into the city. At the gates he was met by Lord Montague with 300 mounted men, representing the queen, and by the Lord Mayor and all the aldermen, who took him through crowded streets to his lodging in Fenchurch Street. At various points on the route he was the recipient of costly presents. Business was not immediately proceeded with, as it was necessary to await the arrival of King Philip from the Netherlands.

At length, on March 25, Osep Nepea had his first formal audience of their Majesties, and the negotiations for a treaty were commenced. It appears from a Venetian report—a source, however, which we have seen to be very untrustworthy in this connexion—that, besides discussing commercial matters, the ambassador requested a loan of artillery and ammunition for the Czar, and that the Swedish ambassador protested strongly, threatening war.[1] No trace of any military question appears in any other evidence as to the negotiations. Among the Cecil papers are some memoranda for a treaty with Russia.[2] The concessions proposed for the Muscovites were very similar to those granted by Ivan to the English; but, in fact, the treaty was rather ornamental than useful.

---

[1] *Venetian Cal.* vi, No. 852.   [2] *Cal. Cecil MSS.*, i, p. 146.

There was no necessity for it, for the simple reason that
no subjects of the Czar were likely to resort to London
for many a year to come.   Russia's sole outlets to the
ocean were at that time the shores of Lapland and the
White Sea ; her sailors were nothing more than fishermen, and their craft were quite unsuited for a voyage
to England, being for the most part undecked rowing-
boats ; while her merchants were landsmen and not
seamen, accustomed to carry their goods for immense
distances over the rivers and plains, but having none of
the knowledge or inclination requisite for a sea-borne
commerce.   Hence the intercourse between the two
countries was necessarily very one-sided, and the privileges
already granted by the Czar were all that was needed in
the shape of diplomatic regulation.   The real utility of
Osep Nepea's visit was to learn something of the power
and civilization of England, and to open up an inter-
change of civilities between the two courts.

An interesting glimpse of the Muscovite at Mary's
court is afforded by a letter from Josse de Courteville,
one of Philip's Flemings, to the President Viglius :

' Je tiens que vous aves esté adverty de l'arrivée du
Moscovitte en ce royaulme, que l'on dict estre passé par
la Mer Froide et que l'on tenoit innavigable.   La royne
l'a faict icy tarder jusques a l'arrivée du roy ; et aujour-
d'huy a-t-il esté mené vers Leurs Majestés, au droict
costel de l'evesque de Londres, accompagné de plusieurs
chevaliers de l'ordre et autres, accoustré, assez à la
turquesque, d'ung habillement long jusqu'en terre, de
velour pourfillé d'or, et sur la teste force pierreryes. . . .
Il y marchoit quatre de ses serviteurs devant luy, ac-
coustrés à l'advenant d'une mesme fachon, et deulx
derrière, qui portiont chascun ung fardeau que aucuns
disiont estre sables, aultres aultre chose, pour en faire

présent à Leurs Majestés. Et, comme je me voulus
enquérir du surplus, j'eus nouvelles du partement de ce
courier, qui ne me sembloit se debvoir oublier; et par
ainsy je suis forcé vous laisser le compte à demy.' [1]

The Company had prepared four ships for the Russian
voyage in the spring of 1557, three of which had already
been used in the voyages to the Guinea coast. They
were the *Primrose*, the *John Evangelist*, the *Anne*, and
the *Trinity*. In the first-named went as admiral Anthony
Jenkinson, who was henceforward to take a foremost
place in the exploration of Russia and Central Asia.
Osep Nepea also took passage in the *Primrose*, bearing
a letter from Philip and Mary to the Czar, together
with numerous costly presents for himself and his master.
Their Majesties' letter gave a summary of the commercial treaty which the ambassador had concluded, and
expressed the customary hopes of amity and good will
between the two nations. The Russian merchants—if
any should ever come to England—should have liberty
to come and go, and carry on their business in all parts
of the kingdom, selling their goods wholesale or retail
without impediment. While in England they should be
under the special protection of the queen, and should
be free from the payment of the taxes and dues which
all other foreigners had to pay. They might set up
warehouses in London and other cities. For their greater
security the Lord Chancellor should be assigned as their
judge and legal adviser, and should decide impartially all
disputes. The letter concluded by giving a testimonial to
the conduct and ability of Osep Nepea, who would be able
to describe at greater length the matters referred to.[2]

---

[1] *Brussels Archives*, Kervyn de Lettenhove, i, p. 61.
[2] *Cotton MSS.*, Nero, B viii, 3.

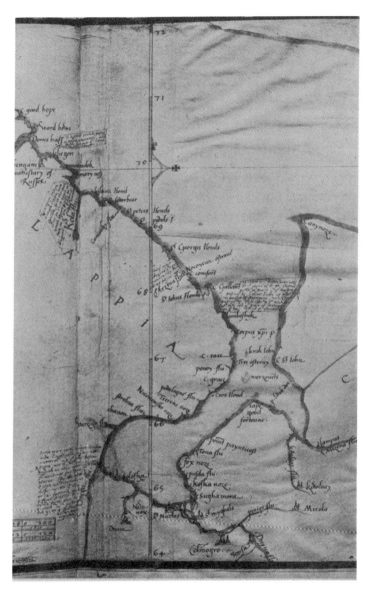

THE ENGLISH DISCOVERIES IN THE NORTH-EAST.
From William Borough's Chart of Northern Navigation,
Royal MS. 18 D. iii. 124.

With the departure of the ambassador and the arrival in Russia of Anthony Jenkinson, the story of the Russia Company enters on a new phase. The business of the Company, in spite of the maritime disasters of its early years, was now firmly established. It had three principal factories, at Colmogro, Vologda, and Moscow; and a third agent, Henry Lane, was sent out in 1557 to assist the two already appointed. Numerous subordinate merchants and apprentices were employed, and crafts-men of various kinds—rope-makers, coopers, skinners—were set to work at the establishments in Russia so that freight might be saved by exporting manufactured goods instead of raw material. A regular service of letters through Poland and Danzig was established.

After Stephen Borough's voyage in 1556 the search for the sea passage to Cathay was for a time discontinued, but the marvellous journeys of Anthony Jenkinson by land more than maintained the reputation of the Com-pany for the promotion of discovery. His adventures, however, and the further history of the Company, fall mainly in the reign of Queen Elizabeth and outside the scope of this work. One point deserves to be emphasized : King Philip, by giving his full countenance and support to the north-eastern discoveries, had tacitly admitted that the papal division of the globe was not by him considered as extending to the Arctic regions. Once the literal interpretation of the great bull was broken down, it was impossible to say where the line should be drawn, and the way was prepared for the retreat of Spain from an untenable position to the more reasonable one of maintaining her monopoly in the lands already colonized by her.

CHAPTER XIII

SHIPS AND MEN. ENGLISH PORTS

The fifteenth and sixteenth centuries witnessed great developments in English shipbuilding. In the former the feeble, untrustworthy vessels of the Middle Ages were improved and strengthened until they were sufficiently sound for regular voyages to all the waters of Europe, the Mediterranean included ; and in the latter an ocean-going type was evolved, capable of keeping the sea for weeks and months at a stretch, and of making such voyages as those of Drake and Cavendish, which constituted an astonishing advance on anything that had previously been possible.

At the commencement of this improvement in shipping England lagged far behind her competitors. The Venetians were regularly voyaging to the North Sea for at least two centuries before there was any established English trade to the Mediterranean. The Portuguese had commercial posts on the Guinea coast a hundred years before Wyndham sailed the first English vessel there ; and their successive advances on the route to India, spread over a long period of years and culminating in Vasco da Gama's arrival at Calicut in 1498, gave them a long start in the acquisition of the experience necessary to the advance of shipbuilding. Yet by the end of the sixteenth century the positions were reversed, and English ships were excelled by none in durability and handiness and general efficiency for the purposes for which they were designed.

It would seem that this rapid advance in excellence was largely due to the interest in the navy displayed by Tudor governments. The development of the warship preceded in most respects that of the merchantman; and, owing to the peculiar conditions of the time, every merchantman which was to be of use for anything beyond mere coasting had to be provided with some fighting gear. For distant voyages in fact, such as those to the Mediterranean, merchants preferred to charter a man-of-war from the State whenever one was available. Throughout the period in question England was exposed to constant wars or threatenings of war with France or Spain, with the result that the improvement of fighting-ships was vigorously pressed. The fleet became a leading care of the State to an extent never before dreamed of; and the mercantile marine, fostered by a system of bounties, shared in the general enlightenment, and steadily extended the scope of its activities to the accompaniment of an unprecedented advance in the construction of ships and the study of all things pertaining to shipping.

Mediaeval vessels fall largely into two classes : the long, low and narrow galley; and the short, broad, almost basin-shaped sailing-ship, propelled usually by a single square sail. In northern waters the galley, common until the twelfth century, gradually gave place to the sailing-ship, on which all progress was concentrated, so that by the close of the Middle Ages the oared vessel was practically extinct outside the Mediterranean. In that sea, however, natural conditions were more favourable to the galley, which survived side by side with the sailing-vessel and which, although costing more in working expenses, was preferred for its swiftness and reliability.

In England the first great improvement of the mediaeval sailing-ship consisted in fitting two or more masts in place of the one which had hitherto been considered sufficient. The exact date of this advance is unknown, but it probably occurred before the beginning of the fifteenth century, when the increasing frequency of voyages to Bordeaux and Iceland began to demand more navigable vessels for their safe accomplishment. A natural concomitant of this change was an increase of length and a modification of the extreme basin-shape of the single-masted cogs, which were only suited for short, fair-wind trips across the narrow seas to France or Flanders. At some time also in the same century occurred the introduction of the lateen sail in place of the square sail on the aftermost mast of the ship. This device doubtless came from the Mediterranean, where small craft were fitted exclusively with such sails.

A modification in the shape of the hull, which was destined to be of long enduring influence, was due to the needs of warfare. In early vessels there was no raised poop or forecastle, but the deck ran in unbroken sweep from prow to stern, at which extremities the timbers of the side curved upwards to a point. For fighting purposes it became customary to fit such ships with raised platforms or castles, built on temporarily at either end, and occupied by archers, slingers, and stone-throwing engines. The latter, from such a high vantage-point, could do great execution on an enemy's decks and could, moreover, assist in repelling boarders from the waist of their own vessel. The efficacy of the new departure was speedily proved, and it became permanently incorporated into the design. Ships were now built with a strong square forecastle and 'summercastle', as the after-edifice was named, as integral parts of the structure. The additional weight thus placed at either end necessitated an increase of length to avoid excessive pitching. The pitching motion was nevertheless very severe, as was proved when a full-sized model of Columbus's caravel, the *Santa Maria*, was sailed across the Atlantic in 1893.[1]

In a late fifteenth-century manuscript in the British Museum,[2] the author of which died in 1491, there are numerous illustrations of ships which may be taken as representing the state of marine construction at the opening of the Tudor period. On folio 5 is a drawing of a sailing-ship, probably the type of vessel with which the longer voyages, such as those to Bordeaux or Spain, were made. She has a platform-shaped forecastle, not of excessive height, and a long poop sloping upwards towards the stern. The masts are three in number, the foremast being very short and the mainmast twice its height. Each of these is intended to carry one square sail, although the mainsail only is shown. The mizen-mast is short and carries one lateen sail. There is a bowsprit but no sprit-sail such as was afterwards used. None of the drawings in this manuscript shows any signs of a sprit-sail yard on the bowsprit; and it is possible that they had not been introduced at that date, although they were in use before the close of the century. The same may be said of top-sails and topmasts; they occur

[1] See *Ancient and Modern Ships*, by Sir G. C. V. Holmes, for an account of this model.
[2] *Cotton MSS.*, Jul., E iv. 6.

nowhere in these drawings, but they were certainly fitted
to warships built for Henry VII not long after his
accession. The drawing on f. 5 has been frequently
reproduced, but generally so badly as to make it appear
that the ship has only two masts instead of three.

On f. 25 of the same manuscript is a very clear drawing
showing a large ship in harbour with sails furled. This
vessel has a short, high forecastle and a long poop rising
in two tiers. The bowsprit and foremast are short. The
mainmast is high and very thick, while there are two
mizen-masts each with a yard for a lateen sail. When
two mizen-masts were fitted to a ship the foremost was
called the main mizen and the aftermost the bonaventure
mizen. This is the earliest drawing showing a four-
masted ship which has been met with. On the other side
of the sheet (f. 25b) the same vessel is shown in a storm
at sea. There are guns on deck in the waist and a row
of oval openings in the poop and forecastle which are evidently intended for ports for smaller pieces. On f. 18b
is a representation of a sea fight, one ship engaging two
others at close quarters. Long-bows, cross-bows, spears,
and stones are the principal weapons used ; and marksmen
are placed in the tops to sweep the enemy's decks. The
mainmasts, and occasionally the other masts, of ships
of the time were fitted with circular tops for fighting and
look-out purposes, and large enough for two or three
men to stand in. At a later period small guns were
mounted in them. All the vessels in this manuscript
show an immense advance on the old mediaeval cog, and
indicate the great improvements which had been going
on during the fifteenth century.

As was natural during a period of more extended
voyages, the size of merchant ships tended to increase.

WARSHIP, c. 1485.
From Cott. MS. Jul. E. iv. 6, f. 25.

Nine vessels trading between England and Spain in the
time of Henry VII, of which the tonnage is mentioned
in the State papers, show an average of 142 tons, the
largest being 220 tons. The Italians generally built
their ships larger than this, and, although we read that
in 1488 there was no ship of 1,000 tons in Venice, the
reference seems to imply that ships of that size were by
no means unknown. The statements as to tonnage must,
however, be taken as of very loose application, the same
ship being sometimes given as 50 per cent. or more larger
than at others. The *Henry Grace à Dieu*, for example,
Henry VIII's great warship, varies between 1,000 and
1,500 tons, and the *Mary Rose*, which was of 400 tons
when built, is described as of 600 three years later. In
English ships the unit of measurement was the tun of
Bordeaux wine, which contained 252 gallons and occupied
about 60 cubic feet of space.[1] When there was a question
of hiring merchantmen for war purposes, for which
payment was made by the ton, the owner's estimate was
apt to differ considerably from that of the government.
In the French war of 1512–13 the navy lists contain
numbers of merchantmen whose tonnage varies so
astonishingly as to suggest that their hulls were capable
of inflation and deflation like balloons.

The cost of building ships was very low in comparison
with modern figures, although it rose rapidly with the
influx of gold from America in the sixteenth century.
Two small warships, the *Mary Fortune* and the *Sweepstake*, were built for Henry VII at a cost of £110 and £120
respectively.[2] At the opening of Henry VIII's reign the
Mary Rose, 400 tons, and the *Peter Pomegranate*, 300,

---

[1] Oppenheim, *Administration of the Navy*, p. 30.
[2] Ibid., *Naval Accounts and Inventories*, Introd., p. xxvii.

together cost £1,016 fully equipped for sea ;[1] while the *Henry Grace à Dieu*, the largest ship of her time, cost £8,708 in 1514.[2] Privately owned ships were chartered by the State at 3*d.* per ton per week.

A French manuscript of 1519[3] affords some information as to the shipping of that date. It is a translation in French of Caesar's wars, to illustrate which a large map of France is provided as a frontispiece. Following the contemporary custom, the cartographer has inserted drawings of ships in the surrounding seas. One of these, placed near the mouth of the Garonne, represents a large merchantman. She has a curved stem and rounded, swelling bows, shaped like a bellying sail and surmounted by a flat, platform-shaped forecastle which overhangs the water. The waist has greater freeboard than that of a warship, and the poop is small and square. No guns are visible, and the hull is evidently designed for stability and carrying capacity rather than speed and fighting convenience. There are three pole masts, each with a round top and one square sail. There are no topmasts and no bowsprit. Three other sailing-ships are shown on the same map. Their hulls are of the same type as the one already described, but they have only one mast each. As this was a work dealing with ancient history it is probable that the artist purposely drew the oldest-fashioned craft he was acquainted with. He had some archaeological instinct, as is evident from the semi-Roman costumes which appear in other illustrations ; and he recognized that it would be inappropriate to place guns in the ships, not one of which possesses them. If this

---

[1] R. O., *Warrants for Issues*, 1 Hen. VIII, No. 121.
[2] Oppenheim, *Administration of Royal Navy*, p. 53.
[3] *Harl. MSS.*, 6205.

view is correct the manuscript is interesting as providing one of the many lost connecting links between the mediaeval and modern types of sailing-ship. Robert Thorne's map of 1527, appended to his book to Dr. Lee, bears a spirited drawing of a sailing-vessel approximating more to the man-of-war type. She has a square, overhanging forecastle, a low waist, and a high, narrow poop. The fore and main masts are lofty, and are each provided with top-sails, while the short mizen has one lateen sail. It is not apparent whether this was intended to represent an English or Spanish vessel. Thorne was an Englishman, but the drawing was made at Seville and is placed in a part of the ocean to which no English ship had then penetrated.

One more example of the none too numerous drawings of merchantmen may be quoted. In a *Book of Hydrography* designed in 1542 by a Frenchman, John Rotz, for Henry VIII,[1] occur numerous beautifully painted maps embracing all parts of the world. On one, representing the North Atlantic, a merchant vessel is seen near the coast of Portugal. The hull, evidently built for carrying capacity, is on very full lines, and the fore and after castles are small in proportion. The mainmast carries two sails, but the fore and mizen masts have only one each, that on the latter being a lateen. There is a bowsprit but no sprit-sail. This may possibly represent a Portuguese carrack of the type with which they voyaged to the East Indies. Such vessels were subsequently developed to (for that time) an enormous size. One captured by the English in 1592, named the *Madre de Dios*, was of 1,600 tons burden.

---

[1] *Royal MSS.*, 20 E ix.

The facts considered above serve to indicate that, although little is known with exactitude about the merchant vessels of early Tudor times, it is at least certain that they were by no means identical in design with the warships. The latter, as will be seen, mounted large numbers of guns—over 100 in many cases—and this fact influenced their design to an extent quite unnecessary in trading craft, which were far less heavily armed. The principal features in the development of the latter from their mediaeval prototypes were : increasing length, relatively small size of the ' castles ', and an increasing number of sails and spars, together with the introduction of topmasts.

The ship's boats were usually three in number, the ' great boat ', the long-boat, and the skiff or jolly-boat. They were probably carried on deck in the waist, and must have been hoisted by tackles from the yard-arms, since davits were not then used for the purpose. The great boat was often towed. Hakluyt gives an account of a voyage to the Mediterranean by the *Matthew Gonson* in 1535, as narrated by one of the crew. He says that they towed their great boat all the way from Chios to the Straits of Gibraltar, implying that she was then hoisted aboard. As this boat was big enough to carry ten tuns of water it is difficult to imagine how it was done.

Although, as we have seen, four-masted ships were known long before the end of the fifteenth century, the merchantman of Tudor times was usually equipped with three. In short vessels the masts were rigged in a fan-shape, the foremast inclining forwards, the mainmast upright, and the mizen raking towards the rear so as to give greater distance between the sails. The latter tended to increase in number, the use of top-sails and

TWO MERCHANTMEN.

1. From Robert Thorne's map, 1527.   2. From
Harl. MS. 6205, date 1519.

sprit-sails beneath the bowsprit becoming common in the reign of Henry VII. An additional spar, projecting from the stern of the ship in the same manner as the bowsprit from the bow, and named the ' outligger ', was fitted to receive the sheet of the lateen sail on the mizen-mast. With top-sails, topmasts were introduced, but the latter were fixtures in the sixteenth century and not strikeable at sea. To diminish rolling in heavy weather it was customary to lower the main- and fore-yards down to the deck, as is depicted in various drawings. Top-gallant-masts and sails were fitted to warships—the *Henry Grace à Dieu* had them on three of her four masts—but it does not appear that any merchant ship had them until a much later date. Although there is some evidence that reefing was known in very early times, it was not extensively practised at the period in question. The purpose of reefing is to reduce the sail area in high winds, but among Tudor seamen a contrary device was favoured. The sails were cut smaller than the maximum size possible, and were lengthened in light winds by lacing to their lower borders additional pieces called bonnets. As many as three bonnets were sometimes supplied for one sail,[1] but two was the more usual number. They were applied to the main- and fore-sails and also to top-sails.[2] Jibs and stay-sails, and fore-and-aft rigging generally, were entirely unknown at this time, the nearest approach to any such thing being the lateen. In consequence it was much harder than at present to make headway against contrary winds, as an example of which the difficulty invariably experienced by English traders in

---

[1] Inventory of the *Sovereign* : Oppenheim, *Naval Accounts and Inventories*, p. 210.
[2] Robert Thorne's drawing, 1527, shows a bonnet on main-topsail.

getting away from the Guinea coast may be cited. The shape of the hulls was such as to offer great resistance to the wind, and the leeway must have been excessive. Towards the middle of the century, when the size of the forecastle had somewhat diminished, it would seem that it was possible to heave the ship to without showing any sail at all : Sir Hugh Willoughby's journal, describing the gale encountered off the Norwegian coast, says, '. . . the wind increasing so sore that we were not able to bear any sail, but took them in, and lay a drift, to the end to let the storm over pass '.

More distant voyages demanded a long-overdue improvement in the science of navigation. The finding of latitude was rendered a comparatively simple matter by the successive inventions of the astrolabe, the cross-staff, and the quadrant.[1] The astrolabe, which came into use prior to the age of the great discoveries, remained in favour throughout the sixteenth century, being described by Martin Cortes in his *Breve Compendio de la Sphera* in 1556. An astrolabe which was used by Sir Francis Drake is preserved in the museum at Greenwich. Cortes's astrolabe consisted of a metal ring, of which 90 degrees were graduated, and a metal pointer turning on a pin in the centre. The pointer had aperture sights at either end, and when moved until the sun could be seen through both apertures it indicated his elevation above the horizon in degrees on the graduated part of the ring.[2] The cross-staff was invented early in the sixteenth cen-

[1] For information on this subject see Laird Clowes, *History of the Navy*, i, chap. xiii.
[2] For detailed description of method of making and using an astrolabe, see Cortes, *Breve Compendio de la Sphera y de la Arte de Navegar*, chap. viii.

tury, but never entirely superseded the astrolabe until both were rendered obsolete by the quadrant, an invention of John Davis at the end of the same century. With these instruments latitude was ascertainable· with fair accuracy ; in skilful hands the error was usually less than one degree. The same could not be said about longitude, in which huge errors were unavoidable by any method then known. Longitude remained then and long afterwards an insoluble problem, and many charts of the time made no effort to indicate it.

Of contemporary foreign vessels the most interesting is the caravel, as being the type with which Columbus made his great voyages across the Atlantic, and which had a considerable influence on the design of the Tudor man-of-war. The caravel, which the Spaniards found most suitable for their early ocean navigations, had little in common with the short, broad merchantmen of the narrow seas. It was built with a high, tapering poop, a low waist, and a high, overhanging forecastle, rectangular in plan, and serving to break the force of a head sea. The high castles and general handiness of design rendered it an efficient fighting vessel, and it was probable, as Mr. Oppenheim has pointed out, that it was for this reason that Henry VII was eager to employ such craft in preference to English-built ships on the rare occasions when he needed to mobilize a naval force.[1] But the caravel, probably as lacking sufficient cargo capacity, did not find favour with English shipbuilders, and as late as 1552 was still distinctively a foreign type. In that year the London merchants who sent out Thomas Wyndham on a trading voyage to Barbary bought a Portuguese caravel of 60 tons to form part of his squadron. The inhabitants

[1] *Naval Accounts and Inventories*, Introduction, p. xxi.

of the Canary Isles, recognizing from a distance that she was not an English ship, made an attack on the expedition as they concluded that she had been wrongfully acquired.

The carrack, unlike the caravel, is not an easily identifiable type, and the word seems to have been applied to any large and bulky vessel. In one navy list the *Henry Grace à Dieu* appears as the 'Imperyall (or Gret) Carrick ',[1] but this is exceptional, and the term was generally used only of foreign ships. In its particular application, if it can be said to have had one, it signified first the trading-ships of Genoa,[2] which ceased to come to England after the fifteenth century, and afterwards the great East Indiamen of the Portuguese. The act granting tonnage and poundage in 1485 provides that if an Englishman ship his goods in a 'carryke or galley ' he shall pay the same duties as a foreigner. The carracks in this case meant Genoese, and the galleys Venetian, vessels.

Another non-English ship was the hulk, the large, clumsy merchantman of the Hanse towns. William Towerson, sailing for Guinea in January 1558, captured two 'hulks of Dantzick ' in the Bay of Biscay. They made no attempt at resistance against his three vessels, and were released as not worth keeping by reason of their poor sailing qualities : ' they sailed so ill that, having all their sails abroad, we kept them company only with our foresails, and without any topsails abroad, so that in every two days sailing they would have hindered us more than one '—which seems to argue that the Germans built

[1] *Letters and Papers*, i, No. 3591.

[2] In Laird Clowes's *History of the Navy*, i. 413, there is an illustration of a Genoese carrack from a drawing said to have been made in 1452 ; but it has every appearance of being at least a century later in date.

TWO CARRACKS.

1. From Royal MS. 20. E. ix.   2. From
Add. MS. 5415. A. 7.

their ships solely with an eye to capacity. Henry VIII
hired several hulks from the Hansa for use against the
French in 1545. His fighting instructions for an antici-
pated action in that year directed that they should be
placed in the front line and used to break up the order
of the enemy before the onset of the men-of-war in the
second line.[1]

Turning to warships, we find ourselves on much surer
ground. Detailed inventories exist of several of the
crack ships of Henry VII and Henry VIII, and carefully
executed drawings of the same period are numerous.[2]
In the evolution of the warship the paramount factor
was the rapid development of artillery. The guns
mounted in ships were at first small and of little penetra-
tive power. Consequently it was essential to place them
where they could do the greatest execution on an enemy's
decks and against his rigging. The tactical idea in the
use of the gun was mainly to employ it in the same way
as the long-bow and the cross-bow ; to kill the enemy's
crew rather than to sink his ship. Hence we find in the
warships of Henry VII large numbers of ' serpentines ',
small guns weighing about three hundredweight and
throwing a half-pound ball, grouped in the castles of the
ship, which were built very high to accommodate them in
two or three tiers. At the same time a few heavier guns,
throwing stone balls, were placed in the waist. These
were too low down to reach the greater part of the hostile
deck at close quarters, and must therefore have been fired
at the hull. The collective weight of all these guns was

[1] *Cal. of Le Fleming MSS.*, p. 8.
[2] See Oppenheim's *Naval Accounts and Inventories of Henry VII* ;
inventory of the *Henry Grace à Dieu* in the same author's *Administration
of the Navy* ; drawings of warships in *Add. MSS.*, 22047 ; *Archaeologia*,
vi. 208 ; Volpe's picture at Hampton Court, &c.

very great and, to secure stability and structural strength, the ship's sides had to be sloped inwards from the water-line so that the weight should be more centrally carried. This ' tumblehome ' in high-built ships was so great that the width of the deck on poop and forecastle was often less than half the width at the water-line. It served another purpose in rendering boarding more difficult, for, even if two vessels were touching at the water-line, their decks were necessarily several feet apart. The most easily accessible part was the waist, which was defended by nettings and by guns placed in the castles on purpose to sweep it with ' hail shot ', the forerunner of grape and canister.

The armament of the *Sovereign*, built in 1488, was as follows : [1] In the forecastle, above deck, 16 serpentines, and below deck, 24 ; in the poop, 20 serpentines ; in the ' somercastle ' (apparently a quarter-deck, one stage lower than the poop), above deck, 25 serpentines, below deck, 21 together with 11 stone guns ; in the waist, 20 stone guns ; in the stern, over the rudder, 4 serpentines. Total, 110 serpentines and 31 stone guns. The *Regent*, built about the same time, was most likely a larger vessel, as she carried 225 guns. In her case their distribution is not known.

Although Henry VII had these two first-class warships built, he did not maintain a large navy, and at his death there were apparently only seven royal ships.[2] His successor, bent on a more adventurous foreign policy, began to strengthen the fleet from the very commence-

---

[1] *Naval Accounts and Inventories*, pp. 216–17. The armament here given is that mounted in 1497 when the ship was chartered for a voyage to the Levant by some merchants of London.

[2] *Administration of the Royal Navy*, p. 35.

ment of his reign. The *Mary Rose* and the *Peter Pome-granate* were built in 1510, and the *Henry Grace à Dieu* was laid down at the end of 1512 to replace the *Regent*, burnt in action off Brest earlier in that year.

An incident which took place in April 1513 probably had a great effect on the armament of the *Henry Grace à Dieu*. The English fleet was blockading the French in Brest and seeking in vain for some means of bringing the enemy to action. As a reinforcement a squadron of six French galleys was ordered round from the Mediterranean under the command of a brave and able officer named Prégent de Bidoux. Three of these galleys, according to contemporary letters, were armed with one heavy gun each, obtained from the Venetians, and of such a size as had never before been seen in France. It was asserted that a single shot from such a gun would be sufficient to send any ship to the bottom. The boast was soon, to a great extent, substantiated. Arriving off Brest on April 22, Prégent made a bold dash through the blockading fleet and succeeding in getting into Blanc Sablons Bay. In the process his formidable guns sank one English ship outright and crippled another, striking her through in seven places so that there was great difficulty in keeping her afloat. This was a minimum estimate of the damage, as admitted by the English themselves; a neutral account stated that two ships were sunk, and Prégent himself claimed to have destroyed four large ships and two transports, which was certainly a gross exaggeration.[1]

---

[1] A. Spont, *Letters and Papers relating to the French War*, 1512–13, pp. 51, 52, 133, 140, 146. This work is a collection from all sources of original documents concerning the war.

As far as can be traced, this is the first occasion on which a ship is recorded to have been sunk by gun fire.

The construction of the *Henry Grace à Dieu* could not
at this date have been at a very advanced stage, since she
was not ready for sea until June 1514 ; and it is fair to
assume that the demonstration of the effectiveness of
a few heavy guns provided by the above action was
responsible for the mounting of several such in the *Henry*.
Be that as it may, the tendency was henceforward to
reduce the number of light pieces carried in the upper
works of a ship and to transfer the weight of armament
to a hard-hitting battery placed on the level of the waist
and in a fighting deck below the waist. The *Henry Grace
à Dieu* is the first ship known to have been provided with
a tier of guns below the main deck. She was armed in
1514 with 136 small guns, and the following heavier pieces,
the exact dimensions of some of which are not ascertainable : stone guns, 4 ; ' great pieces of iron of one making
and bigness,' 12 ; ' great iron guns of one sort that come
out of Flanders,' 4 ; ' great Spanish pieces of iron of
one sort,' 2 ; stone guns on wheels, 18 ; miscellaneous
large guns, 4 ; great brass culverins, 2 ; a great brass
bombard on four wheels ; and a great brass curtall on
four wheels : total, 48 heavy guns.[1] It is doubtful
whether the stone guns should be ranked as heavy
weapons. They were evidently larger than serpentines,
to judge from their position in the *Sovereign's* armament
already described ; but it is unlikely that they were
identical with the ' canon petro ' of the latter half of the
century, which fired a 26 lb. shot. They were probably
in 1514 medium-sized pieces, and if we deduct them from
the above total, the undoubtedly heavy guns of the *Henry*
numbered 26. The culverin was of 5½ inches calibre,

[1] Chapter House Book xiii, printed in *Administration of the Royal Navy*,
pp. 372–81.

and threw an 18 lb. ball ; according to a paper of 1513 the weight of the shot fired by the curtall was 60 lb., while the missile of the bombard was of 260 lb. and required a charge of 80 lb. of powder.[1] It is somewhat hard to believe that the *Henry* ever used such a gun at sea ; and in another list of almost the same date the bombard is omitted.[2] By the end of the reign the *Henry* had been re-armed, her heavy guns then numbering 19, and consisting of 4 cannon, 3 demi-cannon, 4 culverins, 2 demi-culverins, 2 cannon-petro, and 4 sakers.[3] The weight of shot ranged from 60 lb. for the cannon down to 6 lb. for the saker.

The same policy of reducing the number of guns, increasing their weight, and carrying them lower, was pursued in the case of other ships built during the reign, with the consequence that the excessive height of the castles was no longer necessary ; and after 1540 several vessels were built practically flush-decked. These ships, which varied from 150 to 300 tons, were described as galleys, but the word was not intended in its usual sense. They were fully-rigged sailing-ships and, although they may have been occasionally assisted by the use of sweeps, it was not their principal means of propulsion. They probably owed the name to their speed and handiness as compared with the high-built, older-fashioned vessels. An illustration [4] of one of them, the *Tiger*, built in 1546, appears as the frontispiece of Oppenheim's *Administration of the Royal Navy*. She carries about twenty large guns, of which fourteen are placed on the broadsides below the main deck. The king himself was

---

[1] *Letters and Papers*, i, No. 5108.   [2] Ibid., No. 4968.
[3] Pepysian MS. printed in *Archaeologia*, vi. 216.
[4] From *Add. MSS.*, 22047.

greatly interested in the efforts made to improve warships. The following extract from a letter of Chapuys, an eminently reliable authority, demonstrates his responsibility for the innovation just described :

'The King has sent to Italy for three shipwrights experienced in the art of constructing galleys, but I fancy he will not make much use of their science, as for some time back he has been building ships with oars according to a model of which he himself is the inventor.'[1]

The smaller examples of this class were known as ' rowbarges '. They did good service against the French galleys in the war of 1544–6, and were used for policing the Channel in times of peace. They are thus described by Martin du Bellay, a contemporary French writer :

' Il y a une espèce de navires particulières dont usoyent noz ennemis, en forme plus longue que ronde, et plus estroitte beaucoup que les gallères, pour mieux se régir et commander aux courantes, qui sont ordinaires en ceste mer ; à quoy les hommes sont si duits, qu'avec ces vaisseaux ils contendent de vitesse avec les gallères, et les nomment remberges.'

In the larger ships the type of hull gradually developed into that familiar in numerous pictures of the Armada period : low forecastle, very little higher than the waist, and moderately high poop, the guns being mounted on the main deck and in one or more fighting decks below it. This build, although increased in size, remained substantially unaltered in its main proportions until the middle of the eighteenth century.

Although the hulls of ships were undergoing great modifications, the style of rigging warships remained

[1] *Spanish Cal.* vi, part i, p. 342. July 1541.

practically unchanged during the period under review. The *Sovereign* of 1488 had four masts, the fore and main having topmasts and top-sails, and the mizen and bonaventure mizen being rigged with one lateen sail each. A sprit-sail was carried under the bowsprit. The *Sovereign* was in all respects an excellent ship, and probably in advance of the general standard of her time. As late as 1525, when her timbers were old and rotten, the authorities were recommended to have her rebuilt because ' the form of this ship is so marvellous goodly that great pity it were she should die '.[1] Apparently the advice was not carried out, for she disappears from view about this time. The *Henry Grace à Dieu* carried topmasts and topgallantmasts and three sails on the fore-, main-, and mizen-masts, and a topmast and two sails on the bonaventure mizen ; also a sprit-sail under the bowsprit, which, for practical purposes, was a fifth mast.[2] But the *Henry* was exceptional in most respects, and the rigging of the *Sovereign* became the standard type for sixteenth-century warships.

The great picture at Hampton Court depicting the embarkation of Henry VIII at Dover in 1520 shows the *Henry* and several warships of the time, but the technical accuracy of the artist is open to great doubt. Five ships appear on a large scale, and their hulls are all so suspiciously alike that they suggest the idea that they were all drawn from the same original. The only differences are in a few minor details of carving and colouring. Two of the ships carry four masts and the remainder three ; and it is noticeable that not a single lateen sail is shown in the whole fleet, the mizen-masts having square sails like the fore and main. This is almost certainly

---

[1] *Letters and Papers*, iv, No. 1714.   [2] Inventory.

incorrect.[1] Such guns as can be seen are arranged in precisely the same way in every case, and the whole picture gives the impression that the artist was drawing conventional ships without much study of the real thing, and was concentrating his care on the numerous gorgeously dressed individuals who are seen on the decks and in the foreground.

The fighting record of the *Henry Grace à Dieu* is not particularly brilliant. She was completed just too late to take part in the war of 1512-14. In 1522 war was again declared against France, and she was sent to sea in the fleet commanded by Sir William Fitz-William. He reported that she sailed as well and rather better than any ship in the fleet, weathering them all save the *Mary Rose*; and, although it was only the beginning of June, he went on to talk about laying her up for the winter. She was evidently something of a nuisance, and the admiral was anxious to be rid of her. There had been so much boasting about this marvellous ship that the French were certain to make her the especial object of their attacks, and the king would have been furious if she had been lost. On June 8 she lost her bowsprit, foremast, and maintopmast in a gale in the Downs, and a week later was brought round to Portsmouth to be laid up. Special precautions were to be taken against a French raid; two barks were kept scouting round the Isle of Wight, assisted by an elaborate system of beacons, sentinels, &c. Later on 1,000 marks were spent on a dock and fortifications for the *Henry* at Portsmouth, and it

---

[1] A careful reading of the available inventories supports the idea that square sails were not at this period carried on the mizen-masts. The sails on fore and main are described as fitted with two sheets, while those on the mizen had but one.

THE HENRY GRACE À DIEU.

From a MS. at Magdalene College, Cambridge.

does not appear that she went to sea in 1523, after which year the war was virtually over.[1] In 1526, when laid up at Northfleet, it was reported that she was costing £200 a year in wages alone, and more than that in cables, hawsers, and other stores, and that a dock would have to be built at a cost of £600.[2] The next war was that of 1544–6. In the former year the naval operations were unimportant, and the *Henry* took no part in them ; but in 1545 an immense French fleet was collected in the Channel, and for a time England lost the command of the sea. The English fleet was concentrated at Portsmouth, the *Henry Grace à Dieu* being the flagship. The king was dining on board when, on July 19, the approach of the French was signalled. Indecisive fighting at long range took place, and the French then withdrew. Another cannonade, with the like result, took place off the Sussex coast on August 15, and with this the war services of the *Henry* concluded. She was accidentally burnt at Deptford in 1553. Her career was typical of those of most of the large fighting ships of the time. All of them, both English and French, were considered too valuable to be committed to a decisive action, or to be sent to sea in any but the finest weather ; and such exploits as were performed went to the credit of lighter and more easily handled craft.

In the wars of this period the French galleys on more than one occasion proved exceedingly useful to their side ; but all attempts to popularize this type of vessel in England were failures. As has been explained, the numerous craft so described in the navy lists were for the most part not true galleys, but light sailing ships. In

[1] *Letters and Papers*, iii, Nos. 2302, 2308, 2320, 2355, &c.
[2] Ibid., iv, No. 2635.

1544, however, a galley was constructed on Mediterranean lines and named the *Galley Subtile* or *Row Galley*.
She was of 200 tons, carried a crew of 250, and mounted
31 guns.[1] A drawing in the British Museum shows her
fitted with a pointed beak or ram, and one mast with
a huge lateen sail. She served on the Scottish coast in
1544, when Edinburgh was sacked, and in the actions
against the French in the following year.

Artillery in the sixteenth century was in a state of
transition. Originally, after first rudimentary experi-
ments with wood, ropes, and leather, guns were built
up by binding longitudinal strips of metal into cylin-
drical form with numerous metal rings, on the principle
of the construction of a cask. Guns made in this way
were mounted in Henry VII's warships, and the system
continued in vogue until the latter half of the century.
At the same time cast-brass and cast-iron guns were beginning to be made abroad ; many of them were imported
into England, and they were used in forts and ships side
by side with the built-up guns.

Practically all the larger pieces for sea use were loaded at
the breach. The method consisted in having a detachable
section, from one to two feet long, called the chamber,
which was taken off the remainder of the barrel to be
loaded. When charged with powder the chamber was
replaced at the rear end of the barrel and fixed in position
by a wooden wedge hammered in between it and a pro-
jection on the carriage of the gun, the shot having been
previously placed in the barrel itself. The gun was then
fired by means of a linstock and priming powder scattered
over the touch hole. Three chambers were supplied
with each gun in the time of Henry VII, but the number

[1] Laird Clowes, *Royal Navy*, i. 421.

was afterwards reduced to two. The indistinct accounts of naval encounters give the impression that the rate of fire was not nearly so rapid as might have been expected, and the breech-loading system was rapidly displaced by muzzle-loaders towards the end of the sixteenth century. A large built-up breech-loader, recovered by divers in 1836 from the wreck of the *Mary Rose* (1545), is to be seen at the United Services Museum in Whitehall.

Guns of cast brass were said by ancient authorities not to have been made in England until 1521, nor cast iron until 1543, but these dates are probably much too late. In 1516 payment of £33 6s. 8d. was made to John Rutter of London ' for hurts and damages by him sustained in a tenement to him belonging, wherein the King's great gun called the Basiliscus was cast '.[1] If a great gun could be cast in England in 1516 it is reasonable to suppose that some experience had first been gained in casting smaller ones. The wrought guns of this period were embedded in solid elm carriages and fastened down by iron rings ; but several cast metal examples exist which were fitted with trunnions in the modern fashion.

During the war of 1512–14 the Government purchased large numbers of guns at home and abroad. Humphrey Walker, an English gun-maker, supplied fifty pieces in 1512. The principal foreign place of manufacture was Mechlin, where Hans Popenruyter turned out heavy weapons in great quantities. He delivered twenty-four curtalls weighing about $1\frac{1}{4}$ tons each in 1512, also twenty-four serpentines averaging about $\frac{1}{2}$ ton. The individual guns were all of slightly different weights and were all named with such appellations as The Sun Arising,

---

[1] *Letters and Papers*, ii. 1472.

Virago, Mermaid, Rat, Snake, Dragon, &c.[1] The heavier
weapons were for land service, and assisted at the sieges
of Tournay and Terouenne in 1513.

A paper of 1513[2] gives some interesting information
about the various classes of guns in use : A minion fired
an 8 lb. shot ; a lizard, a 12 lb. ditto, with 14 lb. of
powder ; culverins, 'novemburghs', and apostles were
20-pounders ; while a curtall fired a 60 lb. and a bombard
a 260 lb. missile. The latter could only be fired five
times a day, presumably on account of over-heating.
The rates of fire of the others were very slow, none of
them exceeding forty times a day. The powder was
largely purchased abroad, although some was made in
England ; it cost 3½d. or 4d. a pound, and was of very
poor quality. A Venetian description of England in
1557 mentions that there were then 600 iron and 250
brass guns in the Tower.[3] Since the private ownership
of cannon was not encouraged, this fact goes far to
explain the non-success of all rebellions against the
Tudor throne.

The crews both of warships and merchantmen were
much more numerous in proportion to the size of the ship
than they have since become. Many improvements
tending to greater manageability were then unthought of.
On long voyages also, allowance had to be made for
serious sickness and mortality, which was almost invariably
experienced. The *Matthew Gonson* of 300 tons, which
voyaged to the Levant in 1535, carried 100 men, and it
was recorded as remarkable that only one died. On
tropical voyages, such as those to Guinea in the reign of
Mary, it sometimes happened that more than half the

[1] *Letters and Papers*, i, p. 464.　　　[2] Ibid., p. 716.
[3] *Venetian Cal.* vi, App. No. 171.

crew never returned. Overcrowding and poorness of
the victuals were partly responsible. The food supplied
in English warships consisted only of biscuit, beef, fish,
and beer, and it is unlikely that merchantmen were
better found. A French victualling list, however, is
somewhat more varied, including biscuit, fresh bread,
flour, cider, beer, wine, salt and fresh flesh, mutton,
bacon, butter, peas, fish, and verjuice.[1] The wages in
1512 were as follows : Admiral, 10s. per day ; captain,
18d. per day ; lodesman (pilot), 20s. per month ; sailors,
5s. per month and 5s. worth of victuals.[2] The subordinate
officers were paid the same as the sailors and, in addition,
divided among themselves a number of ' deadshares '
proportionate to the size of the ship. In merchant
vessels private trading by all members of the crew, at any
rate on long voyages, was a recognized custom, and they
were allowed a certain amount of space in the hold for
their goods. It is referred to in the charter granted by
Henry VII to the Bristol syndicate in 1501, in the accounts
of the Guinea voyages, and in the instructions to Sir Hugh
Willoughby in 1553.

A large trading-ship was commanded by a captain,
appointed by the merchants owning the cargo, and
having general control over the conduct of the voyage,
the ports of call, dates of sailing, &c, and by the master,
who navigated the ship and controlled the crew. The
captain was not necessarily a professional seaman, as the
master, of course, invariably was. The composition of
the crews in a well-found merchant fleet is illustrated
by Hakluyt's account of Willoughby's expedition. In
addition to the officers above mentioned, the *Edward
Bonaventure*, the largest ship, carried a master's mate,

---

[1] Spont, p. 179.   [2] *Letters and Papers*, i, p. 344.

a minister, a master gunner and his mate, two gunners, a surgeon, a boatswain and his mate, four quarter-masters, a steward and his mate, a cook, a cooper and a carpenter, together with twenty-one sailors. Most merchantmen also carried a purser. The *Matthew Gonson*, in the voyage already referred to, had six gunners and four trumpeters. The officers of the Tudor merchant service were recruited from the more educated seamen, or from boys who went to sea as ' gromals ' or pages, the equivalent of the modern apprentice. Sebastian Cabot's instructions for the North-East voyage enjoin that the boys are ' to be brought up according to the laudable order and use of the sea, as well in learning of navigation, as in exercising of that which to them appertaineth '. The seamen were by no means the most illiterate class of men in the community. Several distinguished men, such as William Borough, rose from the forecastle ; and the numerous relations in Hakluyt by persons in inferior positions indicate a comparatively high standard of education among seafaring men. There were no official certificates or examinations, and a man had to depend for advancement on the reputation he acquired among his fellows. Consequently it was easier for able men to come by their own than in the days of paper qualifications. The level of theoretical knowledge was not, however, very high ; and in this respect England was inferior to foreign nations, which largely accounts for her comparative failure in exploration during the first half of the sixteenth century.

The subject of discipline in merchantmen is somewhat puzzling. The master of a ship had apparently no statutory control over his crew ; his powers of discipline must have been largely those inherent in the cunning of his own right hand. Certain customary punishments, such as putting in irons, seem to have been recognized ; one of Willoughby's men was ' for pickerie ducked at the yard's arm and so discharged ' before the expedition cleared the English coast. But insubordination was common on long voyages, and often forced the captain and master to change their plans and forgo occasions of profit. Even in the navy things were sometimes no better. William Knight, writing in 1512 of the expedition to Spain, complains of ' the ungodly manners ' of the seamen, who robbed the king's victual while the soldiers were sea-sick.[1] The loss of the *Mary Rose* in 1545 was undoubtedly due to the state of anarchy prevailing on board. Her captain, when told of the danger arising from the open ports on the lee side, remarked that he had a set of rascals he could not rule ; the ports were left open, and the sea poured in and sank the ship.

Piracy, the bane of European waters, flourished exceedingly during this period of constant struggle among the western powers. After the peace between England and France in 1514, a joint attempt was made by the two countries to put a stop to it. In 1517 it was arranged that a commission of three or four suitable persons should sit at Calais to hear French complaints, and that a similar court should hear English grievances at Boulogne. Judgement was to go against all persons who should neglect to appear when summoned.[2] Some attempt was made to put the above into practice, but anything short of an international arrangement was foredoomed to failure, for, when hard pressed, the freebooters changed their flag—French pirates pretended to be Scots, and

[1] *Letters and Papers*, i, p. 362.   [2] Ibid., ii, No. 3520.

vice versa—and it was impossible to obtain any redress. The general state of public opinion also rendered it improbable that port officials would be very eager to do justice on their own countrymen in behalf of foreigners.

In England piracies were judged by the Admiralty Court, the tribunal consisting of the Lord High Admiral or his representative, the Master of the Rolls, and another judge, proceedings being opened at the place nearest to that at which the offence took place.[1] An Act of 1536 strengthened the hands of the court, permitting it to pass sentence of death, and depriving pirates of benefit of clergy.

The evil increased as time went on, and during the war of 1544–6 assumed gigantic proportions. Privateers, under pretext of cruising against the enemy, snapped up any neutral vessels of value, and the signing of peace did very little to repress their activities. The weakness of the Government in the next reign encouraged them to greater audacity, and the Lord Admiral Seymour was accused of abetting them. The Act of Attainder by which he was condemned to death [2] stated that he had ' maintained, aided, and comforted sundry pirates, and taken to his own use the goods pyratuslye taken against the laws '. It was not until long afterwards that the Narrow Seas became reasonably safe, for the French wars

---

[1] R. G. Marsden, *Select Pleas in Court of Admiralty*, Introd., p. lvi. The Admiralty Court had other duties : ' All contracts made abroad, bills of exchange (which at this period were for the most part drawn or payable abroad), commercial agencies abroad, charter parties, insurance, average, freight, non-delivery of or damage to cargo, negligent navigation by masters, mariners or pilots, breach of warranty of seaworthiness, and other provisions contained in charter parties ; in short, every kind of shipping business was dealt with by the Admiralty Court ' (Ibid., p. lxvii).

[2] 2 and 3 Ed. VI, c. 18.

of religion, the revolt of the Netherlands, and the Anglo-Spanish war continued to produce hordes of privateers throughout the remainder of the sixteenth century.

During the period 1485–1558 the principal seaports after London were Southampton and Bristol. The customs receipts at Newcastle and Boston were both in excess of those at Bristol, but, as they were mainly derived from the extortionate duties on wool, none of which product was exported by the western city, they over-represent the true volume of traffic at those ports. Throughout the whole of this period the tendency was for London to increase its business at the expense of the other ports, many of which steadily decayed in importance although the volume of the country's total trade was increasing. Since the duties continued practically unchanged, the sums paid at the various ports afford, when certain allowances have been made, a fair means of estimating their trade.

The growth of London as a port is illustrated by the following figures : during the first five years of Henry VII the average annual customs payments, exclusive of wool duties, amounted to £7,274 ; during the last five years of the same reign, £12,359 ; and during the years 1533–8, the last such period in which, for various reasons,[1] a just comparison can be made, £17,962. In half a century, then, the general trade of London was considerably more than doubled. The wool duties show a steady decline, due, not to a smaller output, but to the increase of the home manufacture of cloth which left less raw material

[1] The free trade policy of 1539–46, the troubles with the Hansa under Edward VI and Mary, and the rapid rise of prices during the same two reigns.

available for export. The wool averages for the same three periods were £10,515, £7,206, and £4,217.[1]

Southampton suffered great misfortunes owing to changing conditions. During the latter part of the fifteenth century the town enjoyed great prosperity as the sole English port to be visited by the Flanders galleys of Venice and the great carracks of Genoa, bringing valuable cargoes of eastern goods, and departing with their holds full of English wool. As time went on this traffic almost entirely ceased, and Southampton, unlike London, failed to benefit by the growth of the North Sea trade. Consequently, after enjoying a maximum period of prosperity in the closing years of Henry VII, during which time she bade fair to rival London, the southern seaport experienced a steady and irretrievable decay under his successor. The average receipts at Southampton for 1485-90 were £5,449; for 1504-9, £10,341; and for 1533-8, £3,232. The quantity of wool exported by the Staple from Southampton was very small, and does not appreciably affect the above figures.

So serious had the distress of Southampton become that in 1530 an Act of Parliament [2] was obtained for the purpose of releasing the town from certain dues to the Crown which it found itself unable to continue paying. The preamble sets forth the cause of its decline, attributing it to the cessation of the 'petie custom of merchandise which of old time was accustomed to be levied of the goods of strangers repairing thither in carreckis of Jeane (Genoa), laden with Jean woade; and in

[1] The customs returns for the period are given *in extenso* in Schanz, *Englische Handelspolitik*, ii. 37-156.
[2] 22 Hen. VIII, c. 20.

gallies of Florence and Venyse laden with spicis ; and now by the time of many years past since that Tolowes (Toulouse) woade hath been usually brought into this realm, and that the King of Portugal took the trade of spices from the Venyzians at Calacowte, few or no such carreckis, galeis ne other shippis have repaired unto our said town with woad or spices, nor be like to repair hereafter '. The trade of Southampton, it was stated, had also suffered from the wars with France. Many persons of substance had forsaken the town, and others were preparing to follow. The melancholy state of affairs here described is borne out by the figures and may be taken as correct ; unlike the majority of such preambles, which were very prone to wail about ' change and decay ', and must be received with caution.

Although the great state galleys came no more to England, occasional Venetian merchantmen still continued to make the voyage through the Straits of Gibraltar, more especially after the restriction of the wool export by the overland route in the reign of Mary. In order to help Southampton as much as possible it was ordered that they were to discharge cargoes exclusively at that town. This was opposed by the London merchants, but the privilege of Southampton was successfully upheld. In 1558 the Council further commanded that all malmseys brought to England were to be unloaded there, under penalty of 20s. per butt.[1]

Bristol, whose trade lay principally in the direction of Bordeaux and the Peninsula, missed a great opportunity in not persevering with the explorations of the Cabots and their obscure successors in the time of

---

[1] *Acts of the Privy Council*, vi. 39 and 325 ; *Venetian Cal.* vi, No. 554.

Henry VII. Unlike many lost chances, it presented itself once again, and the days of the town's greatest prosperity came when trade with America was opened up in the following century. During the early Tudor period Bristol fairly maintained its position without experiencing any such fluctuations of fortune as those which assailed Southampton. The average customs receipts for the first and last five years of Henry VII and for the period 1533–8 were respectively £1,175, £1,051, and £1,306. At the commencement of this time Bristol exported considerable quantities of corn to Spain, but as sheep-farming developed the price of food in England increased, and the export had to be restricted. An Act of 1543 permitted it only under certain conditions.[1]

In the Middle Ages a Staple had existed at Bristol; but, although it continued to elect mayors and officials, it had become entirely unimportant by the middle of the fifteenth century.[2] The trade of Bristol, in fact, became free to all individuals, notwithstanding various attempts to form a close corporation to the exclusion of outsiders. In 1500 one such company was formed with Hugh Elyot, the Newfoundland pioneer, as one of its members, but it failed to prosper. Again, in 1552, a charter was obtained incorporating a Bristol Society of Merchant Venturers, to the exclusion of non-members from the use of the port. Being unaccompanied by penalties it proved useless. In 1566 confirmation was obtained, and the monopoly was backed up by an Act of Parliament ; but owing to great opposition the scheme was dropped in 1571.[3] On many occasions Bristol

---

[1] 34 & 35 Hen. VIII, c. 9.
[2] J. Latimer, *History of the Merchant Venturers' Society of Bristol*, p. 15.
[3] *Bristol Charters* (1909), by the same author, pp. 142–7.

displayed a progressive spirit ; it was natural, therefore,
that an attempt to impose mediaeval restrictions on its
enterprise should be successfully resisted.

Of the other seaports, Exeter and Dartmouth, closely
approaching Bristol in importance, and Plymouth and
Fowey, with about half its volume of trade, remained
fairly steady in their returns. Poole, sharing to some
extent the misfortunes of Southampton, declined. Hull,
Ipswich, Newcastle, and Boston, all of which depended
mainly for their revenues on the dwindling export of
wool, show a more or less serious falling-off in their
customs receipts, although, since the cloth export was
on the increase, it is probable that their total bulk of
shipping was undiminished. It must be remembered
that the duties on exported cloth were nothing like so
heavy as those on raw wool. It is certain, however, that
the enormous increase of London's business was partially
at the expense of the prosperity of the smaller ports.
As merchant vessels grew in tonnage and draught they
naturally resorted more and more to the safer harbours,
and many of the minor havens dwindled to the status
of mere fishing villages. An Elizabethan document [1]
gives a list of all the seaports of the country by counties ;
seventeen are enumerated in Sussex alone, where it would
be difficult at the present day to find more than half
a dozen. The same tendency has extinguished numerous
east coast seaports.

[1] *Lansdowne MSS.*, 170, f. 281.

CHAPTER XIV

THE NAVY, 1485–1558

HENRY VII raised himself to the throne at the close of a period of naval decadence which corresponded with that of English commerce and prestige, and which, in common with the last mentioned, was a result of the feudal anarchy characterizing the expiry of the Middle Ages. The rulers of the country during the minority of Henry VI—and for practical purposes his minority lasted until his deposition—sold off the powerful fleet which his father had established, and relied upon hiring vessels for the very modest naval undertakings of the reign. The Yorkist kings never enjoyed sufficient breathing-space from internal disorders to do much for the re-establishment of the nation in its proper place in the councils of Europe, but their intentions undoubtedly outran their accomplishments, and they took some steps towards the acquisition of a royal fleet. Between 1461 and 1485 eleven ships were purchased by the Crown, and one, the *Grace Dieu*, was built. They were mostly of small size and indistinguishable in design from merchant-men, in which capacity the purchased vessels began their careers. They were probably adapted for naval service by the mounting of guns and strengthening of the upper works.

Of these vessels Henry VII acquired six with the crown, the others having disappeared from the navy list before his accession. His òwn reign is not remarkable for important naval operations, and his additions to the fleet, although of unprecedented quality, were not numerous. He built two first-rate ships of large size and heavy armament, the *Regent* and the *Sovereign*, and also two smaller craft, the *Sweepstake* and the *Mary Fortune*, which were provided with numerous oars in addition to a full equipment of masts and sails. They were probably intended for the policing of the Narrow Seas and the extermination of the enemies of commerce. By purchase or capture, Henry VII also acquired three other ships of minor importance.[1]

A short war against the Scots in 1490, in which the enemy captured several hired merchantmen from the English and lost one warship to them ; an expedition under Sir Edward Poynings two years later against a nest of pirates which had terrorized traders and used the town of Sluys as a base ; and a demonstration against the Scottish coast from Berwick to Edinburgh in support of an invading army which penetrated no farther than eight miles from Berwick in 1497, represent the only naval events of the reign. Of the fighting in 1490 no details are known beyond the general result above stated. Poynings' expedition against Sluys was entirely successful, the place falling to the combined attack of the English by sea and the Elector of Saxony, acting in the interest of the Archduke Maximilian, on land. In the Scottish campaign of 1497 the *Regent* and other new ships, besides hired merchantmen, were employed under the command of Lord Willoughby ; but for political reasons the commanders on both sides were unwilling to close, and

---

[1] For full details of naval administration under Henry VII, see M. Oppenheim, *History of the Administration of the Royal Navy*, and *Naval Accounts and Inventories*.

there is no record of any fighting at sea. On land the only result was the destruction of a few border strongholds.

The reign of Henry VIII was destined to be of greater naval importance than any previous one in English history ; and from the date of his accession he set vigorously about building or buying ships in preparation for the reconquest of France which was the dream of his earlier years. Before the end of 1512 eight vessels, large and small, had been laid down, and nine others bought. These, added to the fine ships left by Henry VII, formed a powerful fleet, which was steadily increased in force to the very end of the reign. On the day of Henry's death, the Royal Navy consisted of more than fifty ships averaging over 200 tons in burden.

The first war against France and Scotland was preluded by the celebrated action between Sir Andrew Barton, the Scottish rover, and the brothers Edward and Thomas Howard, sons of the Earl of Surrey. Barton with two ships, the *Lion* and the *Jennet Purwyn,* haunted the trade routes leading to the Flemish ports, and robbed, according to English allegations, all merchants who fell into his hands, although his own profession was that he was simply making reprisals against the Portuguese for injuries inflicted on his father many years before. He was undoubtedly a pirate under very thin disguise. In June 1511, Henry commissioned the Howards to bring Barton to justice, and they put to sea with two ships, of which the names and strength are unknown, for that purpose. There is no strictly contemporary description of the fight which ensued ; the most probable account is that furnished by Hall's *Chronicle,*[1] copied by Holinshed and

[1] 1809 edition, p. 525.

later writers. An Elizabethan ballad, although erroneous
in many details, preserves the spirit of the encounter
amid a mass of legendary embroidery.

Hall states that the Howards sailed in separate vessels
and were parted by chance of weather. Lord Thomas
Howard fell in with Barton in the Downs, and chased
him until he brought him to action. Barton, in the *Lion*,
defended himself bravely, blowing his whistle to encourage
his men ; but at length the English boarded, and the
Scots made their last stand on the hatches. Barton was
taken prisoner, so sorely wounded that he died soon
after, and the remnant of his crew surrendered. In the
meantime Sir Edward Howard had chased and taken
the *Jennet Purwyn*, which surrendered after an equally
desperate resistance. The two prizes were brought to
Blackwall on August 2, 1511, and were both added to
the navy. The prisoners were released on acknowledging their piracy. James IV was ' wonderfull wrothe '
on hearing of this action, and it was one of the causes
which determined him to make war on England two
years later. On the eve of Flodden, Lord Thomas
Howard, who was then serving with the army, sent him
a message to the effect that he had come to render him
an account of the death of Andrew Barton.

In January 1512, king and Parliament decided on war
with France, and preparations for equipping a fleet were
at once entered upon. Its first duty was to keep the sea
passage open for the transit of the land army to the north-
east of Spain, whence it was intended to launch an invasion of Aquitaine. By an arrangement with Ferdinand
of Spain it was agreed that the English Navy should hold
the sea from Calais to Brest, while that of Spain should
blockade the remainder of the western coast of France

down to the Pyrenees. Sir Edward Howard, the younger of the two brothers who had accounted for Andrew Barton, was appointed admiral, his command to consist of 18 ships and 3,700 men.[1] He was under twenty-four years of age and endowed with dauntless spirit and energy, marred, however, by a lack of patience and ability to play the waiting game which circumstances were eventually to demand of him. His subordinate captains were his equals in courage, but, as was inevitable in a hastily improvised force, they did not at all times work in concert ; although the latter defect was not apparently due to any lack of goodwill.

Before the fleet put to sea, the king made a banquet to all the captains, who took oath to perform their duty faithfully.[2] The French were not yet ready, and the first cruise was an unopposed parade through the Channel, resulting in the capture of fishing-boats and merchantmen. In June the army left for Spain under the Marquis of Dorset, Howard proceeding to the neighbourhood of Brest to beat down any attempt at interception. Far from any such intention, the French were unable to preserve their own coast from insult, the English landing and marauding on three successive days. When the army had completed its passage to San Sebastian the fleet returned once more to Portsmouth at the end of July.

By this time the French had made some progress with their preparations, and early in August had concentrated a fleet of twenty-two sail at Brest. Howard sailed again to look for them, and a general action, the only one of the war, took place on August 10, 1512, in Bertheaume Bay. The largest French ships were the *Louise*, in which was the admiral, René de Clermont, and the *Cordelière*,

---

[1] *Letters and Papers*, i, p. 344.   [2] Hall, p. 534.

commanded by a Breton gentleman, Hervé de Porzmoguer. On the English side were the *Regent*, commanded by Sir Thomas Knyvet, with Sir John Carew
as his chief subordinate ; the *Mary Rose*, in which
Howard sailed in person ; and twenty-three others.
After a preliminary cannonade René de Clermont and
the majority of his captains turned tail and fled back to
Brest, only the *Cordelière* and another vessel called the
Nef de Dieppe remaining to retrieve the honour of their
flag. The latter vessel retired after fighting for seven
hours ; but the *Cordelière*, grappled by the *Mary James*,
the *Sovereign*, and the *Regent*, fought to a finish. The
unequal combat was drawing to its inevitable close when
by some means, which eye-witnesses are not agreed upon,
the *Cordelière* took fire. The *Regent*, closely locked with
her foe, shared the same disaster, and the two mightiest
ships of England and France were destroyed together.
Porzmoguer, Knyvet, and Carew all perished, together
with the majority of their men. Of the 700 in the
Regent, 180 were saved ; of the Frenchman's crew,
probably superior in numbers, only six survived. Perhaps
the most intelligible and—from the circumstances of
author and recipient—most trustworthy account of the
affair is that written by Wolsey to the Bishop of Worcester
on August 26 :

' And to ascertain you of the lamentable and sorrowful
tidings and chance which hath fortuned by the sea, our
folks, on Tuesday was fortnight, met with 21 great ships
of France, the best with sail and furnished with artillery
and men that ever was seen. And after innumerable
shooting of guns and long chasing one another, at the
last the *Regent* most valiantly boarded the great carrack
of Brest, wherein were four lords, 300 gentlemen, 800

soldiers and mariners, 400 crossbowmen, 100 gunners (these figures are undoubtedly exaggerated), 200 tuns of wine, 100 pipes of beef, 60 barrels of gunpowder, and 15 great brazen curtaulds with a marvellous number of shot and other guns of every sort. Our men so valiantly acquitted themselves that within one hour's fight they had utterly vanquished with shot of guns and arrows the said carrack, and slain most part of the men within the same. And suddenly as they were yielding themselves, the carrack was (at) once a flaming fire,[1] and likewise the *Regent* within the turning of a hand. She was so anchored and fastened to the carrack that by no means possible she might for her safeguard depart from the same, and so both in fight within three hours were burnt, and most part of the men in them. Sir Thomas Knyvett, which most valiantly acquit himself that day, was slain with a gun. Sir John Carew, with divers others whose names be not yet known, be likewise slain. . . . Sir Edward hath made his vow to God that he will never see the King in the face till he hath revenged the death of the noble and valiant knight Sir Thomas Knyvett.'[2]

There was no pursuit of the remainder of the French, but, although the English had suffered as much material loss as their foes, their command of the sea was assured, and the fruits of victory thus remained with them: After ravaging the environs of Brest and scouring the Channel for prizes, the English fleet returned to port at the end of August, and was for the most part de- mobilized for the winter. In the late autumn Dorset's expedition, having achieved nothing, returned from Spain, again without molestation. Its failure was due

----

[1] Another account says that a gunner of the *Cordelière*, desperate at the approaching surrender, fired the magazine. If the figures as to survivors are correct they give support to the idea that the French ship blew up while the *Regent* burned.

[2] *Letters and Papers*, i, p. 409.

to bad organization, lack of discipline, and the failure of Ferdinand to fulfil the lavish promises which he had made at the commencement of the undertaking.

During the winter some of the minor ships were kept cruising in the Channel, while the dockyards were busy in repairing the remainder and constructing new vessels, one of which was the famous *Henry Grace à Dieu*. The latter was not finished in time to take part in this war. The French also made efforts to strengthen their Channel fleet. At some time in the autumn of 1512 a squadron of galleys arrived at Brest from the Mediterranean, under the command of Prégent de Bidoux. After completing his crews Prégent set out for a raid on the English coast, but was driven by various misfortunes to give up the design and put into St. Malo. While he was still there, Sir Edward Howard put to sea (April 10, 1513) and speedily drove the French sailing fleet into Brest, thus separating it from the galleys.

A strict blockade of Brest was now instituted under circumstances of great difficulty and danger for the English. The fleet was very poorly supplied with food, and the sailing of the victuallers with replenishments was unreasonably delayed. In addition the French were riding securely in the harbour and refused to come out and fight, while reinforcements from other ports, together with Prégent's galleys, were daily expected. Thus at any time the blockaders might find themselves in decisively inferior force. More important still, a strong westerly gale would entail the ruin of the fleet, driving under the guns of Brest such vessels as might escape destruction on the coast. Howard's letters, while exposing to the full the disadvantages under which he laboured, breathe a spirit of confidence and assurance of victory. Hall states, although the story lacks documentary corroboration, that when the French were securely bottled up in Brest, the Admiral wrote to King Henry, ' to come thither in person, and to have the honour of so high an enterprise : which writing the King's council nothing allowed, for putting the King in jeopardy upon the chance of the sea. Wherefore the King wrote sharply to him to accomplish that which appertained to his duty.' [1] True or false, the story is quite characteristic of Howard's temperament. He treated war as the field for the display of the fantastic knight-errantry of the mediaeval romances rather than as the struggle between two nations for material advantages.

As time went on it became apparent that, unless the English could get at their enemy, the unfavourable conditions described above would force them to relinquish the blockade. An attempt was made to sail into the harbour and engage the French even under the guns of the forts ; but one ship was lost by striking a submerged rock, and the others drew back. The captain of the wrecked vessel, Arthur Plantagenet, an illegitimate son of Edward IV, called upon our Lady of Walsingham when in danger of drowning, and made a vow that if he escaped he would eat neither fish nor flesh till he had seen her. As he must have subsisted exclusively on bread and beer if he had remained with the fleet, Howard made him the bearer of dispatches to the king, and thus put him in the way of fulfilling his vow. [2]

The next incident was the sudden appearance of Prégent de Bidoux with his six galleys and four smaller craft. In spite of instructions given in anticipation of

---

[1] Hall, p. 536.   [2] *Letters and Papers*, i, p. 538.

the event, he forced the blockade and made his way, not into Brest itself, but into Blancs Sablons Bay, after sinking one English ship and disabling another. It is evident that the fighting powers of the galleys had been under-estimated. Prégent anchored his galleys in a narrow cove with rocks on either hand. Batteries were mounted on the rocks, and the water was so shallow that only rowing boats could approach. Two plans for capturing this position suggested themselves. The first was the landing of a large force on an unprotected part of the coast, which force should march overland ' and so come unto the backside of the galleys '. Orders had actually been given for this enterprise when a long-expected fleet of victuallers was seen approaching, and the captains, probably because they had no choice in the matter, immediately set their starving men to work in transferring the supplies. For some reason unknown, Howard did not return to his original intention, but decided instead to make a frontal attack on the galleys by dashing into the narrow bay with all the small craft and ships' boats at his disposal. Once in, he relied upon his luck and his leadership to expel the enemy from their ships, to get the latter under way, and to bring them out in the teeth of the cross-fire from the batteries. Without a full knowledge of all the conditions it is unjust to condemn him for rashly giving away his life and those of his men. Much more impossible-sounding things have been done by English sailors, achievements which have owed their success to their very audacity, but it must be admitted that in Howard's case there is ground for suspicion that pique rather than sober judgement actuated him. An English captain tried to dissuade him, while a Spaniard, Alfonso Charran, urged him on ;

and one can imagine that Howard's fiery temper may have been stung by an insinuation that the English dared not do what Spaniards had the courage for.

On Sunday, April 25, the attack was made, the large ships in the meantime continuing the blockade of Brest. Howard himself went in a rowbarge with Charran and eighty men. Other boats were commanded by Lord Ferrers, Sir John Wallop, Sir Henry Sherburne, Thomas Cheyne, and Sir William Sidney. At four o'clock in the afternoon they pulled in, Howard's boat leading by a considerable distance. In spite of a storm of arrows and shot from the batteries he reached Prégent's galley and climbed aboard. His men threw an anchor into the galley and so held on, but before more than sixteen persons had had time to follow the Admiral, the cable parted and the boat drifted away. Those who had boarded were killed or jumped overboard, and Howard was seen alone on the galley's deck, waving his arm and crying: 'Come aboard again! Come aboard again!' Then seeing that there was no hope he took his whistle from about his neck and hurled it into the sea; and immediately afterwards the pikes thrust him against the rail and so overboard. The Spaniard Charran, his evil councillor, shared his fate. The men in the first boat, dismayed by what had occurred, made no further effort. The remaining boats arrived after Howard's death, which, in the smoke and confusion, they had not perceived. They made a gallant though ill-combined attack, and lost many men. Sir Henry Sherburne and Sir William Sidney boarded Prégent's galley, but were driven off. Then, seeing the Admiral's boat retiring, and supposing him to have abandoned the attack, they drew off like-wise, and only on reassembling outside did they discover

their loss. Next day some of the captains went ashore
with a flag of truce and parleyed with Prégent : what
he told them destroyed the hope that the Admiral was
taken prisoner, and rendered his death indisputable.[1]
The words of Sir Edward Echyngham, one of his
officers, constitute his best epitaph : ' Sir, when the
whole army knew that my lord Admiral was slain, I trow
there was never men more full of sorrow than all we
were ; for there was never noble man so ill lost as he
was, that was of so great courage and had so many
virtues, and that ruled so great an army so well as he
did, and kept so good order and true justice.'
Lord Ferrers succeeded temporarily to the command,
and led the fleet back to Plymouth before a week had
passed. The retirement would have been inevitable even
had Howard lived, for the shortage of provisions had now
become unendurable, and sickness had also broken out.
Discipline, never very strong in an irregular force, went
utterly to pieces ; for, after the Admiral, there was no
other officer combining rank and character in a sufficient
degree to exercise real command. The king was very
angry at the failure, and wrote a severe letter to the
captains. He appointed Lord Thomas Howard Admiral
in succession to his brother, and ordered him to return
at once to the Breton coast. Lord Thomas reported
that his men were in great fear of the galleys and ' had
as lief go to Purgatory as to the Trade (Brest water) '.
However, he promised to lead them there if victuals
were forthcoming. After a month's delay it was decided
not to return to Brest, but to keep a select force in the

[1] Echyngham's account. Prégent's own description of the fight tallies
with the above. The English loss was about 120 killed, number of
wounded unknown.

Narrow Seas for the preservation of the communications
of Henry's army invading the north of France. In spite
of their misfortunes, the English had demonstrated their
superiority to the French at sea, and it would have been
folly to have wasted more ships and men in continuing
to blockade Brest without a chance of bringing the enemy
to action. After the loss of the *Cordelière* the French
sailing fleet never showed the least inclination to leave
the shelter of its ports and contest the command of the
Channel.

There was a promise of some revival of naval interest
in the war in the latter half of 1513, when, after Henry
had commenced his Continental campaign, James IV of
Scotland declared war and allied himself with France.
The small Scottish fleet was sent southwards and joined
that of France, but their combined operations were
ineffectual, and most of the Scottish ships returned to
their own country after a few weeks had expired. The
small naval force which England had kept afloat for the
guarding of the Straits of Dover was deemed sufficient
to deal with the allies; and the Lord Admiral did not
think it necessary to go to sea, fighting instead on land
at Flodden.

In the spring of 1514 Prégent de Bidoux raided the
Sussex coast with his galleys. Landing by night he
burnt Brighton, which the chronicler calls 'a poor
village', but which a contemporary drawing[1] shows to
have been something more. The drawing in question
was thought by the editor of the *Letters and Papers of
the Reign of Henry VIII*[2] to represent Prégent's raid,
although it is inscribed with the date 1545 in a sixteenth-

---

[1] *Cotton MSS.*, Aug. I. i. 18.   [2] Vol. xx, Preface.

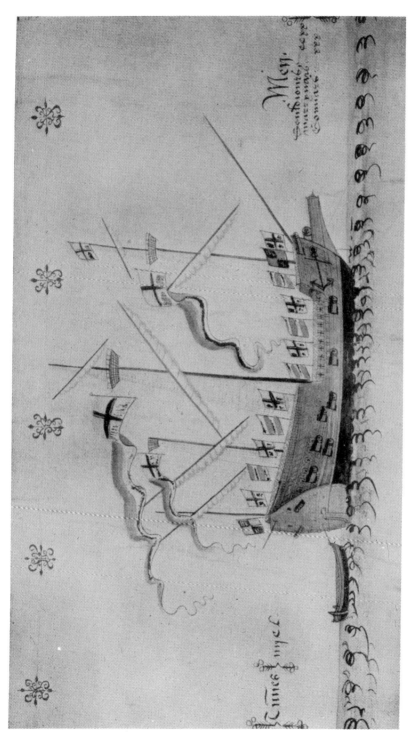

THE *GRAND MISTRESS*, BUILT 1545.
From Add. MS. 22047.

century hand. It represents the town of Brighton in the form of a hollow square, with a green in the middle and houses on three sides of it, the shore forming the fourth. To the west is the village of Hove, separated by an intervening stream. The French galleys are thrust ashore on the open beach, where also the fishing-boats of the natives are seen in flames. Numerous French warships are cruising near the coast, doubtless to cover the landing of the galleys. The town is partly on fire, but reinforcements appear marching down a high road from the interior, summoned by the smoke of the beacon blazing in the ' towne fyre cage '. The whole is beautifully drawn and coloured, and seems to be the work of a sailor. The details of the ships are minutely correct, and the artist does not commit the error, almost invariably made by the landsman-limner of the period, of making the wind blow two ways at once. Holinshed says that Prégent was finally driven off by a force of archers, losing one of his eyes as the result of an arrow wound. Although, apart from the above manuscript, there is no contemporary description of the burning of Brighton, it undoubtedly took place, since there is a reference to avenging it in a letter of June 5, 1514. The revenge consisted in a similar raid by Sir John Wallop on the coast of Normandy, in the course of which, with a force of only 800 men, he burnt twenty-one towns and villages and numerous ships.

This was the last act of the war, peace being signed shortly afterwards. On the whole the English had no reason to be ashamed of the deeds of their youthful navy. The right spirit was in the officers and men, although inexperience had betrayed them into many errors, and the business organization, in spite of Wolsey's talent, had been lamentably weak. Prégent's galleys had certainly borne off the palm for general efficiency and enterprise. The secret of their success was to be found, not in any advantages which might be possessed by the galley itself, but in the exceptional ability of their commander. On later occasions galleys failed to come up to the expectations which had been formed of them on the experience of this campaign. As to the behaviour of the French sailing-ships, it had been, with one or two brilliant exceptions, beneath contempt.

For the ensuing eight years, Wolsey's policy was supreme in the State, and peace reigned between France and England. During this time the navy was strengthened by the completion of the *Henry Grace à Dieu* and other first-class vessels.[1] In 1522 Henry, in spite of his gorgeous conference with Francis II at the Field of the Cloth of Gold, entered into an alliance with the new Emperor Charles V. On May 29, while Charles was in England, war was again declared on France ; and soon afterwards the Emperor, secure in the knowledge that the English fleet would ensure him a safe passage, set sail for Spain. Lord Thomas Howard, now Earl of Surrey, and later, by the death of his father, Duke of Norfolk, still filled the office of Admiral, although a great part of the operations of the fleet were conducted by the Vice-Admiral, Sir William FitzWilliam. The fact that Surrey was invested with the supreme command of the Imperial fleet as well as of that of England testifies to the prestige the navy had gained in the previous struggle with France.

---

[1] The *Great Elizabeth*, 900 tons, bought 1514 ; the *Katherine Pleasance*, 100, built 1518 ; the *Mary Gloria*, 300, bought 1517 ; the *Mary and John*, bought 1521 ; the *Mary Imperial*, 120, built 1515 ; the *Trinity Henry*, 250, built 1519.

The war of 1522-5 produced no such stirring incidents as had that of 1512-14. The English fleet, coupled with the marine forces of the empire, was so immeasurably superior to that of its enemies that the latter did all in their power to avoid an engagement. Large numbers of French and Scottish merchantmen were captured or burnt, and a very imperfect blockade of the northern ports of France was maintained. It was fortunate for the allies that the Government of Francis I had allowed the French navy to fall into decay, for on the English side, although the country had never before possessed so many powerful fighting ships, there was the utmost slackness and inefficiency in the civil administration of the fleet. Although the war had been reckoned as a certainty for quite a year before it actually broke out, the naval preparations were hopelessly inadequate. Not only was there a deficiency of accumulated provisions, but also of such essentials as casks and rigging, without which no fleet could remain at sea for more than a few days at a time.[1] All food, both solid and liquid, had to be carried in casks, of which an enormous number was required. Yet such was the confusion in the administration that some time after war had been declared Surrey was complaining that he could not move, as some of his ships had victuals for only eight days, and the majority for not more than a fortnight.

The French, however, missed their opportunity, and did nothing in the Channel. In July 1522 Surrey got to sea, and sacked Morlaix. In August he landed at Calais and ravaged the Boulogne district to the accompaniment of horrible atrocities. Every farm, village, church, and castle in the Boulonnais was destroyed.[2]

[1] *Letters and Papers*, iii, Preface, p. ccxvi.   [2] Ibid., p. ccxix.

But for Francis the main interest in the war was elsewhere, and there was practically no opposition. In spite of this Surrey was unable to capture Boulogne itself. By the middle of October the raid was over, and he was back at Calais.

In 1523 the fleet was better able to keep the sea, and in the autumn another feeble invasion of Picardy was attempted, this time under the king's brother-in-law, the Duke of Suffolk. After a perfectly futile march into the interior, ending in the capture of an unimportant town, which could not be permanently held, Suffolk returned as Surrey had done in the previous year. Scarcely ever has the military art descended so low in England as during this war of 1522–5. Meanwhile Henry and Wolsey had been experiencing the greatest difficulty at home in raising money for the inefficient army. After 1523 the war, as far as England was concerned, perished of sheer inanition. The one side was supreme at sea, but weak on land, the other was able to fight on land, but powerless at sea; and neither possessed the means of bringing its strength to bear upon the other. In 1524 nothing was done; and in 1525 peace was signed with France, bringing to a close the most purposeless war in English history.[1]

The third and final maritime war of Henry's reign opened with hostilities against Scotland in 1543. In the latter half of that year naval actions occurred in the North Sea involving the capture of several merchantmen. War with France was also imminent. In April Henry refused licence for twenty shiploads of wine to pass from Bordeaux to the Netherlands; but serious fighting did not take place until 1544. In May of that year a great

---

[1] *Political History of England*, vol. v, pp. 250–1.

English fleet under Lord Lisle, with land forces commanded by Hertford, appeared in the Forth. It took and burnt Leith and disembarked the army, which thereupon captured and partially destroyed the city of Edinburgh, although the castle held out. Scotland being thus for some time to come put out of action, Henry himself crossed to France with a large army. Assisted by Lisle's fleet, he laid siege to Boulogne, which surrendered in September. Desultory naval operations continued in the Channel almost to the end of the year.

But the English were not to hold undisputed the command of the sea. For the first time in modern history, France made a supreme effort and, by the summer of 1545, had concentrated in the Channel a fleet which was indubitably stronger in material than that of her enemy. All the fighting ships, both royal and private, of the northern and western coasts of France were collected in the Seine ports, and a strong squadron of twenty-five galleys was ordered round from the Mediterranean. The admiral of the whole fleet was Claude d'Annebaut, Baron de Retz, the galleys being commanded by Polain, Baron de la Garde, and Strozzi, Prior of Capua. England was certainly in a critical position, for Charles V, who had been her ally in the previous year, had made a separate peace with France at about the same time as Boulogne fell, and was now, owing to the irrepressible activity of the English privateers, distinctly hostile in his attitude. In retaliation for depredations suffered by his subjects at sea he had ordered the arrest of all English merchants and ships in his dominions.

The French plan was to sweep the Channel by superior force, to occupy the Isle of Wight, and use it as an advanced base for the blockade and destruction of Portsmouth and with it the English fleet. In the meantime Francis I himself with the land forces of France was to retake Boulogne, cut off in this manner from all hope of succour from England. If Boulogne fell, there appeared to be nothing to prevent a similar reduction of Calais and the enforcement of a humiliating peace upon England. The destination of the great armament was kept secret : Henry could not guess whether it was intended for Scotland, the Thames, Portsmouth, or any intermediate point on his coast. Consequently he was obliged to disperse his forces over the whole country and postpone concentration until the blow actually fell. With regard to Scotland he was particularly uneasy, more especially as a strong body of French troops had already been sent to that country to operate upon the northern border of England. It has been calculated that the land troops under arms in England during the summer of 1545 numbered more than 120,000 men.[1]

The weather during the early summer was rough and stormy and unsuited for the use of the great ' highcharged ' battleships which formed the principal hope of England's defence. Indeed, until the French should put to sea, there was no service upon which they could be wisely employed ; for the casualties inevitable in a sustained blockade of the Seine would but increase their original inferiority in numbers, and such a blockade would not have prevented the great French fleet from leaving harbour when ready. Accordingly, the king's ships were concentrated at Portsmouth, while the lighter and more seaworthy privateers of the western ports

---

[1] Froude, *History of England*, iv. 419.

ranged the Channel and the Bay of Biscay down to the coasts of Spain itself. Their commissions empowered them to ' annoy the enemy ', which they did very effectively, almost contriving in the process to convert the neutral Spaniards and Netherlanders into allies of the French. Only one enterprise was undertaken by the regular navy against the fleet in the Seine, and that— an attempt to damage it by means of fireships—failed owing to misadventures and change of weather.[1]

At length the French armada was complete. It set sail from Havre on July 16, after losing one of its greatest ships, the *Caraquon*, by an accidental fire.[2] Martin du Bellay, a contemporary observer, says it consisted of 150 ' gros vaisseaux ronds ', 60 auxiliary craft, and the 25 Mediterranean galleys. In addition to the normal ships' companies, there were a number of soldiers for the occupation of the Isle of Wight, and of siege troops presumably for use against Portsmouth.

In England the fleet had been made ready with the greatest energy, although the unexpected defection of the emperor in the previous year had left it to face a foe conscious of superiority and certain of victory. A list of ships drawn up in April 1545 shows that there were then available twenty-nine king's ships, five prizes taken in the Narrow Seas, two ships belonging to Lord Lisle and one to Sir Thomas Seymour, and twenty hired merchantmen, of which three were supplied by the Reneger family of Southampton.[3] This total of fifty-seven sail had been increased by the middle of July to about eighty. The imperial minister, writing on July 24,

[1] *Letters and Papers*, xx, part i, Nos. 987, 1023, 1101.
[2] Martin du Bellay, *Mémoires*, ed. Michaud et Poujoulat, 1838, p. 553.
[3] *Letters and Papers*, xx, part i, No. 543.

says there were that number at Portsmouth, forty of them being 'large and beautiful'.[1] Thus the French armament, exclusive of the galleys, was quite double as strong as that of England ; and in certain circumstances, as the event was to prove, the galleys were capable of hitting very hard.

At the time the French set sail the weather fell very calm and hot, and so continued for several days. On the evening of the 18th they were seen sailing round the eastern end of the Isle of Wight, the galleys in advance and the sailing-ships behind. Four of the galleys were sent forward to reconnoitre, but were driven back by a force of small craft sent out from Portsmouth. The French then anchored for the night, most probably in the neighbourhood of Ryde. The position occupied by the English is somewhat difficult to determine. There are two detailed accounts of the battle of the following day ; one, written from the French side, by Du Bellay, and the other from the English, by Van der Delft, the imperial ambassador. In addition there is an engraving in the British Museum from a contemporary painting, now destroyed, giving a panoramic representation of the scene.[2] From these sources it would appear that the English fleet was at anchor outside the inner harbour of Portsmouth, in a position covered on the left by forts and batteries on the shore towards Southsea, and on the right by shoals. The only approach was from the front by a narrow channel.

On the morning of July 19 there was no wind, and the French galleys were sent forward to cannonade the

[1] Du Bellay says the English had only sixty ships on July 18.
[2] Brit. Mus. Maps, 3, Tab. 24, No. 2. The original painting was at Cowdray House, Midhurst, and was burnt with that building at the end of the eighteenth century.

anchored English fleet. Some of them entered the outer harbour and for more than an hour kept up a hot fire, doing considerable damage. Du Bellay claimed that the *Mary Rose* was sunk by their fire, and that the *Henry Grace à Dieu* was so knocked about as to be kept afloat with difficulty. Neither of these statements was correct. The *Mary Rose* was sunk by accident, and the *Henry* was at sea shortly afterwards none the worse for the fight. But undoubtedly the situation, if prolonged, would have been most serious for the English. Their ships were becalmed at anchor, while the galleys, with free power of movement, were extremely difficult to hit. The method of mounting the big guns of the time allowed for very little lateral adjustment, and no elevation or depression, so that unless the ship could be manœuvred the enemy might take up a position in which it would be impossible to bring guns to bear on him. Fortunately a land breeze sprang up and the lighter English sailing craft immediately dashed out upon the galleys. The latter had outstayed their welcome, and just missed suffering severely for it. The English row-barges were among them before they could get clear of the harbour. Once a sailing craft could range alongside a galley, that galley was doomed, for her oars would be smashed without the least damage to her opponent. Accordingly, there was nothing for it but instant flight. Since the galleys carried no guns pointing astern, they were at a great disadvantage, and the French sailing fleet had to advance to their rescue.

Lord Lisle now saw the chance of fighting a battle on his own terms, in which his smaller fleet would be assisted by the fire of the land batteries. His heavy ships immediately moved out to join action with the

French. In the process occurred one of the famous disasters of the English Navy. The *Mary Rose*, the vice-admiral, having discharged her guns on one side, went about to fire the other broadside, and, the ports on the discharged side not having been closed, as apparently they should have been, their lower edges dipped below the water as the ship heeled. In a moment the catastrophe happened; the sea poured in and heeled the ship still further until she capsized and sank so rapidly that only some thirty of a crew of five hundred were saved. Sir George Carew, the captain, was among the lost. A trustworthy authority states that the need for closing the lee ports was well known, but that owing to indiscipline no one thought proper to attend to it.

Undismayed by this disaster, the English presented a bold front to the enemy, and showed perfect willingness to continue the action. But d'Annebaut was not prepared to fight both fleet and forts at the same time, and, having rescued the galleys, the French retired to their former anchorage off the Isle of Wight.[1] The action was renewed at long range on the following day, but neither side would surrender the advantage of position and consequently there was no decisive result.

There was now no doubt as to the intentions of the French, and every nerve was strained to concentrate decisive forces at the point of danger. The king and the Privy Council had already moved down to the neighbourhood of Portsmouth before the French had arrived, and the king was aboard the *Henry Grace à Dieu* when their approach was first signalled. On July 20 orders were

---

[1] Froude, iv. 425–6; Van der Delft to Charles V, *Spanish Cal.* viii, No. 101; Du Bellay, p. 554. Froude's account is based mainly on Du Bellay; Van der Delft's letter was unknown at the time he wrote.

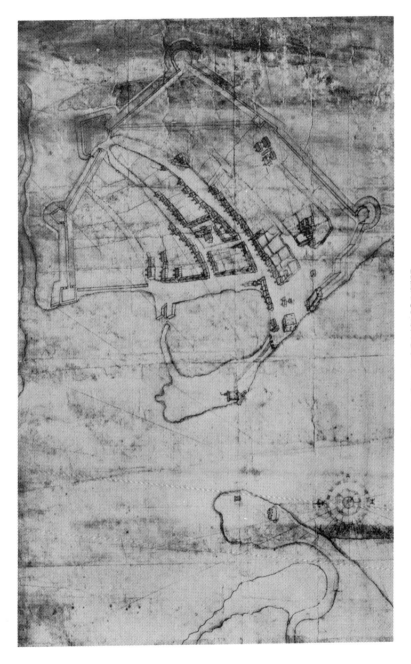

PLAN OF PORTSMOUTH, c. 1545.
From Cott. MS. Aug. I. ii. 15.

sent to the western privateers to make all speed to
Portsmouth.¹ Some sixty sail of small but active fighting
ships would thus be added to the English strength. At
the same time the officials at the Tower were instructed
to send down all the large ordnance and ammunition in
that fortress.² The levies of the southern shires were
also set in motion, but, as the event fell out, their services
were not needed, and before long they were met by orders
to disband, as the danger had passed away.

Time was now in favour of England. If a week were
allowed to elapse in inaction on the part of the French,
Portsmouth would be safe and the invasion would have
failed. On the French side other factors pointed to the
same conclusion. Disease in its most terrible forms had
broken out in their crowded ships, and the maintenance
of a blockade long enough to allow of the capture of
Boulogne was an impossibility. Already the great ship
Maitresse, strained by the seas and shaken by the discharge of her own guns, had been beached and abandoned
to save her from the fate of the *Mary Rose*. D'Annebaut
was not the man to hold on in face of difficulty as Howard
had done at Brest in 1513. He seems to have realized
that prompt action was the only alternative to eventual
failure, and, after vainly seeking to draw the English
into the open by landing and burning villages in the
Isle of Wight, he proposed the desperate plan of sailing
his whole fleet into Portsmouth harbour and attempting
to carry the town by a *coup de main*. His pilots represented to him that the thing was an impossibility, that
his ships, passing the narrow entrance in single file,
would be smashed by the fire of the batteries on their
flank, and that tides and shoals would prevent any

¹ *A. P. C.*, i. 212.   ² Ibid., p. 215.

retreat. After sending in a boat party to assure himself of the truth of these arguments, he submitted to the inevitable and began to think of withdrawal.[1]

Meanwhile there had been sharp skirmishing in the Isle of Wight. The smoke of the burning villages could be seen from Portsmouth, but the French were by no means unopposed. Small bands of native archers, perfectly acquainted with the country, ambushed them in the woods. Reinforcements were sent across, apparently by favour of the negligence of the French fleet, until 8,000 English troops were in the island, and a large force would have been necessary for its conquest.

D'Annebaut's next move was to leave the Isle of Wight on July 21 and anchor his fleet along the western shore of Selsey Bill. His reasons for this move are not clear. It would seem that his original position was more advantageous until he should be forced by necessity to retire to France. He has been criticized for not permanently garrisoning the Isle of Wight, since he had a large number of supernumerary troops on board his fleet. But he was probably justified in not doing so. With no strong, well-provisioned fortress in which to hold out, the most powerful force imaginable would have been driven to surrender in course of time when deprived of the support of the fleet. With the imperfect firearms of that day improvised earthworks were not a sufficient defence, especially within a few miles of such an arsenal as Portsmouth.

Lord Lisle detected the weakness of the French anchorage off Selsey Bill and made plans to attack when the first south-westerly wind should place the enemy on a lee shore.[2] But he was preoccupied with attempts to

---

[1] Du Bellay, pp. 555-6.   [2] *Letters and Papers*, xx, part i, No. 1237.

refloat the *Mary Rose*, and, before the plan could be put into execution, the French received warning and slipped off in time to escape annihilation. D'Annebaut sailed for Boulogne, and landed his troops to assist in the siege, which was making very poor progress.

The great plan had now definitely failed, and its failure was undoubtedly due in the first place to the terrible mortality 'from plague, typhus, and kindred scourges, which afflicted the French crews, packed to suffocation as they were in their narrow quarters in sultry weather, and most probably badly fed. In a lesser degree the failure was ascribable to admirable leadership on the English side, although this would not have availed to save Boulogne if the French had been in a state to maintain a blockade for the necessary time. The Fabian conduct of the English fleet was exactly suited to the occasion ; and the credit for it is due rather to Henry VIII himself than to his Admiral, who did nothing of his own initiative if he could by any possibility obtain instructions from the king.

D'Annebaut, after landing his sick and provisioning his fleet, was soon at sea once more. But by this time the West of England ships had come in,[1] and Lisle was at the head of a fleet strong enough to go in search of the French. On August 11 he received orders to put to sea, the French being reported to be off Rye to the number of 200 sail. The two fleets sighted each other on the 15th off Shoreham. As before, the galleys formed the advanced guard of the French, and were engaged by the lighter English sailing craft. The English fleet was drawn up—if a set of fighting instructions dated a few days earlier was followed—in the manner of a land

---

[1] *Letters and Papers*, xx, App. No. 27.

army of the period : the first-class ships in the centre,
preceded by a line of armed merchantmen, and guarded
on either flank by the auxiliaries. The merchantmen
thus answered to the cannon in a land battle, breaking
the enemy's ranks in preparation for the advance of the
main body—the infantry on land—behind. The light
craft on the wings played the part of cavalry, guarding
the flanks of their own fleet and taking advantage of
confusion among the enemy. The plan was very pretty
on paper, but it is doubtful if it would have stood the
test of practice by a fleet untrained to manœuvre in
concert, and a much simpler procedure was actually
adopted in the Armada fights in 1588.[1] In the present
instance, the battle was never fairly joined. The galleys
maintained a brisk cannonade against the row-barges and
privateers, getting, on the whole, the worst of the
encounter. The French ' great ships ' held off, hoping
that the galleys would do all the work. Towards evening
the weather became worse and the galleys were much
knocked about. Both fleets anchored for the night
within a league of one another ; and next morning at
dawn Lisle saw his enemies' topsails disappearing beneath
the horizon. Finding the galleys useless in anything but
a calm, they had decided to give up the enterprise and
retire to Havre.[2]

The English made sail to the Narrow Seas, and a few
days later Lisle, apprehending no further danger for the
moment, quitted the fleet. He was present in person
at a meeting of the Council at Woking on August 24.
In September he raided the Normandy coast, burning the

[1] See J. S. Corbett, *Drake and the Tudor Navy*, for tactical formations
employed in the sixteenth century.
[2] Froude, iv. 435-6 ; Du Bellay, p. 559.

town of Tréport and thirty ships, and retiring without molestation. Thus the French, for all their superiority of force, had again surrendered the command of the Channel. But the victory had not been attained without great sacrifice. The fishermen of all the southern shires had been impressed into the service, and were now dying by hundreds from the same epidemics which had scourged the French. Their wives and daughters were obliged to take the boats out ·in search of a living ; and it was a common occurrence for a boat ' manned ' by a dozen women and a boy to be chased into port by a French privateer. The mortality in the fleet was so great that, as soon as it was ascertained that the French acknowledged defeat, haste was made to discharge the majority of the crews. The privateers compensated by their energy for the timid tactics of the great ships. They scoured the Channel and the neighbouring seas and were seldom scrupulous as to the ownership of the property they took. Privateering as a lifelong profession dates from this war. It was never thoroughly put down until the following century.

In 1546 naval operations were renewed, centring principally round the siege and relief of Boulogne ; but the French were relatively much weaker than in the previous year, and the captured fortress remained in English hands. The war terminated in June with a French acknowledgement of powerlessness to do anything further.

On a general view it is evident that Henry VIII's naval policy was justified by success. If it was his object to create a fleet sufficiently powerful to render England immune from invasion and to secure respect for her sea-borne commerce, it must be admitted that that object was gained. Although the Continental powers were very much more formidable than they had been at the opening of his reign, he was generally able to take the offensive and to fight on the enemy's ground. Scotland, too, was rendered easier to deal with by the vulnerability of Edinburgh to a stroke from the sea ; and the oft-dreaded Franco-Scottish combination was seldom effective owing to the interposition of an English fleet between the allies. Henry died in January 1547, and a list [1] made a year later shows that there were then in the navy 6 ships of 500 tons and over, 19 between 200 and 500 tons, 4 between 100 and 200, and 24 of less than 100. The total tonnage of the 53 vessels was 11,268, and they carried between them 7,780 men and 2,087 guns. If the total of guns seems disproportionately large, it must be remembered that many of them were small weapons such as swivels and hailshot pieces, which might almost be reckoned as small arms.

During the eleven years covered by the reigns of Edward VI and Mary, the history of the navy shows a steady decline, not so much in strength of ships and guns as in leadership, administration, and the moral qualities making for success. On paper, especial'y under Edward VI, this decline is not evident ; indeed, a list of 1552 shows that only five of Henry VIII's ships had dropped out, while others had been acquired in their places. But a formidable roll of battleships was of little value if the ships themselves were allowed to rot untended in docks and harbours, or were chartered by merchants for twelve-months' voyages to the Levant or the African coast. This charge of improvidence against the administration is fully borne out by its inability, increasing as

[1] *Archaeologia*, vi. 218.

time went on, to send large fleets of first-class ships to
sea as Henry VIII had done. Details of deterioration
are wanting, and it can only be deduced from its results;
but it is certain that in the last eighteen months of
Edward's reign, three large fighting ships were sent on
distant commercial ventures, and it is probable that
other transactions of the same kind took place, of which
the evidence has perished. The three ships referred to
were the *Jesus of Lubeck* (700–800 tons) and the *Mary
Gonson* (600), chartered for a Levant voyage in February
1552 [1]; and the *Primrose*, which, together with the
Moon (pinnace), was lent to Thomas Wyndham and his
co-adventurers for their Guinea expedition in 1553.[2]

To the credit of Edward's guardians, on the other
hand, must be placed the establishment of the rudiments
of a naval base in the Medway, afterwards Chatham
dockyard, and the inauguration of a special department
for victualling the ships of the fleet.[3]

At the outset of Edward's reign, the Protector Somerset [4] determined on a fresh invasion of Scotland for the
purpose of securing the consent of the Scots to a marriage
between their infant queen and the young king of
England. The expedition was on a more ambitious scale
than that of 1544, consisting of a fleet under Lord Clinton
keeping pace with a marching army under the Protector.
The latter routed the Scots at Pinkie (September 10,
1547) and again took Leith and Edinburgh; while the
fleet ravaged the coast and destroyed all the Scottish
shipping it could find. But the political result of the
invasion was failure, for the young queen was sent off

---

[1] *Journal of Edward VI*, p. 61.   [2] Strype, *Memorials*, ii. 504.
[3] Oppenheim, *Administration of the Royal Navy*, p. 101.
[4] The Lord Hertford who had commanded the land forces at Leith
and Edinburgh in 1544.

to France by way of the Irish Sea in the following summer, and her escort succeeded in eluding the English who were keeping strict watch in the North Sea and the Channel.

During these events France, in a state of scarcely veiled hostility, had maintained a fleet of galleys under Strozzi in her northern waters. The war became regularized when the French began to raid the Sussex coast and to concentrate troops in the neighbourhood of Boulogne in 1549. In consequence of the former operations instructions were given to Thomas Cotton, in May 1549, to patrol the Channel. With the commission of Vice-Admiral he was to take six small craft of the row-barge type and one shallop, and with them to drive the enemy from the Sussex coast, to 'traverse the seas' between the Isle of Wight, Portland, and the Channel Islands, to supply the latter with munitions of war, and to keep watch on Brest, where great preparations were said to be in progress. He was particularly enjoined not to molest neutral shipping.[1] Early in August a sharp action was fought in the neighbourhood of the Channel Islands, but whether by Cotton's squadron or not is not clear. It is vouched for by Fox the Martyrologist and by the writers of chronicles of the time, but has left no trace in official documents, either English or French. The substance of the accounts is that a fleet of French galleys was sent to reduce the Islands and that it was beaten back by an English squadron with the loss of 1,000 men.[2] Boulogne was able to hold out until the spring of 1550. By that time the English Government,

---

[1] R. O., S. P. Dom., Ed. VI, vol. vii, Nos. 9 and 12.
[2] Fox, *Acts and Monuments* (ed. G. Townsend, 1846), v. 741 ; Holinshed, iii. 1055.

hampered by lack of money and by anarchy at home, had come to the conclusion that its retention was not worth the efforts involved. In March they agreed to surrender the fortress for a large money payment, and peace was restored between England and France for the next seven years.

A feature of the naval history of this period was the series of changes in the chief command of the fleet. During Edward's reign the office of Lord Admiral was successively held by Warwick (formerly Lord Lisle); Seymour, brother of the Protector Somerset (executed March 1549); Warwick again, and Clinton. Mary on her accession appointed Lord William Howard, who held office until 1558, when he was superseded by Clinton. One of the charges against Seymour was his connivance at piracy. In this connexion a letter addressed to him in September 1548, by John Graynfyld, a privateer captain, is of some interest. At the date mentioned war had not been declared with France, and the man was legally a pirate. He describes how his bark and three others had sailed from the Cornish coast to that of Brittany, and had there separated ' each to seek their adventure, as the manner is of venturers '. Graynfyld himself, being alone within half a league of Pointe de Penmarch, sighted twenty-seven sail of Normans and Bretons. Nothing dismayed by the odds, he gained the wind of them, waited until twelve of them had passed, and then set on the thirteenth, which was armed with six pieces of ordnance. She only escaped him by going ashore in Audierne Bay. He served two others in the same way. While thus engaged, another of the enemy, of 95 tons and with a crew of twenty-six men, got to windward of him. But Graynfyld rose to the occasion, boarded the French ship and took her, after slaying her captain in the fight.[1] A more convincing testimony to the reckless audacity of the sixteenth-century privateers would be hard to find.

Under Mary the navy sensibly decreased in strength and efficiency, and it may safely be said that it had never since the beginning of the Tudor period passed through such a period of discouragement as that of the years 1557–8. Even the paper strength of the fleet was not maintained. The *Henry Grace à Dieu* was accidentally burned at Woolwich on August 25, 1553. The *Primrose* was sold in 1555, together with nine smaller craft, some of them fetching such ridiculous prices as £8 and £10 apiece,[2] showing the utter state of decay into which they had been allowed to fall. Other ships disappeared also in the reign with the net result that, although six new craft were acquired, there were at Mary's death only twenty-six royal ships with a total tonnage of 7,110, a decrease of 36 per cent. from Henry VIII's total. Mr. Oppenheim does not agree with censures on Mary's naval administration. He points out that thirteen of the ships left by Henry VIII were row-barges of 20 tons, and that it was mainly this class of vessel which was disposed of. But the fact remains that England lost command of the sea in the winter of 1557–8, at a time when the French had no overwhelming force afloat, and that the failure to relieve Calais was due to the fact that not one of the ' great ships ' officially borne on the strength of the fleet was in condition to put to sea at the time of need.

War with France opened in the summer of 1557. In that year Lord William Howard cruised in the Channel

---

[1] *R. O., S. P. Dom., Ed. VI*, vol. v, No. 3.   [2] Oppenheim, p. 109.

with a fleet including six ships of 200 tons and over, the largest being the *Jesus of Lubeck*, described as of 700 tons.[1] His proceedings were uneventful, and all the large vessels were laid up at the beginning of winter. At the end of the year disquieting news began to arrive with startling suddenness in England. On December 22 Lord Grey of Wilton reported from Guisnes that French preparations were on foot, although their object was not ascertainable. On the 26th Lord Wentworth, the commander at Calais, wrote that five French warships, with forty other sail and large numbers of troops, were gathering at Boulogne and Abbeville. On the last day of 1557 Calais, with its garrison of 800, was invested by 30,000 men.

The Government had taken the alarm by the 29th of December and, if the Narrow Seas had been held by such a force as Henry VIII had been accustomed to keep there in the winter, would have been in time to relieve Calais, which held out until January 8. But such force was lacking : a paper of December 29 shows that the ' Ships and Barks already in the Narrow Seas ' were five in number, their combined crews numbering only 400 men.[2] It is true that instructions were given for the immediate preparation of eight other vessels with crews amounting to 1,000 men,[3] but it was too late. The unready ships could not be rigged and manned in time, and their commander, Sir William Woodhouse, only received his final sailing orders on the very day the French entered Calais.[4] In the meantime the Earl of

---

[1] *R. O., S. P. Dom., Mary*, vol. x, No. 67. This paper is small and mutilated, but does not look as if any large portion were missing. It may or may not represent a complete list of the ships employed.

[2] Ibid., vol. xi, No. 65.   [3] Ibid.

[4] Ibid., vol. xii, No. 12.

Rutland had collected a few hoys and fishing boats at Dover, and in them had attempted to transport reinforcements to the beleaguered town. But the French covering fleet beat them off, and he was obliged to leave Calais to its fate.[1]

Calais had been lost by default of those responsible for the naval and military administration of the country. A fortnight after its fall the queen sent orders to Lord Howard to put the navy into an effective state, equipping the regular ships and forcibly borrowing the services of as many merchantmen as he should require. Howard was superseded by Clinton early in 1558, and by midsummer the latter was at sea. He made the usual raid on the Brittany coast in July, burning Le Conquêt and effecting nothing against Brest. At the beginning of August he was back at Portsmouth. On July 13 a squadron detached from his fleet had interfered with decisive effect in a battle fought on the shore at Gravelines between the French and some of Philip's Netherland troops. The ships stood in and played with their heavy guns upon the French until the latter gave way. But this was the only event to lighten the gloom of the close of Mary's reign, and was a trifling exploit as compared with the fall of Calais. Fortunately the depression of English affairs proved to be only temporary, and with a new sovereign and a wiser government misfortunes were retrieved, and the nation was able in the years to come to make triumphant progress along the path mapped out for it by the first two Tudors.

[1] Froude, vi. 500.

INDEX

INDEX

Chancellor, Richard, 238, 313–
333 ; sails with Willoughby,
1553, 317 ; captain of the
Edward Bonaventure, 314 ;
separated from Willoughby,
318 ; reaches Vardo, 322 ; dis-
covers Archangel, 323–4 ; visits
Moscow, 324–5 ; returns to
England, 1554, 326 ; second
voyage to White Sea, 1555,
327–9 ; second visit to the
Czar, 328 ; obtains grant of
privileges, 328 ; remains in
Russia, 1555–6, 329 ; sails for
England, 1556, 332 ; wrecked
and drowned, 333.
Channel Islands, naval action
near, 1549, 402.
Chapuys, Eustace, Imperial ambassador, 131, 132, 143, 268 ;
letters from, 130, 265, 269.
Charles V, Emperor, 125, 126,
130, 131, 132, 170, 185, 186,
187, 191, 195, 220, 224, 389 ;
diplomatic struggle with, 130–2,
223 ; in England, 1522, 386.
Charran, Alfonso, Spanish captain, 381–2.
Chaucer's Shipman, 211.
Chester, Thomas, merchant, forbidden to trade with Guinea,
296.
Chilton, Leonard, English captain trading with Mexico, 226.
Chios, English trade with, 229,
230, 231, 232, 235–8 ; English
factors at, 230 note ; English
consul at, 231.
Chronicle, anonymous (Cotton
MSS. Vit. A. xvi), 61, 69–70.
Cipango (Japan), 57, 77–8, 80, 84.
Clermont, René de, French admiral, 376–7.
Clinton, Lord, Lord Admiral,
401, 403, 406.
Cloth export, 33–6, 40, 42, 126–7,
129–30, 135, 145, 147, 171–3,
192 ; laws relating to, 152–4,
157 ; suspension of laws, 145,
162, 170–1. See also Merchant
Adventurers.
Cloth manufacture, English, 16,
36, 134–5, 147, 152–3 ; Netherland, 20, 32, 33, 36.
Cockeram, Martin, mariner, 266.
Coinage, debasement of, 163.
Coke, John, Secretary of Mer-
chant Adventurers, 188.

Columbus, Bartholomew, 71.
Columbus, Christopher, 71, 73.
Commerce, general development
of, 13–50, 120–51 ; Acts re-
lating to, 124, 124-5, 134–5.
Cooper, Richard, Governor of
English merchants in Spain, 218.
Cordelière, French warship, burn-
ing of, 376–8.
Corte Real, Gaspar and Miguel,
Portuguese explorers, 106, 116.
Cortes, Martin, writer on navigation, 348.
Cosa, Juan de la, map of, 82–3.
Cotton, Thomas, vice-admiral,
402.
Crespi, treaty of, 224.
Crisis, international, 1538–9,
125–6.
Cromwell, Thomas, 125, 128, 262,
268 ; policy of, 127 note, 140.
Customs duties, tonnage and
poundage, subsidies, wool duties,
22, 33, 36–40, 46–7, 123, 136 ;
schedules of, 37, 40 ; Acts
relating to, 38, 123, 150–1, 161 ;
proclamation relating to, 1539,
126–7, 128, 130–2 ; frauds on,
162 ; receipts, 131, 367–71.

Danzig, English merchants at,
44, 129, 158, 178, 197–8.
Dawbeny, Oliver, participator in
1536 expedition, 263.
Denmark, trade with, 41, 129, 197.
Dorset, Marquis of, 120–1, 378–9.
Dudley, John, Viscount Lisle,
Earl of Warwick, Duke of Northumberland, 146, 162, 164, 403 ;
commands fleet against French
and Scots, 1544–6, 389–99 ;
sacks Leith and Edinburgh,
1544, 389 ; action at Portsmouth, 1545, 392–7 ; action off
Shoreham, 1545, 397–8 ; raids
French coast, 398–9 ; policy of,
162, 163, 165 ; project for a
voyage to Peru, c. 1552, 310.
Durforth, Cornelius, master of
the *Bona Confidentia*, 314.

Easterlings. See Hansa.
Eden, Richard, historian, 52, 90,
241–2, 245, 278, 279, 283, 284,
285.
Edward VI, general character
of his reign, 146–7 ; naval
administration under, 400–1 ;
death of, 170.

Oxford : Horace Hart M.A., Printer to the University